# Mastering Unity 2D Game Development

Become an expert in Unity3D's new 2D system, and then join in the adventure to build an RPG game framework!

**Simon Jackson**

BIRMINGHAM - MUMBAI

# Mastering Unity 2D Game Development

First published: August 2014

Production reference: 2211014

Published by Packt Publishing Ltd.
Livery Place
35 Livery Street
Birmingham B3 2PB, UK.

ISBN 978-1-84969-734-7

www.packtpub.com

Cover image by Simon Jackson (darkside@zenithmoon.com)

# Credits

**Author**

Simon Jackson

**Reviewers**

Trond Abusdal

Ben Beagley

Fredrik Kellermann

Wei Wang

Simon Wheatley

**Commissioning Editor**

James Jones

**Acquisition Editor**

James Jones

**Content Development Editor**

Priyanka S

**Technical Editors**

Novina Kewalramani

Humera Shaikh

**Copy Editors**

Roshni Banerjee

Mradula Hegde

Gladson Monteiro

Adithi Shetty

**Project Coordinator**

Kartik Vedam

**Proofreaders**

Simran Bhogal

Maria Gould

Ameesha Green

Paul Hindle

**Indexers**

Hemangini Bari

Mehreen Deshmukh

Tejal Soni

Priya Subramani

**Graphics**

Valentina D'silva

Disha Haria

Yuvraj Mannari

**Production Coordinator**

Adonia Jones

**Cover Work**

Adonia Jones

# About the Author

**Simon Jackson** has been a tinkerer, engineer, problem solver, and solution gatherer ever since his early years. In short, he loves to break things apart, figure out how they work, and then put them back together; usually better than before.

He started way back when with his first computer, the Commodore Vic20. It was simple, used a tape deck, and forced you to write programs in basic or assembly language; those were fun times. From there, he progressed through the ZX Spectrum +2 and the joyous days of modern graphics, but still with the 30 minutes load times from a trusty tape deck. Games were his passion even then, which led to many requests for another gaming machine, but Santa brought him an Amstrad 1640, his first PC. From there, his tinkering and building exploded, and that machine ended up being a huge monstrosity with so many add-ons and tweaked fixes. He was Frankenstein, and this PC became his own personal monster crafted from so many parts. Good times.

This passion led him down many paths, and he learned to help educate others on the tips and tricks he learned along the way; these skills have equipped him well for the future.

Today, he would class himself as a game development generalist. He works with many different frameworks, each time digging down, ripping them apart, and then showing whoever would listen through his blog, videos, and speaking events on how to build awesome frameworks and titles. This has been throughout many generations of C++, MDX, XNA (what a breath of fresh air that was), MonoGame, Unity3D, The Sunburn Gaming Engine, HTML, and a bunch of other proprietary frameworks—he did them all. This gives a very balanced view of how to build and manage many different types of multiplatform titles.

He didn't stop there as he regularly contributed to the MonoGame project, adding new features and samples, and publishing it on NuGet. He also has several of his own open source projects and actively seeks any new and interesting ones to help with.

By day, he is a lowly lead technical architect working in the healthcare industry seeking to improve patients' health and care through better software (a challenge to be sure). By night, he truly soars! Building, tinkering, and educating while trying to push game titles of his own. One day they will pay the bills, but until then, he still leads a double life.

# Acknowledgments

I would like to thank my family above all, my wife, Caroline, and my four amazing children (Alexander, Caitlin, Jessica, and Nathan) for putting up with me and giving me the space to write this title as well as my other extravagances—they truly lift me up and keep me sane. They are my rock, my shore, my world.

I would also like to thank Jamie Hales of PixelBalloon who generously donated some content for the Appendix and gave me new ideas and insights to look in to.

A big shout out to all the guys who ran and helped me out with the Unity porting events, which I supported throughout the course of this book, namely Lee Stott, Simon Michael, Riaz Amhed, Louis Sykes, Ben Beagley, Josh Naylor, Mahmud Chowdhury, and Michael Cameron. Also, the Unity evangelists who were badgered throughout the events and were pumped for hidden details: Joe Robins and Andy Touch. Truly a great crowd to get game developers energized and their titles onto as many platforms as possible. Lots of weekends lost to writing, but the book was better, for it was with so many different experiences.

Finally, thanks to the reviewers of this title who kept me grounded and on target, although that didn't help to keep the page count low—thanks for your support guys.

# About the Reviewers

**Trond Abusdal** first got into programming when writing a modification for Quake2 with a childhood friend, but has been interested in computers since his parents bought him and his brother a C64 in the early 90s.

This interest lead to a Bachelor's degree in Computer Science in 2006, after which he started working for Terravision, a company that uses game technologies as a tool for education and visualization. In 2008, he first got introduced to Unity, which is still his main game development tool, although the knowledge of other technologies and tools often come in handy.

Since 2010, he has been a programmer and more recently a partner at Rock Pocket Games, which makes games for a variety of different platforms, both client projects and internal projects.

**Ben Beagley** is a game development student at the University of Portsmouth, specializing in programming with some design. Currently, he is in his final year after being placed as a member of a small indie development company, the Chromium Gamesroom, that uses Unity as their primary development tool. He also works with Microsoft, promoting development for Windows 8 / Windows Phone 8 with Unity, regularly attending events and helping other Unity developers port their titles. When not working, he enjoys quiet nights in with his girlfriend watching Netflix and getting beaten in all his favorite video games. He has a new development blog where he posts about current projects and uploads old ones at www.benbeagley.com.

**Fredrik Kellermann** is the owner and founder of the independent game development studio CasualGames.nu. He has been involved with the Windows Phone platform since it was released in 2010 and has also been a beta tester of the early version of Unity3D for the Windows Phone platform. Casualgames.nu has since released a number of successful games on the Windows Phone platform reaching more than 4 million downloads.

**Wei Wang** made his first iOS casual game with Unity3D while in his college, which was a huge success with more than 5 million downloads over the world. Since then, he discovered that it is a great thing to create great games. After earning his Master's degree from Tsinghua University (one of the best universities of China), he joined a game company in Japan, and now he is trying to create interesting games with Unity3D.

Right now, he is a skilled engineer and always eager to learn more. He now lives in Kawasaki with his wife. You can know more about him from his project page http://project.onevcat.com or find him on his blog at http://onevcat.com (Chinese). You can also follow him on Twitter at @onevcat.

# www.PacktPub.com

## Support files, eBooks, discount offers, and more

You might want to visit www.PacktPub.com for support files and downloads related to your book.

Did you know that Packt offers eBook versions of every book published, with PDF and ePub files available? You can upgrade to the eBook version at www.PacktPub.com and as a print book customer, you are entitled to a discount on the eBook copy. Get in touch with us at service@packtpub.com for more details.

At www.PacktPub.com, you can also read a collection of free technical articles, sign up for a range of free newsletters and receive exclusive discounts and offers on Packt books and eBooks.

http://PacktLib.PacktPub.com

Do you need instant solutions to your IT questions? PacktLib is Packt's online digital book library. Here, you can access, read and search across Packt's entire library of books.

## Why subscribe?

- Fully searchable across every book published by Packt
- Copy and paste, print and bookmark content
- On demand and accessible via web browser

## Free access for Packt account holders

If you have an account with Packt at www.PacktPub.com, you can use this to access PacktLib today and view nine entirely free books. Simply use your login credentials for immediate access.

# Table of Contents

# Preface

Unity3D has long been viewed as a massive 3D game-making middleware system, with lots of power and an easy-to-use editor. Now, with 2D games back in fashion, Unity has created a 2D toolset for developers with the know-how to create great, customized games.

If you are looking for a book that will show you how to make a fully functional, customizable game product with popular game functionality, then this is the book for you. You will learn how to build an RPG game framework, learning lots of tips and tricks along the way, from advanced C# scripting to getting the most out of Unity's built-in features such as Mecanim and curves, but in ways you may have not even considered.

While creating your own character with its very own little village, you will come to learn about all the new 2D features and how to make the most out of them. Then, you will dive into the big wild world with your character, discovering how to manage different types of scenes, scripting random events, and the dreaded encountering of enemies. You will learn how to make your character ready for battles (with a little shopping) and engaging hordes of angry creatures just rumbling for a fight; how they react is completely up to you.

The one thing this title doesn't cover is audio, as this hasn't changed in Unity 4.3. With so much preparation for Unity 5, it's fair to say that big things are coming; however, there is more than enough to really sink your teeth into.

By the end of this book, you will be able to architect, create, deploy, and integrate your game with all of your intended platforms, and you'll also have the knowledge to build and customize the Unity editor and the games you create with confidence. You will also be schooled with tricks of the trade on marketing and monetization, as well as targeting as many platforms as possible, with a keen focus on how to best profit from your title.

The lessons you will learn in this book will also set you in a good stead for Unity 5 as everything has been checked in the latest beta's. In fact, there is only one slight code change required at the time of writing (which is highlighted in *Chapter 9, Getting Ready to Fight*).

The screens may change slightly, but it all just works. This is both a testament to Unity 5's ability to upgrade projects and that the 2D system is rock solid; everything you learn now will be valid for Unity 5.

*No goblins were hurt during the production of this title; however, a few were extremely grumpy about their poor working conditions.*

# What this book covers

*Chapter 1, Overview*, starts with a look at what Unity has brought to the table from Version 4.2. In this chapter, we will have a walkthrough of the new 2D system and other new features.

*Chapter 2, Character Building*, involves rolling up our sleeves as we dig in and start working with 2D assets and sprites, thereby uncovering the sprite editor and a host of other interesting features.

*Chapter 3, Getting Animated*, introduces that animation is a key in any 2D title; you need more than just a picture to tell a story, so we delve into the new and improved Unity animation system and dope sheet. Beware, curves ahead.

*Chapter 4, The Game World*, explains that with the basics in hand, we will build our home town and let our character run free within it.

*Chapter 5, NPCs and Interactions*, explains that an RPG game without people to talk to would be kind of dull. Here, we will build messaging and conversation systems, readying ourselves to leave the nest and venture beyond. Advanced coding, engage.

*Chapter 6, The Big Wild World*, widens the scope of what we can see, and discusses art and assets, building a map view for the player to navigate in. If you look closely, you can just about see your house from here.

*Chapter 7, Encountering Enemies and Running Away*, discusses that the world is a big and scary place; you stumble upon a crowd of goblins snacking on their latest meal (who knows what's in that pot), and then get scared and run away. Here, we go through building a battle scene, including setting up Mecanim as a state and AI machine.

*Chapter 8, Shopping for Weapons*, dives into lots of shiny things! Leveraging our 2D skills, we build a simple shop scene, reusing our messaging system to add interactivity and expand the player's structure adding an inventory. Plus, we look at the other graphical ways of displaying the player's inventory with a cool command bar implementation.

*Chapter 9, Getting Ready to Fight*, makes us ready to rumble! We have a battle scene but no battle engine yet. Now, it's time to expand on what we have created with a turn-based battle engine, flexing Mecanim's muscles in ways you probably haven't considered.

*Chapter 10, The Battle Begins*, depicts us opening fire (or at least the axe or sword we came with) on the unsuspecting goblins and shattering their tiny bodies with a gratuitous blood scene (PEGI rating pending). From here, it's up to you how you wish to proceed.

*Chapter 11, Onward Wary Traveler*, describes that we have a game framework—all it needs is content and some packaging. So, we'll look at what's involved in finishing your game. Not stopping there, we will look at how you can extend the editor to tame this wild beast to work for us and make it build our content for us (or at the very least, make it a whole lot easier).

*Chapter 12, Deployment and Beyond*, covers the time taken to tackle the last piece of the puzzle, putting your game on a device. We walk through what it means to be multiplatform and build a trustworthy save/load system that will work on multiple platforms, not just one. We finish with a handy marketing section, aimed to arm you and help make your final product successful in the marketplace.

*Appendix, Additional Resources*, has a heap of assets, links, and information resources to help you with your game building travels.

# What you need for this book

In order to follow this book, you will need the Unity 3D software available at `http://unity3d.com/unity/download`.

You can use any version of Unity from Version 4.3, but I recommend the latest 4.x version, which at the time of writing was Version 4.5 (all screenshots have been updated to this version).

You must be familiar with Unity's basic workflow: the words GameObject, components, and Editor/Inspector should be familiar to you.

All the code pertaining to coding skills are available here and explained and commented where appropriate. So, if you are not familiar with them, you will still be able to understand them.

While working with this book, we will be using several freely available assets from the Web, plus a few I cobbled together myself (using my poor programmer art skills). All of these are available as a separate package download along with the book's code downloads mentioned further.

# Who this book is for

Whether you are a beginner starting to work with Unity 3D, an intermediate, or a professional developer looking to make use of the new 2D features of Unity, this book is for you.

The book also covers some intermediate and advanced coding topics, which are explained for developers of any level such that they are easy to follow.

# Conventions

In this book, you will find a number of styles of text that distinguish between different kinds of information. Here are some examples of these styles, and an explanation of their meaning.

Code words in text, database table names, folder names, filenames, file extensions, pathnames, dummy URLs, user input, and Twitter handles are shown as follows: "Using a path-like name such as `playerScene1BounceToWallScript`."

A block of code is set as follows:

```
void OnSceneGUI()
{
  CameraLookAt targetScript = (CameraLookAt)target;
  targetScript.cameraTarget = Handles.PositionHandle
    (targetScript.cameraTarget, Quaternion.identity);
  if (GUI.changed)
  EditorUtility.SetDirty(target);
}
```

When we wish to draw your attention to a particular part of a code block, the relevant lines or items are highlighted:

```
void OnSceneGUI()
{
  CameraLookAt targetScript = (CameraLookAt)target;
```

```
targetScript.cameraTarget = Handles.PositionHandle
    (targetScript.cameraTarget, Quaternion.identity);
Handles.SphereCap(0, targetScript.cameraTarget,
Quaternion.identity, 2);
if (GUI.changed)
EditorUtility.SetDirty(target);
}
```

New terms and important words are shown in bold. Words that you see on the screen, in menus or dialog boxes for example, appear in the text like this: "You can easily change the profile that the editor is using at any time by navigating to **Edit | Project Settings | Editor** and changing the **Default Behavior Mode** option."

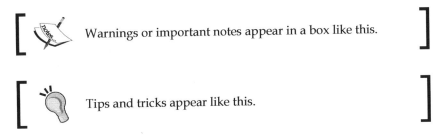

Warnings or important notes appear in a box like this.

Tips and tricks appear like this.

# Reader feedback

Feedback from our readers is always welcome. Let us know what you think about this book—what you liked or may have disliked. Reader feedback is important for us to develop titles that you really get the most out of.

To send us general feedback, simply send an e-mail to feedback@packtpub.com, and mention the book title via the subject of your message.

If there is a topic that you have expertise in and you are interested in either writing or contributing to a book, see our author guide on www.packtpub.com/authors.

# Customer support

Now that you are the proud owner of a Packt book, we have a number of things to help you to get the most from your purchase.

# Downloading the example code

You can download the example code files for all Packt books you have purchased from your account at http://www.packtpub.com. If you purchased this book elsewhere, you can visit http://www.packtpub.com/support and register to have the files e-mailed directly to you.

Additionally, the author has provided a support forum for the book. This forum provides direct support from the author on your queries and any forthcoming announcements regarding the title. You can find this forum at `http://bit.ly/MasteringUnity2DForums`.

# Downloading the color images of this book

We also provide you a PDF file that has color images of the screenshots/diagrams used in this book. The color images will help you better understand the changes in the output. You can download this file from: `https://www.packtpub.com/sites/default/files/downloads/7347OT_Graphics.pdf`.

# Errata

Although we have taken every care to ensure the accuracy of our content, mistakes do happen. If you find a mistake in one of our books—maybe a mistake in the text or the code—we would be grateful if you would report this to us. By doing so, you can save other readers from frustration and help us improve subsequent versions of this book. If you find any errata, please report them by visiting `http://www.packtpub.com/submit-errata`, selecting your book, clicking on the **errata submission form** link, and entering the details of your errata. Once your errata are verified, your submission will be accepted and the errata will be uploaded on our website, or added to any list of existing errata, under the Errata section of that title. Any existing errata can be viewed by selecting your title from `http://www.packtpub.com/support`.

# Piracy

Piracy of copyright material on the Internet is an ongoing problem across all media. At Packt, we take the protection of our copyright and licenses very seriously. If you come across any illegal copies of our works, in any form, on the Internet, please provide us with the location address or website name immediately so that we can pursue a remedy.

Please contact us at `copyright@packtpub.com` with a link to the suspected pirated material.

We appreciate your help in protecting our authors, and our ability to bring you valuable content.

# Questions

You can contact us at `questions@packtpub.com` if you are having a problem with any aspect of the book, and we will do our best to address it.

# 1
# Overview

Arguably, the most important part of any project is knowing where to start and what tools you have in your war chest before setting out to make your game. Here, we will walk through all the new features of the 2D system that were introduced in Version 4.3 of Unity.

Since this is the first chapter, let's cover how this book is structured. The main aim of this book is to build a fully functional **Role Playing Game (RPG)** style game framework and cover all the main aspects of any good and well-rounded RPG game, including the following features:

- Character development and setup
- Building your main game view
- A wider world view
- Events and encounters
- Shopping and inventory systems
- Battles
- Skills, experience, and leveling

We will be visiting places such as the following:

- Your home town, as shown in the following screenshot:

- The local shop, as shown in the following screenshot:

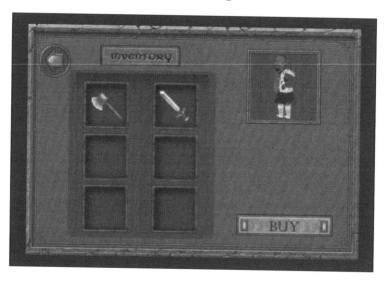

- The outside world, as shown in the following screenshot:

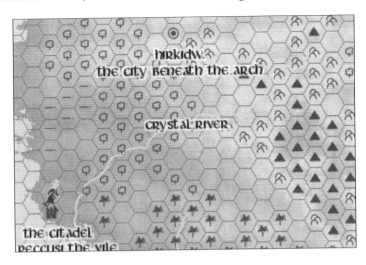

- Battling goblins in the dark forest, as shown in the following screenshot:

In this chapter, we'll walk through what's available in the new 2D toolkit and also what else Unity added to the toolset in 4.3. Then, kick off the next chapter with building the foundations of our project with some of the best practices in the industry, including guidance from the Unity team themselves (either direct from team members or from responses in the forums).

The following topics will be covered in this chapter:

- Overview of the new 2D system
- Rundown of the additional improvements in 4.3

# Getting assets

Since creating games can become quite expensive these days, we'll use some of the best free assets out there. There are plenty of resources available to the game developers these days either as placement assets for the developer's use, whether they are full assets, or just a framework that you can tweak to get your desired result. There are a multitude of options.

> In the code bundle of this book, you'll get all the assets that you need to follow on during the creation of the game, and the site where it is available online will be listed with the instructions.

Some of the best sites to gather assets are described as follows:

- **Art**: Art, especially 2D art, is generally easy to find on a budget; particularly for the placeholder art until you buy or create your own for the finished product (although I've seen many games created with some of these assets). Some good sites to start with are `http://opengameart.org/` and `http://open.commonly.cc/`.
- **Audio**: Right sound is a lot trickier to get. Free sites are okay, but they generally don't have the right sound you will want or you will end up digging through hundreds or more sounds to get a close match. A good website to start is at `http://soundbible.com/`.

> We won't actually be covering audio as part of this title, as not much has changed since the introduction of Unity 4.0. There are also some larger changes being introduced in Unity 5.0 to look out for, so keep your eyes peeled.

# Collection of sites

Some sites just hold a general collection of assets instead of specializing in specific areas. The best site for this, as everything is almost guaranteed to be free, is `http://search.creativecommons.org/`.

For an even wider list of resources, refer to the following blog post that is updated frequently with what's out there:

```
http://darkgenesis.zenithmoon.com/monster-set-of-free-resources-for-
game-design/
```

# Welcome to 2D

Welcome to 2D, as you might say, Unity v4.3 has brought 2D into its primary toolset a huge range of features to make 2D development a lot simpler and more integrated with its editor environment.

What follows is a brief rundown of the entire primary enhancement and a walkthrough of some of the other important improvements brought in with v4.3.

## The new 2D mode

When creating a new Unity project, you now have the option to select whether you want to treat assets as normal 3D assets or use the new 2D import wizards, as shown in the following screenshot:

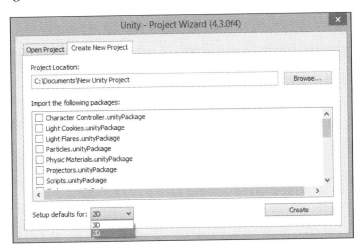

The main difference is the way assets will be imported into your solution and the default camera is set up. You can easily change the profile that the editor is using at any time by navigating to **Edit | Project Settings | Editor** and changing the **Default Behavior Mode** option. This is shown in the following screenshot:

Changing the **Mode** setting will not affect the running of your game. This setting is only used while importing new assets and adding them to your scene as to whether they are imported as textures or sprites.

# Sprites

In 2D, sprites are simple images that generally depict a single object (for example, a character) or scene (for example, background). Several sprites can also be made for a single object in the individual frames for that, as shown here:

At the core of the new 2D system is the new sprite texture importer, which imports your texture assets and prepares them as sprites in your project folder. When dragged on to your scene, they are automatically given a new **Sprite Renderer** object (refer to the next section) that is ready to be displayed in your game; no additional lighting or work is required.

As you would expect, you can alter most of the characteristics of your sprite, including the following characteristics:

- Scaling
- Pivot point
- Sprite region on texture

All of the previous characteristics can be modified straight from the editor or at runtime through code or by using the new animation dope sheet (Unity's new animation editor control).

By default, each texture is imported as a single sprite; however, by using the **Sprite Editor** (refer to the *Sprite Editor* section), you can change this in various ways. These are covered in the next sections.

# Sprite Renderer

The Sprite Renderer is the new 2D renderer to draw sprites to the screen, much in the same way as other Unity renderers draw currently. Refer to the following screenshot:

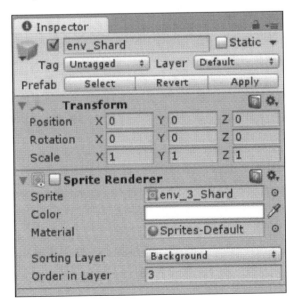

The main difference with the Sprite Renderer object is that you do not need to set up a separate material manually (it is assigned automatically) and the default shader does not require any additional lighting (single vertex lighting is used). You can enhance beyond this by adding your own materials and lighting if you wish; there are certainly no limits here.

The Sprite Renderer, like the other renderers, also supports dynamic batching with uniform scaling as well.

## Sprite Editor

The new **Sprite Editor** object is Unity's way of viewing and manipulating the sprite texture assets once they have been imported into Unity.

The sprite editor window showing a single sprite

The editor allows some basic manipulations to happen to a sprite. For example:

- Changing the Alpha color
- Altering the sprite's pivot position
- Splicing the texture to identify the sprite region (this is also used for spritesheets; refer to the next section)

# Spritesheets

Spritesheets are a core part of any 2D system, especially with 2D animation. Unifying all textures into a single larger texture means greater performance when sending the sprites to the graphic cards in a single texture, which is a lot faster than sending lots of smaller files. Refer to the following screenshot:

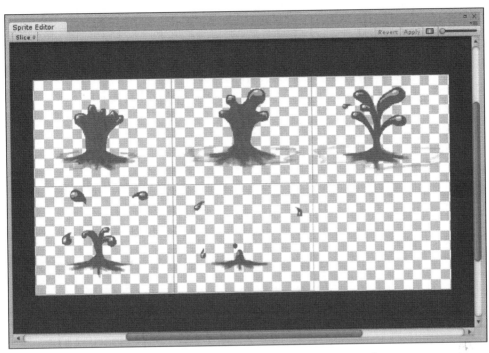

Sprite editor window showing multiple sprites in a grid

The traditional way of forming spritesheets is to put sprites into specific regions on a single image, and then identify the box regions where the individual sprites lie. These regions form individual frames in the sprite animation. As you can see in the preceding screenshot, you have six sprites arranged horizontally in two rows to form a single splash animation. The sprites could have also been arranged in a single row or a single column; it doesn't matter. It's just how the artist best packs the spritesheet for the animation. Unity can handle just about any arrangement you wish to throw at it. Just set the width and height of each texture region and the Unity **Sprite Editor** will do the rest.

# Texture atlases

Akin to spritesheets, texture atlases are a more efficient way of packing textures into a single texture. Refer to the following screenshot:

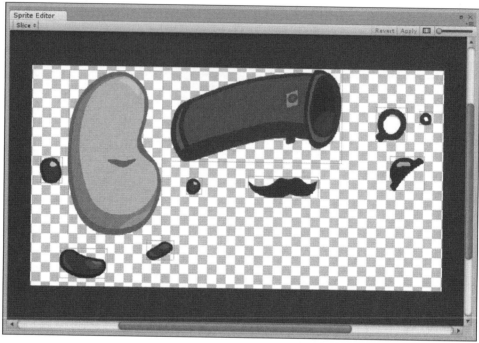

A selection of separate textures that have been automatically packed, example from Unity's platformer sample

Unity has added a very clever texture cutting and edge detection to make this work very well and identify specific regions on the texture for each sprite. You can also change the selection areas if Unity is too optimistic when selecting the texture regions.

If you have the Pro edition of Unity, the editor can also generate these texture atlases for you from many other sprites very efficiently. This saves hours in asset generation.

# Sprite meshes

In Unity Pro, the engine also has the capability to turn your 2D texture asset into a 2D static mesh, which allows you to have greater control over the display and modification of the original texture at runtime. Refer to the following screenshot:

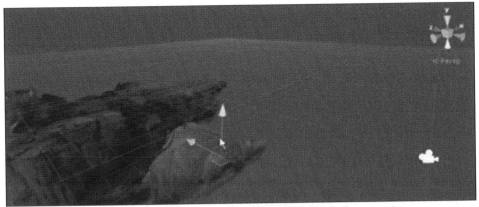

Image sprites that have been converted into 2D meshes in the scene view

You have several options with the mesh feature, and you can decide whether you want a mesh for the entire texture or a single tight mesh for the sprite in parts only (effectively, creating a flat 2D mesh just for your sprite).

This also would enable the ability to rig your sprites and alter their shape during the course of the game.

# The Box2D physics system

For those who have tried (or have created) physics systems in a 3D world of a 2D game, it's always been troublesome to just restrict one of the physics axes; it basically just doesn't work very well and is not as performant as it could be due to all calculations still being in 3D. Refer to the following screenshot:

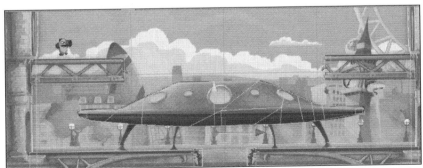

Example of Box2D 2D colliders used in the Unity platformer example to surround walkable elements

More often than not, developers create their own much more simple physics systems (which usually accounts for a high percentage of bugs in games if done wrong).

Unity recognized this limitation while building their 2D system and has pulled in another world class physics system for 2D, called **Box2D**.

> Games such as Angry Birds and Cut the Rope make heavy use of the 2D physics systems to handle a lot of on-screen animation for free using physics.

Box2D has already been used and ported for many other platforms (including XNA), so it makes complete sense for Unity; in most 2D games, you'll see a 4 times increase in the physics performance. Care should be taken, as with every physics system; don't expect it to solve all your problems. Code well and make sure that the standing objects generate interactions.

> If you want to see a great comparison between the 2D and 3D physics systems, refer to this excellent post at http://x-team.com/2013/11/ unity3d-v4-3-2d-vs-3d-physics/.

Through Box2D, Unity adds several new physics collision options. They are as follows:

- **Rigidbody 2D**
- **CircleCollider 2D**
- **BoxCollider 2D**
- **PolygonCollider 2D**
- **EdgeCollider 2D**

Unity also adds the following 2D physics joint options to control how two physics bodies bond together:

- **Distance Joint 2D**
- **Hinge Joint 2D**
- **Slider Joint 2D**
- **Spring Joint 2D**

Similar to the 3D system, you can also apply the physics materials to your 2D objects using **Physics Material 2D**. This allows greater control over an object's physics interactions, such as friction and bounciness.

# The new animation Dope Sheet

The new animation **Dope Sheet**(animation editor) is effectively a second version of the original animation **Dope Sheet**. This area has received a complete overhaul and has now been tightly integrated with the **Mecanim** system. Refer to the following screenshot:

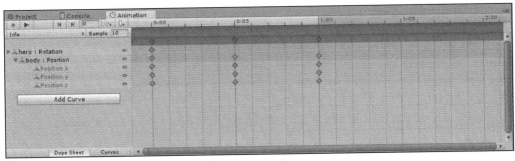

The animation editor **Dope Sheet** window showing a single animation over time

When the recording mode is enabled (it is a small record button at the upper-left of the **Dope Sheet** tab), simply changing any value in the editor while in animator view will create new properties in the animation. These animations can then be enhanced with curves for tweening/lerping support and can have the length of the animation controlled much more easily.

You can also manually edit the **Dope Sheet** tab without the recording mode enabled by adding the curves (the **Animation** properties) and selecting the property on the attached object that you wish to animate.

For extra visibility, there is a **Preview** window next to the **Animator** controls. So, you can see a close up of the effects of the changes you make to the animation.

In the 2D system, animations automatically generated from the spritesheets lean very heavily on this feature, making it very powerful for 2D.

We will cover the animation **Dope Sheet** system in *Chapter 3, Getting Animated*, so stay tuned.

# Other Unity 4.3 improvements

Unity 4.3 was not just about the new 2D system; there are also a host of other improvements and features with this release.

The major highlights of Unity 4.3 are covered in the following sections.

# Improved Mecanim performance

Mecanim is a powerful tool for both 2D and 3D animations. In Unity 4.3, there have been many improvements and enhancements, including a new game object optimizer that ensures objects are more tightly bound to their skeletal systems and removes unnecessary transform holders. Thus making Mecanim animations lighter and smoother. Refer to the following screenshot:

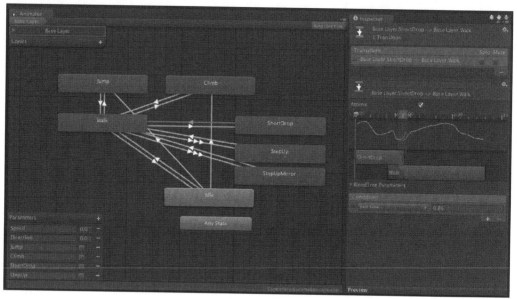

The Mecanim Animator window showing an example animation tree

In Unity 4.3, Mecanim also adds greater control to blend animations together, allowing the addition of curves to have smooth transitions, and now it also includes events that can be hooked into at every step.

# The Windows Phone API improvements and Windows 8.1 support

Unity 4.2 introduced Windows Phone and Windows 8 support, since then things have been going wild, especially since Microsoft has thrown its support behind the movement and offered free licensing for the existing Pro owners. Refer to the following screenshot:

Unity 4.3 builds solidly on the v4 foundations by bringing additional platform support, and it closes some more gaps between the existing platforms. Some of the advantages are as follows:

- The emulator is now fully supported with Windows Phone (new x86 phone build)
- It has more orientation support, which allows even the splash screens to rotate properly and enabling pixel perfect display
- It has trial application APIs for both Phone and Windows 8
- It has improved sensors and location support

On top of this, with the recent release of Windows 8.1, Unity 4.3 now also supports Windows 8.1 fully; additionally, Unity 4.5.3 will introduce support for Windows Phone 8.1 and universal projects.

## Dynamic Nav Mesh (Pro version only)

If you have only been using the free version of Unity till now, you will not be aware of what a Nav Mesh agent is. Nav Meshes are invisible meshes that are created for your 3D environment at the build time to simplify path finding and navigation for movable entities. Refer to the following screenshot:

| Nav Mesh Agent | |
|---|---|
| Radius | 0.5 |
| Speed | 3.5 |
| Acceleration | 8 |
| Angular Speed | 120 |
| Stopping Distance | 0 |
| Auto Traverse Off Mesh Link | ☑ |
| Auto Braking | ☑ |
| Auto Repath | ☑ |
| Height | 2 |
| Base Offset | 0 |
| Obstacle Avoidance Type | High Quality |
| Avoidance Priority | 50 |
| NavMesh Walkable | Everything |

You can, of course, create the simplified models for your environment and use them in your scenes; however, every time you change your scene, you need to update your navigation model. Nav Meshes simply remove this overhead. Nav Meshes are crucial, especially in larger environments where collision and navigation calculations can make the difference between your game running well or not.

Unity 4.3 has improved this by allowing more runtime changes to the dynamic Nav Mesh, allowing you to destroy parts of your scene that alter the walkable parts of your terrain. Nav Mesh calculations are also now multithreaded to give an even better speed boost to your game. Also, there have been many other under-the-hood fixes and tweaks.

## Editor updates

The Unity editor received a host of updates in Unity 4.3 to improve the performance and usability of the editor, as you can see in the following demo screenshot. Granted most of the improvements are behind the scenes.

The improved Unity Editor GUI with huge improvements

The editor refactored a lot of the scripting features on the platform, primarily to reduce the code complexity required for a lot of scripting components, such as unifying parts of the API into single components. For example, the **LookLikeControls** and **LookLikeInspector** options have been unified into a single LookLike function, which allows easier creation of the editor GUI components. Further simplification of the programmable editor interface is an ongoing task and a lot of headway is being made in each release.

Additionally, the keyboard controls have been tweaked to ensure that the navigation works in a uniform way and the sliders/fields work more consistently.

## MonoDevelop 4.01

Besides the editor features, one of the biggest enhancements has to be the upgrade of the **MonoDevelop** editor (http://monodevelop.com/), which Unity supports and is shipped with. This has been a long running complaint for most developers simply due to the brand new features in the later editions. Refer to the following screenshot:

MonoDevelop isn't made by Unity; it's an open source initiative run by Xamarin hosted on **GitHub** (https://github.com/mono/monodevelop) for all the willing developers to contribute and submit fixes to. Although the current stable release is 4.2.1, Unity is not fully up to date. Hopefully, this recent upgrade will mean that Unity can keep more in line with the future versions of this free tool.

Sadly, this doesn't mean that Unity has yet been upgraded from the modified V2 version of the **Mono** compiler (http://www.mono-project.com/) it uses to the current V3 branch, most likely, due to the reduced platform and the later versions of the Mono support.

## Movie textures

Movie textures is not exactly a new feature in Unity as it has been available for some time for platforms such as Android and iOS. However, in Unity 4.3, it was made available for both the new Windows 8 and Windows Phone platforms. This adds even more functionality to these platforms that were missing in the initial Unity 4.2 release where this feature was introduced. Refer to the following screenshot:

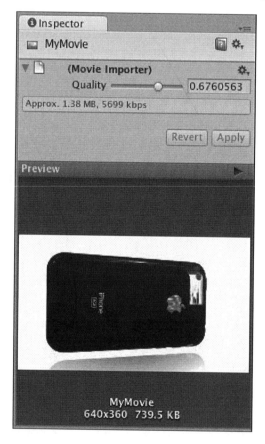

With movie textures now added to the platform, other streaming features are also available, for example, webcam (or a built-in camera in this case) and microphone support were also added.

# Summary

So, now you can see what all the excitement is about with the new Unity 4.3 release. Unity has gone a long way to address the gaps in their product and added some new bells and whistles to boot. You should also watch the keynotes at `http://unity3d.com/unite/archive`, especially to see what else is coming up (such as the new GUI system coming in Version 4.6).

We covered the objective of the book, the paths to get the assets needed for the sample project, a detailed analysis of the new 2D features added in Unity 4.3, and a rundown of the additional features in 4.3 for reference.

Are you seated comfortably? Well keep your arms and legs in the ride at all times and prepare yourself for a high-speed ride.

# 2
# Character Building

It's time to start putting in the building blocks that will make up your game, starting with setting up the project and then on to main character. It's an important first step as most of your game's core logic and framework generally centers on the main protagonist and highlights exactly how the player will interact with the game.

Here, we are aiming to create a 2.5D style in-game world where the player can explore each town and have random encounter scenes to fight off those pesky bad guys. So, first we need to get our character in and moving.

The following is the list of topics that will be covered in this chapter:

- Designing a good class structure
- Planning and designing behaviors
- Importing sprites
- Setting up user control effectively

For this game, we will use the excellent, free **Unity games starter kit** resources, which can be found at `http://wootstudio.ca/win8platstarter` (towards the bottom of the page).

There are several different themed sets of assets for use in any game (commercial or otherwise). For the purpose of this book, we will use the **Fantasy** pack and its associated **Backgrounds**.

Additional assets that I have created myself will be included with the associated code bundle of this title.

# Getting your project started – the right way

Before you start your project for real, you should consider how you intend to set it up and architect your project in the long term. I've looked at or worked with far too many projects that have created problems for themselves by just diving in rather than designing the outline for the project at the start.

Your game and your assets are not the only things to consider when starting a fresh project. Sure, you can start importing assets, creating scripts, and getting things running; most **Proof of Concept (POC)** projects start this way. Once your project is of a sufficient size and you start expanding on your initial concept, you'll realize that you have issues with regards to picking up items and putting them together. Then, you will start devising new ways to organize your project and eventually find that it's an unmanageable mess; nevertheless, you will stride on, taking longer and longer to produce new content or add new features.

The best advice one can give is to think about your entire project and how you organize it as an asset in itself, and accordingly, design it correctly from the beginning. So, what follows are a few short tricks that you can learn to get started on the right foot.

Architecture is a point that is often missed out in any game development and should not be overlooked. What follows are some of the best practices you can use from day 1 to design your game and thereby save a lot of time to fix or change and reorder things later. These lessons will be used throughout the course of the book wherever applicable.

 As this chapter focuses on the implementation of the 2D sprite system, we will return to these lessons later in *Chapter 5, NPCs and Interactions*; however, they are critical at this juncture, that is, before we write the code.

# Structure

When building games with Unity, especially when you are prototyping, you will find that most projects have all their assets in the root of their Unity project folder or are organized by how your game works. This isn't particularly wrong, but as your project gets larger, this will eventually cause problems.

The best way in which Unity advises you to organize your project (as also shown in all of their own examples) is to group objects by their type in the root `Assets` folder, as shown in the following screenshot:

This ensures that you will find assets for your entire project that are ready for reuse in every scene or level according to the type of object. You can then subdivide these appropriately depending on their use, such as the following:

- Separating animation clips from all the controllers that may act on them or on your models:

- Grouping audio by its intended use in your game, such as enemies, special effects, and background music:

- Grouping prefabs by layer or their intended use:

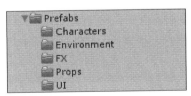

- Sprites can also be structured in the same way; you can order them according to how they should be used in your project:

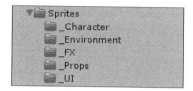

By following the preceding patterns, you are organizing your project effectively in the same way Unity itself does under the covers and guides you to use a more component-based design. Each scene is built up of many components through the lifetime of your project, so organizing your assets this way will help in the long run.

You can set this level of subgrouping for scripts, scenes, fonts, materials, and so on. However, as these are generally distinct things that apply to every component, there is no need to divide them further.

# Object naming

There are no specific patterns for how you should name each object/component in your asset library as such. Generally, this is left to your preference, and more importantly, how you recognize each part of your game. There is no need to give something a really long and complicated name in the preceding structure, only so long that you can find it later.

Many of the other tutorials I have read or watched tend to lean on a few patterns for naming, most of which seem to follow the usual coding standards such as the following:

- Prefixing the name with a three letter acronym for its type: scn for a scene, efx for an effect, and so on

- Suffixing an underscore plus the same three letter acronym to the end of an asset's name

- Using a path-like name such as playerScene1BounceToWallScript

From experience, these are useful, but my advice is to name things plainly based on what it is. Using the structure mentioned earlier, you have already organized your assets to overcome a lot of the issues that the preceding patterns try to solve.

Plan ahead before you even start your game and set a standard that works for you. You should be able to identify what each asset is and what it does just by looking at the name. However, remember that each asset will most likely be used many times on many different game objects, so plan accordingly. Add prefixes and suffixes only when a script or asset is intended to be limited to a certain type of game object.

The Unity examples are another good place to look for inspiration here. See the following screenshot and decide whether you can tell what these scripts are and what they are used for just by looking at them:

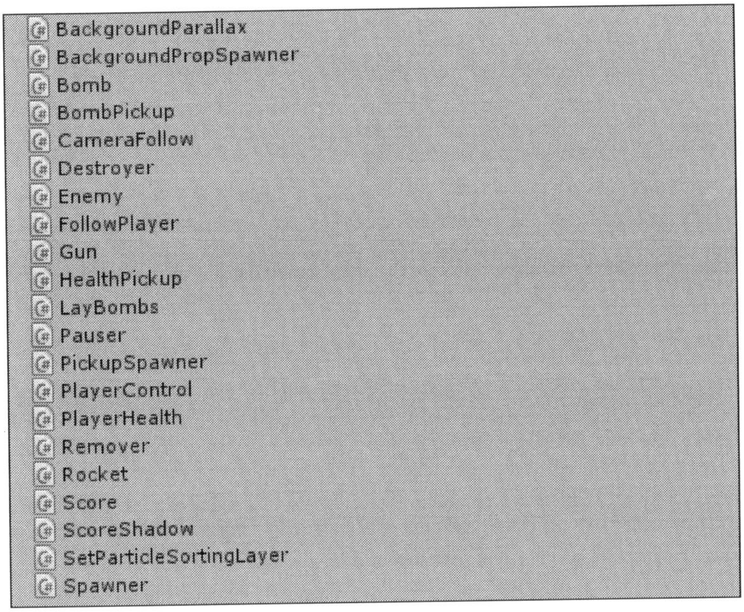

# Understanding components

Components in Unity are the building blocks of any game; almost everything you will use or apply will end up as a component on a `GameObject` inspector in a scene.

Until you build your project, Unity doesn't know which components will be in the final game when your code actually runs (there is some magic applied in the editor). So, these components are not actually attached to your `GameObject` inspector but rather linked to them.

# Accessing components using a shortcut

In most Unity examples, you are shown how to access components through scripts by using shortcuts to the MonoBehaviour class that the game object inherits from. Accessing the components with the help of the following code:

```
this.renderer.collider.attachedRigidbody.angularDrag = 0.2f;
```

 If you need any help with this title or have any suggestions on it, join in on the support forum for the book at http://bit.ly/ MasteringUnity2DForums. The forum will also keep you updated on any announcements on the title, so check it often.

What Unity then does behind the scenes for you is that it converts the preceding code to the following code:

```
var renderer = this.GetComponent<Renderer>();
var collider = renderer.GetComponent<Collider>();
var rigidBody = collider.GetComponent<Rigidbody>();
rigidBody.angularDrag = 0.2f;
```

The preceding code will also be the same as executing the following code:

```
GetComponent<Renderer>().GetComponent<Collider>().GetComponent<Rig
    idbody>().angularDrag = 0.2f;
```

Now, while this is functional and working, it isn't very performant or even a best practice as it creates variables and destroys them each time you use them; it also calls GetComponent for each component every time you access them. Using GetComponent in the Start or Awake methods isn't too bad as they are only called once when the script is loaded; however, if you do this on every frame in the update method, or even worse, in FixedUpdate methods, the problem multiplies; not to say you can't, you just need to be aware of the potential cost of doing so.

# A better way to use components – referencing

Now, every programmer knows that they have to worry about garbage and exactly how much memory they should allocate to objects for the entire lifetime of the game.

To improve things based on the preceding shortcut code, we simply need to manually maintain the references to the components we want to change or affect on a particular object. So, instead of the preceding code, we could simply use the following:

```
Rigidbody myScriptRigidBody;
void Awake()
{
  var renderer = this.GetComponent<Renderer>();
  var collider = renderer.GetComponent<Collider>();
  myScriptRigidBody = collider.GetComponent<Rigidbody>();
}
void Update()
{
  myScriptRigidBody.angularDrag = 0.2f * Time.deltaTime;
}
```

This way the `Rigidbody` object that we want to affect can simply be discovered once (when the scripts awakes); then, we can just update the reference each time a value needs to be changed instead of discovering it every time.

## An even better way

Now, it has been pointed out (by those who like to test such things) that even the `GetComponent` call isn't as fast as it should be because it uses C# generics to determine what type of component you are asking for (it's a two-step process: first, you determine the type and then get the component).

However, there is another overload of the `GetComponent` function in which instead of using generics, you just need to supply the type (therefore removing the need to discover it). To do this, we will simply use the following code instead of the preceding `GetComponent<>`:

```
myScriptRigidBody = (Rigidbody2D)GetComponent
    (typeof(Rigidbody2D));
```

The code is slightly longer and arguably only gives you a marginal increase, but if you need to use every byte of the processing power, it is worth keeping in mind.

If you are using the "." shortcut to access components, I recommend that you change that practice now. In **Unity 5**, they are being removed. There will, however, be a tool built in the project's importer to upgrade any scripts you have using the shortcuts that are available for you. This is not a huge task, just something to be aware of; act now if you can!

# Creating the project

First things first! To ensure that you have all the bases covered, you need to start a new project. For 2D, however, you need to ensure that you start the project using the *2D game template* in the Unity New Project wizard, as shown in the following screenshot:

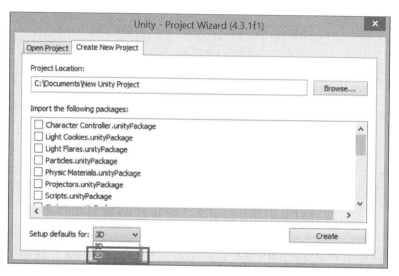

If you accidentally leave the 3D option set (which is the default) as is, don't worry! You can change this at any time for your project through **Editor Settings**. To open **Editor Settings**, simply navigate to **Edit | Project Settings | Editor**, as shown in the following screenshot:

Lastly, let's create the folder structure for the project, as shown in the following screenshot, using the guidance provided earlier:

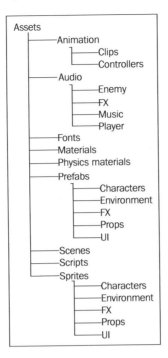

At this point, it's important to note that we will most likely not use all of these folders during the course of the book. Nevertheless, it is a good working practice to get these set up for every project just so that you have a standard template.

 This book will cover the process of creating your own project template later in *Chapter 12, Deployment and Beyond*, which will create a standard asset for our folder structure to import the setup of the project's framework automatically; let's get on and start populating it.

# Classes

Architecting the core of your game from the beginning is an often-skipped process. Because we're too eager to just get on and build our game, let's jump straight in and start placing assets in a scene, adding them as we go. This kind of practice is fine for prototypes (mostly, however, even with prototypes, a level of architecture is usually required). When building your actual product, however, without setting up a proper architecture from the beginning, you are heading toward a world of utter mess.

When we say architecture, it doesn't mean that you need to design everything (but it helps). You just need to ensure that you plan what you are going to build before you build it instead of thinking about stuff and checking Google for information on how to do it. Even if you are using some kind of an agile method, you should have a good framework and goal for each sprint as you plan for each sprint. This will guide you on what should be done and when, not just designing the project on the fly.

# The object-orientated design

Unity in itself is a fully **object-orientated** (OO) system with strict interfaces to ensure that the engine knows what to expect and when, so why shouldn't your game follow the same pattern? Unity is also component-based, which is something else to take into account while designing how your game will be put together.

At the core of any object-orientated design, the focus is on reusability. If a set of attributes is repeatedly used across multiple objects, then they should be separated into one common class and shared in much the same way we do with code refactoring; in addition to this, you should also reduce the amount of code that is lying about doing the same job. This means that we can more easily make changes to this base set without having to re-edit all the classes that might need those attributes. The following diagram shows two approaches of using a base class to define common attributes over multiple code implementations:

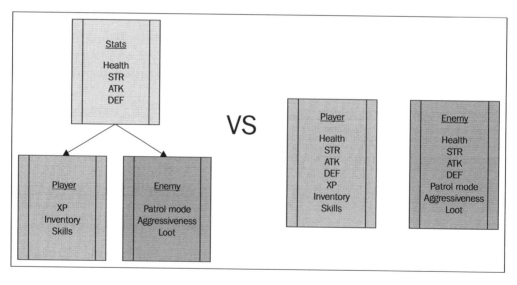

Another facet of OO is to employ interfaces to govern exactly how a class should look if you have multiple objects of the same type. For example, you have an `Enemy` class structure that defines how enemies in general should work; then, using that same structure, you specify all the enemy implementations, such as zombies, spiders, and white-fanged rabbits. Interfaces can also define behaviors or methods on a class, so you can ensure that all the classes that implement that interface will always have the same common abilities, such as all the enemies will have `patrol`, `Fight`, and `run away` methods. This means that if you have an enemy object, it will always have those methods attached to them when you refer to them in the code.

The following diagram shows how you can plan for multiple inheritances, allowing you to add a common behavior pattern to each group of entities:

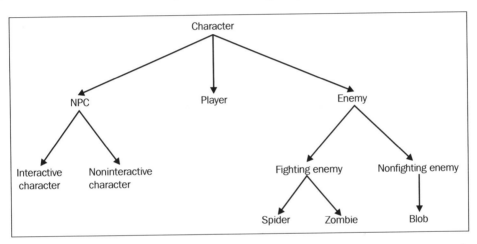

Knowing this helps us design our game effectively and ensures that we architect it correctly from the beginning.

We'll discuss these patterns in more detail when we implement them in the following sections.

# The game structure

To keep in line with the preceding architecture set, we'll design the layout of the class to support a flexible structure that will be easily extended in the future.

# The common game object

As almost every entity in our game will have statistics and some basic behaviors, we start with a generic object (Entity) to define the attributes that all the entities in our game will have. As there is only one entity type, we don't need to set up an interface for this object as all the other game objects will just use this one definition, as shown in the following diagram:

This shows that we have several common attributes for things such as health and strength. This Entity object is implemented in the code as follows in a C# script called **Entity** in the Assets\Scripts folder:

```
using UnityEngine;
public class Entity : ScriptableObject
{
    public string Name;
    public int Age;
    string Faction;
    public string Occupation;
    public int Level = 1;
    public int Health = 2;
    public int Strength = 1;
    public int Magic = 0;
    public int Defense = 0;
    public int Speed = 1;
```

```
public int Damage = 1;
public int Armor = 0;
public int NoOfAttacks = 1;
public string Weapon;
public Vector2 Position;
}
```

 The entity class is inherited from a specialized class called `ScriptableObject`. This is essential to know how we will use it in the game. We will cover `ScriptableObject` in more detail in *Chapter 5, NPCs and Interactions.*

## The player object

Basing the player's character on the `Entity` object makes the definition of the player a lot simpler. So, you only need to focus on what is specific to the player's character itself, that is, the differences between the player and all the other game entities.

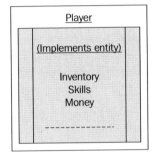

So, the player character we see here is the only one who has **Inventory, Money,** and **Skills** since they are specific to our hero's work in our game. This is implemented in the following code with the player inheriting all the properties from the `Entity` class in another new C# script called **Player** in the `Assets\Scripts` folder:

```
using UnityEngine;
public class Player : Entity
{
  public string[] Inventory;
  public string[] Skills;
  public int Money;
}
```

Preferably, all the attributes of any class should be of the read-only type outside of the class itself (unless there is a very good reason for it). This is to ensure that you don't mistakenly change a class's value without knowing why. It might sound easier to just keep updating everything, but at some point, while you are debugging, you will want to know why things are changing. If any code updates these values, then you will literally spend hours trying to find why. If you need to change values, then you need to implement behaviors (see the following sections).

## More later

To show you how to build the architecture progressively in this project, we will add more classes to each section; we'll keep things simple and build the project with a strong foundation.

We already have our base entity in place from which all the game entities as well as our player are driven, so let's look at implementing them further.

# Planning behaviors

Behaviors are just a fancy way of saying *things or interactions that will happen in the game*. Breaking down these actions or reactions in this way helps to componentize how we think our game will work. Stopping and thinking about this from the very beginning means we won't get too many surprises later on. (There are always surprises after a good night's sleep.)

For example, behaviors can take the following forms:

- Attacking another entity
- Taking damage
- Collecting the loot, which could be money or items
- Teleporting to another land

It is also important to note that visual effects as the result of a behavior or action are different to those that affect the characteristics of the game's object. You may have a visual representation as the result of a behavior or action (for example, a particle effect when taking damage or the character swinging their sword to attack), but in Unity especially, you have to keep these separate. We will cover more on this later.

> In traditional games that are built using other systems, bundling visual interactions or audio with behaviors is quite common. However, Unity forces you to think differently; it recommends you to work with the system, not against it.

Behaviors on classes should only affect the class that it is defined on. If you are going to affect another class's attributes, it should be through another behavior on that class.

It is far too easy to simply perform `player.health = 10` rather than `player.damage(10)`; this way any side effects or saves from damage can be taken into account within the class itself. Read on!

# Behaviors for the common game object

As we have an existing class for common game objects (`Entity`), we can start to define some behaviors that are common to all the characters in our RPG game, namely, the following objects:

- `TakeDamage`: This is an object where a character can be damaged. Keeping this object as common ensures that the calculation of damages is the same for all.

- `Attack`: This is an object where a character can attack another character; if successful, it deals with damage, or in rare occurrences, it makes characters hurt themselves. Again, having one way to calculate this helps in battle games so that attacks are balanced.

So, if we add these behaviors to our `Entity` object, we get something that looks like the following screenshot:

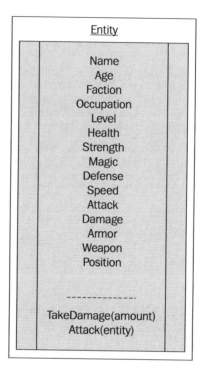

The behaviors shown in the preceding screenshot would add the following to the `Entity` class code:

```
public void TakeDamage(int Amount) { Health -
  = Mathf.Clamp((Amount - Armor),0,int.MaxValue);}

public void Attack(Entity Entity)
  { Entity.TakeDamage(Strength); }
```

We'll not implement these actual behaviors in the code just yet as we will cover them in more detail when we visit the battle system. For now, we are just setting the ground work for what we expect to use in the game.

# Behaviors for the player's character

For now, we won't add any further behaviors to the player; we will simply evolve it as we require it.

If you are feeling adventurous using what was previously detailed, try sketching out what kind of behaviors a player's character might have and then compare/test them against future chapters.

# Introducing the Unity sprite system

Armed with the data we need for our player character in our game world, let us now turn to the visual side of things and get our first 2D visual elements into our game, starting with our hero.

Before the new 2D system was implemented in Unity 4.3, setting up a 2D-rendering system was a tortuous affair that required importing texture assets, creating a 2D-fixed camera system, implementing 2D lighting and a rendering pipeline, and either constraining a physics system to just two dimensions or building your own. It didn't stop there as there was a lot more to contend with, including an endless Z-order fighting to draw the textures correctly (which the new 2D-sorting layers resolve quite nicely). Most developers just ended up using one of the many 2D asset packages from the store to solve a lot of these issues, but it was still a huge challenge to get them right.

Now, with Unity's 2D pipeline, things are a lot simpler. I almost envy new developers who come to the platform for the extra free tools they wish to arm themselves with to build their projects. Unity doesn't stop there though as there are many more new developments heading our way, such as the new UI system that was introduced at the Unite keynote in Vancouver.

 If you haven't done so already, I recommend that you at least watch the keynotes from Unity's Unite conferences at http://Unity3D.com/unite. Watch more if you can as they will provide you with a keen insight into what is to come and also how to use it in advance in most cases.

Some sessions will also show you how to better use the existing features as a lot of the sessions are created from the leading issues in the forums.

# Importing sprites

When a Unity project is in 2D mode, the first change you will notice is that when new images are imported into the project, they are configured as sprites instead of just normal textures, as shown in the following screenshots:

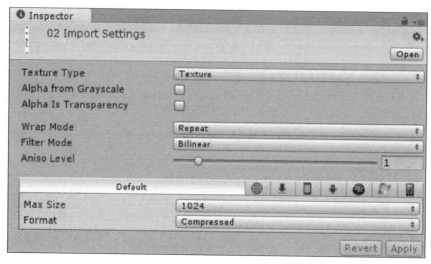

Imported texture properties

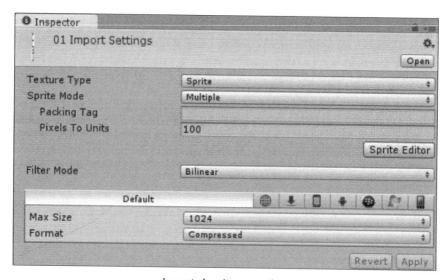

Imported sprite properties

So, let's go into a bit more detail as to what these new properties mean.

# Texture type – sprite

Setting this option changes the import settings for the asset. Note the changes that take place when you click on **Apply** or **OK** on the **Import Settings** change dialog.

# Sprite Mode – single/multiple

This setting tells Unity whether there is a single sprite or multiple sprites within the imported image. In Unity 4.3, only after you select **Multiple** will the **Sprite Editor** become available, however in later versions, the Sprite Editor is always available.

# Packing tag

This is a customizable option that lets you set groups to pack sprites into texture atlases. By setting this up, it tells Unity to group all the objects with the same tag under a separate texture atlas/sheet together, thereby overriding the default behavior of placing all the assets on the same atlas. Any assets without a tag will be grouped onto the default atlas.

Texture Atlas packing is a Unity Pro feature that will not be covered in this book. You can read more about it at `http://docs.Unity3D.com/Documentation/Manual/SpritePacker.html`.

If you don't have access to Unity Pro, there are a few texture packing tools out in the wild that prepack the assets for you (such as Nvidia's texture asset tools available at `https://developer.nvidia.com/legacy-texture-tools`). Once there, Unity will automatically split them up for you; more on this later.

# Pixels to units

This option is just a setting that allows you to scale the image asset at import time, the default being 100 pixels per unit (or scaled up to 100 percent).

This setting is important because it sets the relative scale of the assets you will import to your defined game units. This is just as important in 2D as it is in 3D. Your base game unit guides you on how all the assets will scale appropriately to each other, and more importantly, to the camera.

You can manage the game scale through this setting, or you can handle this scale through the original texture's sizes; the choice is up to you.

# The Sprite Editor button

When **Sprite Mode** is set to **Multiple**, the button to open the editor (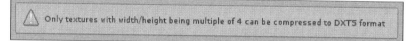) becomes available.

Once you click on the **Sprite Editor** button, you will be presented with the new **Sprite Editor** main window.

All the other settings under the sprite **Inspector** are pretty much the same with the exception of the texture compression setting.

 When the sprite texture type is selected, you will get warnings if your image is not using a power of 2 size texture; this means that the height must be a multiple of 2 against the image's width, so W2/H4 is a power of 2 whereas W3/H4 is not. This is not critical as Unity will still make best efforts to compress the image; it just won't be as small as it should be. Unity will warn you about this with the following information box in the inspector:

> ⚠ Only textures with width/height being multiple of 4 can be compressed to DXT5 format

 If your sprites look blocky or blurry on screen, be sure to check your sprite texture's import compression level. If the texture's resolution is higher than your import setting, then Unity will do its best to compress the texture (scale it down), which can cause some weird onscreen artifacts (especially if the difference is large, for example, a 4KB texture compressed down to 1KB). Make sure this is what you want or resize your original textures.

# Sprite Editor

Sprite Editor, as the name suggests is Unity's new tool to allow the carving up of spritesheets and texture atlases to identify individual sprites for use in your game; also, it comes with several simple yet powerful features to control how the individual sprites will be imported, as shown in the following screenshot:

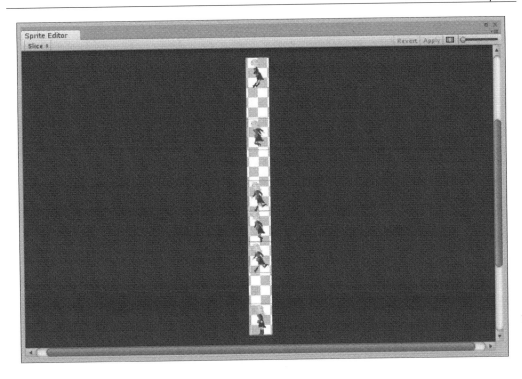

In the editor, you have two sets of functions: the sprite splitter and the view controls.

# Sprite splitter (slicer)

The splitter or slicer has two modes, automatic and grid (manual), in which it can carve up your spritesheet to create individual images for use in your game.

## Automatic

Unity has put some very smart logic into its automatic sprite carving system that can quite easily identify regions in your spritesheet where your images are packed. Plus, you have some advanced options to guide the system to make it fit for your game, as shown in the following screenshot:

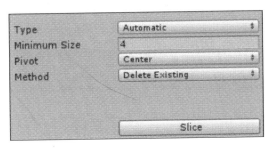

The carving is based on the alpha regions within the texture, so bear this in mind. The following are the advanced options provided by Unity:

- **Minimum size**: Setting the minimum size of the sprite defines the smallest pixel-grouping size on the image to select a single sprite. Setting this to a larger value constrains the selection logic to look for larger groups of sprites. It can also be viewed as the minimum space between the sprites on the sheet.

- **Pivot**: As the name suggests, it allows you to set the default pivot position at import time for the sprites that it creates by default.

- **Method**: This option has the following options to guide the selection logic to identify sprites:

  ○ **Delete existing**: Selecting this option will clear all the existing sprite ranges from the sheet.

   This is the default option and Sprite Editor will not select any sprites until you select one of the sprite identification methods.

  ○ **Smart**: This option will try to identify common patterns in the sprites from the sheet meant for selection. In some cases, it is able to identify groups that make up a single sprite together.

  ○ **Safe**: This option focuses on tighter regions around each element it identifies on the spritesheet, thereby making the edges as close as possible.

## Grid (manual)

The grid option is a lot simpler with no complex logic. It simply allows you to define (as the name suggests) a grid over the spritesheet with defined cell sizes by setting the height and width options, as shown in the following screenshot:

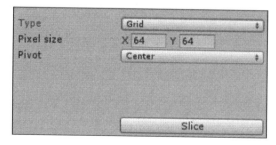

Unity will then automatically identify sprites based on that grid. Note that it will also ignore any blank areas on the spritesheet by default, so keep this in mind if you need them.

If you do not see a selection box around your sprites, then check your height and width settings against the original size of the spritesheet. Normally, you will not see anything if the sizes are too big.

My advice is to start with a smaller size where the grid shows up and alter the width and height settings upwards until you are happy with the selection on the entire sheet, especially if you are unsure of the dimensions of each sprite.

# View controls

The view controls simply change or affect what you are viewing in **Sprite Editor**, as shown in the following screenshot:

The following are the view controls provided by Unity:

1. **Revert**: This control simply resets the texture back to the original settings the editor had when it was opened or when the apply option was used to save. Note that this is not simply an undo button as it completely resets the editor back to the beginning.

2. **Apply**: As the name suggests, this applies any changes you have made in the editor. If you close the editor and keep the changes pending, you will be prompted to apply the changes. Note that once you apply your changes, these *cannot* be undone, so when you click on apply, be sure that the changes refer to what you actually want.

3. **Alpha/Color**: This control simply changes the view between fully textured sprites or just the alpha regions. It is useful if you want to see what the automatic splitting options are using to identify individual sprites.

4. **Zoom slider**: This control is used to zoom in and zoom out. Need I say more?

# Sprite region manipulation

Once you have your individual regions identified on the spritesheet, you can still further change the import settings for each sprite as if they were imported individually; this is shown in the following screenshot:

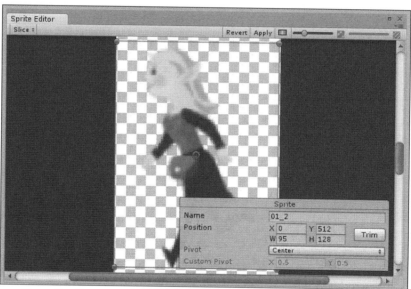

The sprite editor zoomed in on a single sprite from the spritesheet shown earlier

In the preceding screenshot where a single sprite is selected, you can clearly alter the name, the position of the spritesheet the sprite is picked from, its width and height, and also the pivot point using the sprite selection inspector.

Additionally, you can use the selection box surrounding the sprite to alter the settings graphically using the hook points in each corner or by dragging the pivot circle to the center to alter the pivot's rotation point.

The settings you will change with a single sprite selected will only affect that sprite and not the rest that are on the spritesheet, so keep this in mind if the sprite you are editing is part of an animation.

# Putting it together

So now that we have understood how to import our 2D assets into our project and how the sprite system works, let's look at building our game with it.

**Downloading the example code**

You can download the example code files for all Packt books you have purchased from your account at `http://www.packtpub.com`. If you purchased this book elsewhere, you can visit `http://www.packtpub.com/support` and register to have the files e-mailed directly to you.

I'm going to talk about the usual thought process that is used to build such systems and highlight issues that you might commonly face and how to resolve them, rather than just pointing out fingers and saying do this and that.

The lessons learned in the *Classes* section are very important lessons to learn early on as we are just starting out with the 2D features. We won't use them just yet but refer to this again when we hit *Chapter 5, NPCs and Interactions*, and start implementing them fully.

# Importing our main character

So with what we have learned, let us get our main character imported into our game.

Select the image titled `01.png` from the `01_characters` folder under `FANTASY_PACK` from the free game art pack, then drag it to the `Characters` folder under `Assets\Sprites\` in your Unity project, as shown in the following screenshot:

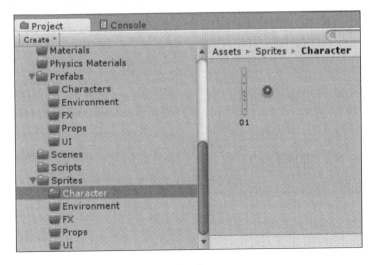

Next, as our image contains all the frames of the sprite's animation for our main character, we need to break it up. So select the image from the project view and change **Sprite Mode** in the **Inspector** to **Multiple**, as shown in the following screenshot:

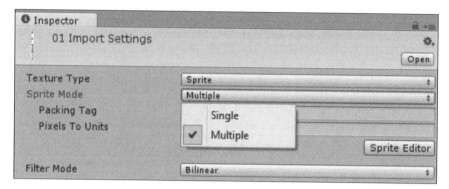

You should now see that the **Sprite Editor** button is now enabled; click on it to bring up the **Sprite Editor** window, as shown in the following screenshot:

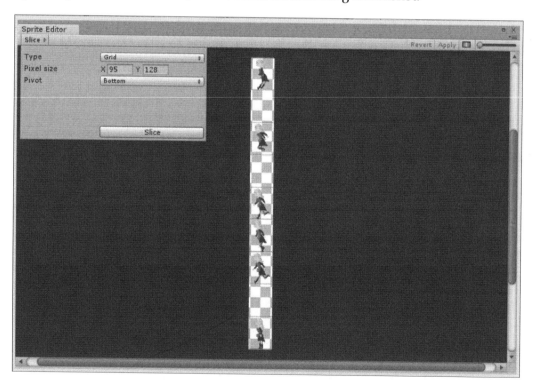

To carve up our sprites, change the slicing options to Grid and enter a width of 95 and a height of 128; then, click on **Slice**, as shown in the preceding screenshot. Leave the **Pivot** point as Bottom.

Now, click on **Apply** and close Sprite Editor. Upon returning to the project view, you should now see an arrow symbol next to the image asset we imported; clicking on it will show you all the individual sprites that were identified, excluding any blank spaces on the sheet as shown in the following screenshot:

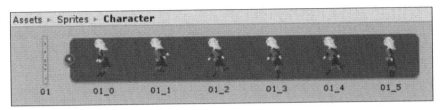

Now that we have our character in our project and it is properly imported, let's put our hero into the scene.

# The hero

Earlier, we imported our hero character's spritesheet into our project and carved up the sprites from that sheet to ensure they are ready to use. So, let's first just get him or her into the play area.

As with most things in Unity, there are two ways in which we can do this; first, we'll do this manually and then show you a shortcut route. The following steps describe the manual procedure:

1. Create an empty game object in our game's hierarchy for our hero (by navigating to **GameObject** | **Create Empty** in the menu) and name it Player.

2. Add a sprite renderer component to the player's game object by navigating to **Add Component** | **Rendering** | **Sprite Renderer**.

3. Expand the 01 asset in the Sprite folder so that you can see all the sprites in that spritesheet.

4. Drag the sprite named 01_5 (the idle sprite) to the Sprite parameter of the sprite renderer on the player's game object.

Be sure to set your transform values for the new game object to 0 or it will create issues later with the animation. Always define animations with objects set at the center to avoid confusion; you can always move/place them later.

You should now have the same screen as shown in the following screenshot:

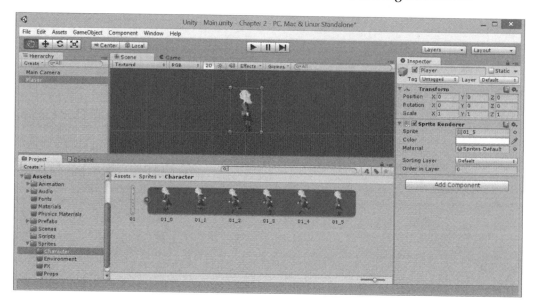

 Alternatively, you can just drag the individual sprite on to the project hierarchy to achieve the same effect.

# Controlling the hero

A sprite that only stands on the screen isn't going to make much of a game, so we'll add a script to allow the player to move the hero to the left or right.

First, we'll add the physics component to control the movements related to our hero; we don't need anything heavy, just a rigidbody so that we won't pass through other objects in the world and a collider so that we know when we bump into things:

1.  Add a `Rigidbody2D` component by navigating to **Add Component | Physics2D | Rigidbody 2D** in the player's `GameObject` inspector.

2.  Set the **Gravity Scale** parameter to `0` (as we are not using gravity), and check the **Fixed Angle** checkbox (as we want the player to always remain in the standing position).

3.  Next, add a `BoxCollider2D` component by navigating to **Add Component | Physics2D | Box Collider 2D**, and scale down the **Size X** parameter to `0.41` (just to narrow the collision box to the width of the hero).

This should give you the following view in the inspector:

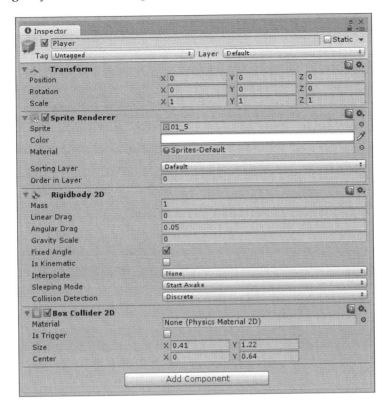

 As we are only setting up the basic physics and collisions, we won't be using the full range of Rigidbody 2D settings. For more details on what the rest of the Rigidbody 2D properties do, check the Unity Rigidbody video at https://www.youtube.com/watch?v=rq6c2B_socs.

To finish off this chapter, add a new C# script to the Scripts folder by navigating to **Create | C# script** in the project window and saving it as Assets\Scripts\ CharacterMovement.cs. Open the script in the editor and replace its contents with the following script:

```
using UnityEngine;

public class CharacterMovement : MonoBehaviour
{
```

```
// RigidBody component instance for the player
private Rigidbody2D playerRigidBody2D;

//Variable to track how much movement is needed from input
private float movePlayerVector;

// For determining which way the player is currently facing.
private bool facingRight;

// Speed modifier for player movement
public float speed = 4.0f;

//Initialize any component references
void Awake()
{
  playerRigidBody2D = (Rigidbody2D)GetComponent
    (typeof(Rigidbody2D));
}

// Update is called once per frame
void Update () {
  // Get the horizontal input.
  movePlayerVector = Input.GetAxis("Horizontal");

  playerRigidBody2D.velocity = new Vector2(movePlayerVector *
    speed, playerRigidBody2D.velocity.y);

  if (movePlayerVector > 0 && !facingRight)
  {
    Flip();
  }
  else if (movePlayerVector < 0 && facingRight)
  {
    Flip();
  }
}

void Flip()
{
  // Switch the way the player is labeled as facing.
  facingRight = !facingRight;

  // Multiply the player's x local scale by -1.
  Vector3 theScale = transform.localScale;
  theScale.x *= -1;
  transform.localScale = theScale;
}
```

The script is fairly basic; it simply has some parameters to control the speed and its facing direction. The `update` method checks if the player is controlling the game using the default horizontal keys (left and right) and then applies force to move the hero accordingly. Finally, we check which way the hero is facing, and based on the direction the player has pressed, it will flip the sprite to face the correct direction.

 The `scale` parameters are a common way to swap which way a sprite is drawn toward. This means you don't need sprites for every single angle of your game; you can just flip or rotate them.

To finish off, add the script to the player's game object by either dragging it to the object in the hierarchy or navigating to **Add Component | Scripts | Character Movement**.

 You should note that this very simple controller code only uses a keyboard input. For touch-only-based platforms such as iOS, WP8, and arguably Android, you would need to include touch controls or use the accelerometer.

If you run the project now, you should see our hero on the screen, and using the left and right arrows on the keyboard, we will move the player to the left or right.

 An alternative approach to writing your own controller code is to make use of the built-in `Character controller` components of Unity. These components help you reduce the amount of code you need to control a player's movements and also add other recommended components such as physics.

You should also check out Unity's enhanced **Sample Assets Beta**, which introduces a new true multiplatform singular control system complete with touch controls. Check out `http://blogs.unity3d.com/2014/01/17/new-sample-assets-beta/` for more details.

# Going further

If you are of the adventurous sort, try to expand your project by adding the following:

- Add a few more characters from the pack and get them rigged up
- Play with some of the other assets in the FANTASY_PACK and tackle automatic and grid-based splicing

# Summary

We have certainly covered a lot in this chapter simply because there is a lot to say about the new sprite rendering system, and we will not be stopping at this. In later chapters, we will extend this further.

Until now, we have covered the following topics:

- The basics of game design and structure
- An overview of all the main sprite components (sprite / sprite renderer)
- Importing new sprites
- Carving up individual sprites from spritesheets
- Adding sprites to your game

Buckle up your seatbelts; there's more to come!

# Getting Animated
# 3

In Unity V4.x, the new Mecanim animation system was introduced, bringing with it a whole raft of new features to the already feature-packed Unity editor. With Unity 4.3 (and beyond), this system has had an overhaul for the new 2D animation system to give developers even more fine-grained control along with many fixes, tweaks, and performance improvements.

In this chapter, we will walk through all the features that are important to the new 2D system and go over several tips and tricks to irk the most out of what is available.

 This chapter isn't going to cover everything you can do with the Mecanim system as it needs an entire book in its own right. In fact, there is one in the PacktPub library already, namely, *Unity Character Animation with Mecanim, Jamie Dean*.

The topics that will be covered in this chapter are as follows:

- Sprite animation
- State machines and Mecanim
- Curves and fine control

## Sprite animation

Besides the 2D sprite system, Unity has created and updated their animation to handle 2D. With a greatly enhanced dope sheet animation/clip controller and full integration with the Mecanim state management system, there is a boundless world of choices available that are easy to use once you get to grips with them.

# Animation components

All of the animation in the new 2D system in Unity uses the new Mecanim system (introduced in Version 4) for design and control, which once you get used to is very simple and easy to use.

It is broken up into three main parts: animation controllers, animation clips, and animator components.

## Animation controllers

**Animation controllers** are simply state machines that are used to control when an animation should be played and how often, including what conditions control the transition between each state. In the new 2D system, there must be at least one controller per animation for it to play, and controllers can contain many animations as you can see here with three states and transition lines between them:

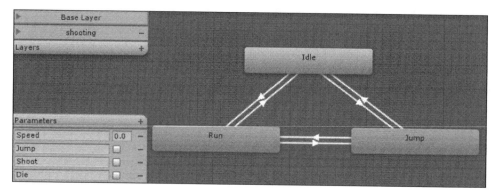

## Animation clips

**Animation clips** are the heart of the animation system and have come very far from their previous implementation in Unity. Clips were used just to hold the crafted animations of the 3D models with a limited ability to tweak them for use on a complete 3D model:

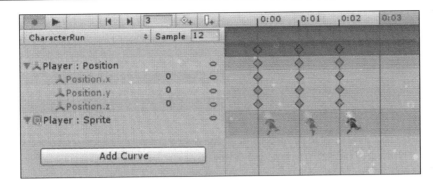

The new animation dope sheet system (as shown in the preceding screenshot) is very advanced; in fact, now it tracks almost every change in the inspector for sprites, allowing you to animate just about everything. You can even control which sprite from a spritesheet is used for each frame of the animation.

The preceding screenshot shows a three-frame sprite animation and a modified **x** position modifier for the middle image, giving a hopping effect to the sprite as it runs. This ability of the dope sheet system implies there is less burden on the shoulders of art designers to craft complex animations as the animation system itself can be used to produce a great effect.

 Sprites don't have to be picked from the same spritesheet to be animated. They can come from individual textures or picked from any spritesheet you have imported.

## The Animator component

To use the new animation prepared in a controller, you need to apply it to a game object in the scene. This is done through the **Animator** component, as shown here:

The only property we actually care about in 2D is the **Controller** property. This is where we attach the controller we just created.

 Other properties only apply to the 3D humanoid models, so we can ignore them for 2D. For more information about the complete 3D Mecanim system, refer to the Unity Learn guide at `http://unity3d.com/learn/tutorials/modules/beginner/animation.`

Animation is just one of the uses of the Mecanim system; we'll explore other uses of it in *Chapter 7, Encountering Enemies and Running Away, Chapter 9, Getting Ready to Fight*, and *Chapter 10, The Battle Begins.*

## Setting up animation controllers

So, to start creating animations, you first need an animation controller in order to define your animation clips. As stated before, this is just a state machine that controls the execution of animations even if there is only one animation. In this case, the controller runs the selected animation for as long as it's told to.

 If you are browsing around the components that can be added to the game object, you will come across the **Animator** component, which takes a single animation clip as a parameter. This is the legacy animation system for backward compatibility only. Any new animation clip created and set to this component will *not* work; it will simply generate a console log item stating **The AnimationClip used by the Animation component must be marked as Legacy**. So, in Unity 4.3 onwards, just avoid this.

Creating an animation controller is just as easy as any other game object. In the **Project** view, simply right-click on the view and select **Create | Animator Controller**.

Opening the new animation will show you the blank animator controller in the Mecanim state manager window, as shown in the following screenshot:

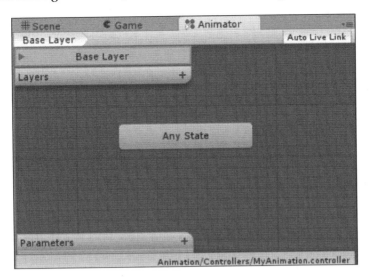

There is a lot of functionality in the Mecanim state engine, which is largely outside the scope of this book. Check out for more dedicated books on this, such as *Unity 4 Character Animation with Mecanim, Jamie Dean, Packt Publishing*.

If you have any existing clips, you can just drag them to the Mecanim controller's **Edit** window; alternatively, you can just select them in the **Project** view, right-click on them, and select **From selected clip** under **Create**. However, we will cover more of this later in practice.

Once you have a controller, you can add it to any game object in your project by clicking on **Add Component** in the inspector or by navigating to **Component | Create** and **Miscellaneous | Animator** and selecting it. Then, you can select your new controller as the **Controller** property of the animator. Alternatively, you can just drag your new controller to the game object you wish to add it to.

Clips in a controller are bound to the spritesheet texture of the object the controller is attached to. Changing or removing this texture will prevent the animation from being displayed correctly. However, it will appear as it's still running.

So with a controller in place, let's add some animation to it.

 If you are using the automatic clip creation technique detailed in the next section, you can skip this step as it also generates the animation controller for you.

# Setting up animation clips

Unlike the 3D system in Unity where animations are defined in modeling programs and bound to certain model types and poses, there are actually two ways in which animations (or clips) can be created in the new 2D system. This is because Unity controls the creation of an animation, not an external tool.

## Manual animation clip creation

Let's start off by creating some animation clips manually. It is a slightly lengthier task than the automatic route, but it is good to understand what the automatic system is actually doing for you. This helps you choose which route to take depending on the kind of animation you want to create.

To start, first we need to create a game object in the hierarchy with an animator component and controller attached to it so that we can add a reference to the spritesheet. Perform the following steps:

1. Drag either the spritesheet (with the regions defined) or any single sprite to the scene hierarchy in the scene view. This will create a new game object with **Sprite Renderer** for the assigned texture.

2. Add the **Animator** component to the game object.

3. Create a new animator controller by clicking on **Animator Controller** in the **Project** view.

4. Drag the new animation controller to the game object, or set it to the **Controller** property in the inspector panel for the animator.

Now, if you open the **Animator** window (**Window | Animation**) with the new game object selected, you will get a blank animation with no clips defined, as shown in the following screenshot:

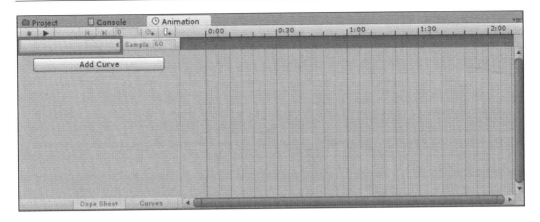

To create your first clip, simply click on the clip selection drop-down menu and click on **[Create New Clip]**, as shown here:

From here, you can either drag individual sprites onto the timeline at the points you want to show a sprite from in your animation, or you can alter the properties in the **Inspector** pane to animate how the sprite should look on the screen. You can even preview the animation by clicking on the play button in the **Animation** tab and it will display the running animation in the **Scene** view window:

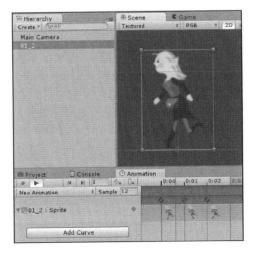

From the preceding screenshot, you will notice that I have moved the **Animation** window to a separate part of the screen (just drag the tab and move/dock) so that both the **Project** and **Animator** windows are placed side by side. This makes it easier to drag the sprites on to the dope sheet.

Now, you can have ultimate control over your animation as it plays out on the screen. The next section will go into more detail on the dope sheet system and what it has to offer.

Note that you are not limited to the whole character animation with the new animation system; you can also construct characters from several sprites and animate them individually. The best example of this is Unity's own 2D platform sample, which is available at the Unity **Asset** store (http://bit.ly/UnityPlatformer2D):

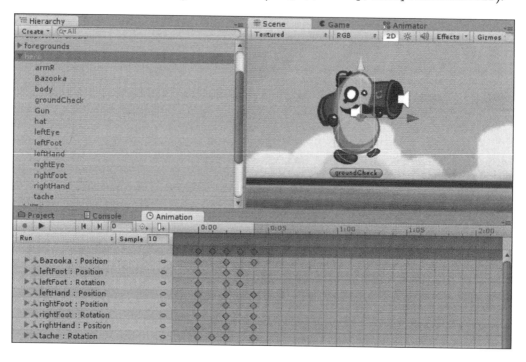

In the screenshot, you can see all the parts of the hero in the hierarchy, such as the body, tash, feet, and bazooka as separate sprites; then, in the animation dope sheet, the **Run** animation alters the position of each of these sprites to emulate a fast walking effect. This feature can be used in a powerful way once you get your head around what is possible.

# Automatic animation clip creation

The approach I'd always recommend (especially for beginners) is to let Unity create the animation clips for you. The automatic routines are well equipped to understand your animations, and they set the various properties for you very well. You can always tweak it later.

The process is very simple, and you can even create the default animation controller in the process by performing the following steps:

1. First, delete the example you created previously, just to avoid confusion.

2. Browse to the spritesheet that is in the `Assets` folder structure in the **Project** view.

3. Expand the discovered sprites by clicking on the arrow next to the spritesheet's image.

4. Select all the sprites for a single animation.

5. Drag the selection to the **Scene** view hierarchy (*not* the **Game** view).

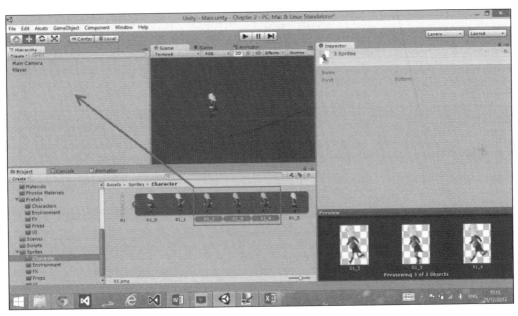

Dragging multiple sprites to the scene to make an animation

6. You will then be prompted where to save the new animation clip:

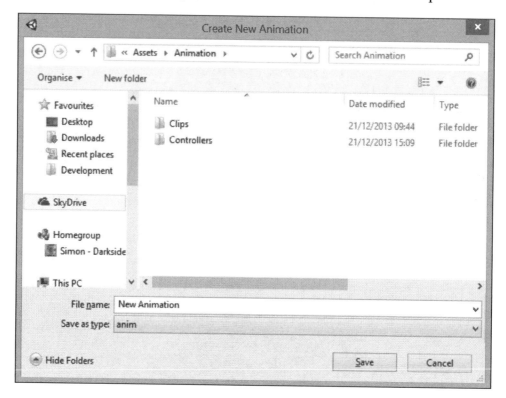

 The animation controller that is automatically created will have the same name as the first sprite in your animation. Be sure to rename it if you wish.

7. Save it to `Assets\Animation\Clips` and you are done.

 If you perform the preceding steps for every animation, just remember to delete any controllers it creates that you do not intend to use. Time and experience will help you find the right path that fits your needs.

Once saved, be sure to sort your controllers and clips in the correct folder of your project, or leave them where they are until you are happy.

If you examine your new game object in the **Inspector** pane, you should find a new sprite created with an **Animator** component along with the new controller you saved, shown in the **Inspector** pane as you can see here:

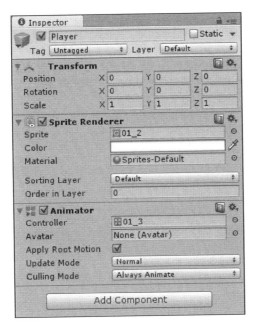

Now, if you double-click on either the new controller in your `Project` folder or the **Controller** parameter in the **Animator** controller component in the **Inspector** pane, you will see the new single state animation that was generated for you, as follows:

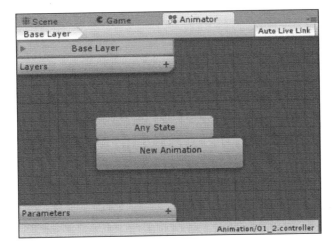

If you also want to check out how the animation looks like, select your new object in your **Project** hierarchy and open the **Animation** view by navigating to **Window | Animation** in the menu. Once open, you should see the animator **Dope Sheet** view (as shown in the following screenshot) for the currently selected game object with the current animation clip in view (as highlighted):

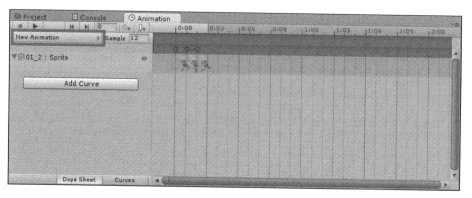

Here, you can see the simple sprite animation expressed in the **Dope Sheet** view with the timings for when the sprite's image will change. By default, this will be in an eternal loop from start to finish.

Any changes that you make at this point with **Dope Sheet** open in the **Inspector** pane will be recorded at the selected time in the animation, so be careful about what you click on. We will cover more on the dope sheet system later.

## Animator Dope Sheet

The new and improved animation **Dope Sheet** has a growing set of features to make the animation easier and yet more powerful:

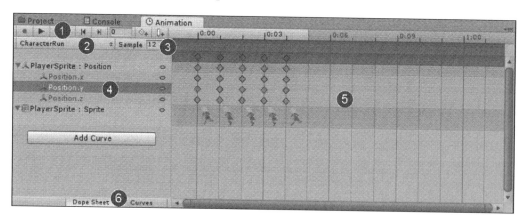

The features aren't limited to the new 2D system for use, but they do make a lot of 2D tasks a lot simpler to implement.

Navigating round the Animation editor (as shown in the previous screenshot), we have the following sections:

# (1) The time/recording controls

The time controls let you play or step through your recorded animation to see how it flows. This is especially useful when combined with the active play in the **Scene** and **Game** views.

The record button determines whether the changes in the **Scene** or **Inspector** panes will affect the **Animation** properties and will add new ones if a property has not been touched yet.

There are also the buttons to add new **KeyFrames** (specific point on the timeline at the currently selected time) or **Animation Events** (script launching points based on time).

# (2) Selecting the animation clip

This is a simple list of all the clips in the current animation set/controller. It also has the facility to add more clips directly from this drop-down menu.

# (3) The sample rate (frames per second)

The sample rate sets the number of frames per second that are available in the timeline. It controls the number of key frame points possible between time intervals.

# (4) Animation properties

Animation properties list all the different **Inspector** properties that are being controlled by this animation clip. If a property is touched in the editor while the record mode is active, it will create a new property in the animator or alter the existing property at the current time.

Currently, the animations have one limitation. If a property is part of a construct such as `vector3` and even if you only change one part of that construct, say the X value, it will set the other parts to their default values.

Animating the *x* axis on a position property, for instance to 0.1, at a specified time will also set the Y and Z values to 0; this overrides any script, changing those values. Keep this in mind while animating similar properties.

While in the record mode, *any* change in the editor will be captured. This includes any child game object properties that you change. This becomes very useful if your animated objects comprise multiple sprites in the child game objects.

## (5) Timeline

The timeline window shows all the key frames being animated over the lifetime of the animation. Setting the sample rate higher and lower will control how many key points/frames will be available between time units.

You can also use the following keyboard shortcuts to navigate between the frames on the timeline:

- Press comma (,) to go to the previous frame
- Press period (.) to go to the next frame
- Press *Alt* + Comma (,) to go to the previous key frame
- Press *Alt* + Period (.) to go to the next key frame

## (6) Dope/curve view

The timeline view has an alternate view mode to add finer control and curves between the key frame animations, as shown in the following screenshot:

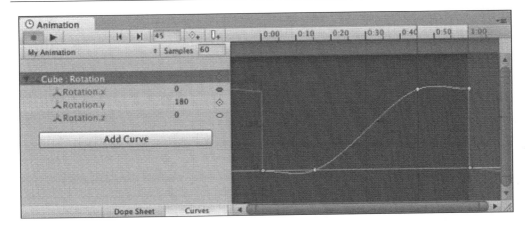

Editing the curves takes a little finesse but makes for a better-looking transition than the default `Boolean` (on/off) effect.

You can further control the curves by setting the inbound and outbound tangents of the curve, setting either a smooth (linear), sharp (constant), or free-form curve. Simply play with these settings until you have the kind of curve you want.

> Curves can also be used for just about anything and from anywhere in the code. So, if you are using a separate library or complex math to emulate curves or tweening, stop and have a serious look at the animation curves. We will cover more on this later.

We'll cover curves in *Chapter 5, NPCs and Interactions*, where we'll learn a few of the slightly more complex curves and animations.

# Putting it together

So far, our hero can move to the left and right of the screen, but it is a little flat. As we have some animation in our spritesheet, let's put that into action.

As described earlier, in order to get the animation running, we will need the following prerequisites:

- An **Animator** component in our game object

- An **Animator** controller to manage our animation that is bound to the animator

- At least one animation clip to play in the controller

# Setting up the animation controller

To get started, first we need to add the **Animator** component to the player's game object by navigating to **Add Component | Miscellaneous | Animator** in the **Inspector** pane. Leave all the other options alone for now.

Next, create a new animation **Controller** in `Assets/Animation/Controllers` by navigating to **Create | Animator Controller** in the **Project** window (or by right-clicking on it while viewing the folder). Then, drag the new controller to the **Controller** property in the **Animator** component we just created.

You should now have something that looks like the following screenshot:

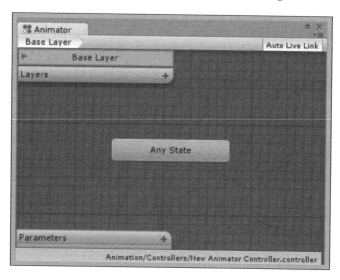

Now, we just need to add our animation clip. Open the new animation **Controller** (if you haven't done so already) by double-clicking on it, then open the **Animation** window by navigating to **Menu | Window | Animation** (or press *Ctrl* or *Command 6*).

You may have to rearrange your Windows at this point, as the default location for the **Animation** window is next to the **Project** view. I recommend moving it next to the main window so you can see both the Project folder and the **Animation** window at the same time.

This is easily done by dragging the tab for the **Animation** window to the desired point. When it gets near a point in the editor where it can dock, it will do so automatically.

# Adding your first animation clip (idle)

To add your first animation clip, create a new clip by opening the clip selection drop-down menu and selecting **[Create New Clip]** (as shown earlier in the *Animator Dope Sheet* section, marked as item 2). This will prompt you for a location to save the new clip. Save it under `Assets/Animation/Clips` as `CharacterIdle.anim`.

For the idle animation, we only need to add one sprite to show the hero standing at rest, so drag the sprite named **01_5** onto the timeline at position **0**, as shown here:

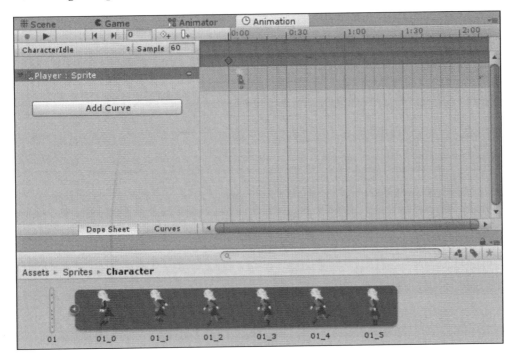

The **Animation** controller should now look like the following screenshot, with a single state for the idle animation (highlighted in orange to denote it is in the default state):

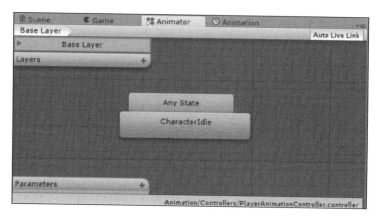

# Adding another animation clip (run)

To add the running animation, you'll need to add another clip. This time it is called `CharacterRun`, and instead of just dragging a single sprite, we will add three sprites to form one animation set. First, set the **Sample** rate to `12` in the **Animation** window; select the **01_2**, **01_3**, and **01_4** sprites together and drag them to the timeline window, which will order them on the timeline appropriately as shown in the following screenshot:

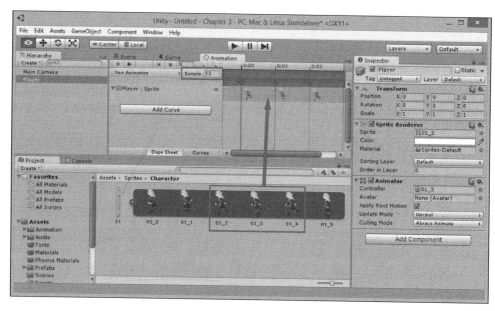

Looking at the **Animation** controller now, you will see that an additional state is added to the view; the main difference being that it is gray (as it's not the default), and at this point, nothing connects the two states together:

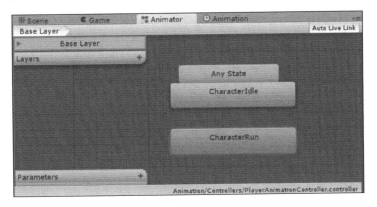

 You can also create the animation clips with multiple sprites by selecting the sprites in the **Project** view and dragging them together to the **Scene** or **Project** hierarchy. This will automatically create a new game object complete with **Sprite Renderer**, **Animation** component, **Animation Controller**, and **Clip** for the set. If you start this way and add an idle animation clip later, just be sure to check which state is the default state.

There is a lot of power in Unity to automate the creation of animations.

# Connecting animation states

At the moment, our two states are not connected. So when we run the project, the hero is always idle (lazy guy); let's change that.

To tell the controller to move between the two states, we need the following prerequisites:

- A transition link between the two states
- A parameter or event to activate the transition
- Something to change the value of that parameter, usually in a script

So, first we create the transition between the default idle state by right-clicking on the **CharacterIdle** state and selecting **Make Transition**. This will change the mouse cursor to an arrow. Then, click on the state we want to transition to, which in this case is the **CharacterRun** state. Clicking on the new transition shows you the properties of that transition in the inspector, as shown in the following screenshot:

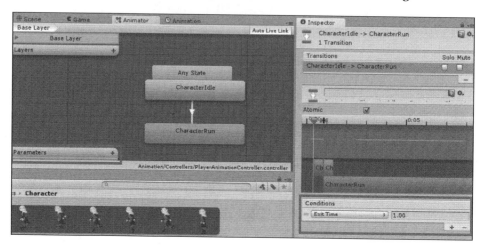

As shown in the **Inspector** pane, at the lower-right corner, by default, the new transitions are controlled by a single parameter called **Exit Time**, which simply means that when the first animation ends, it will transition to the second. We don't want that here as we want to control when the **Run** animation is activated.

First, we need a new parameter, which we will be able to access later from our character controller script. So click on the + symbol as indicated in the parameter section of the animation controller and add a new **Float** parameter called speed.

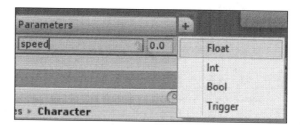

Now in the **Inspector** pane, change the **Exit Time** parameter by clicking on it and selecting the new **speed** parameter; give it a value of 0.1. This tells the animator that when the speed is greater than 0.1 units, it will transition from the idle state to the run state.

Next, repeat the process and add a transition from the **CharacterRun** state back to
the **CharacterIdle** state, choosing the same parameter value; however, this time, set it
to **Less** with a value of `0.1`, as shown in the following screenshot:

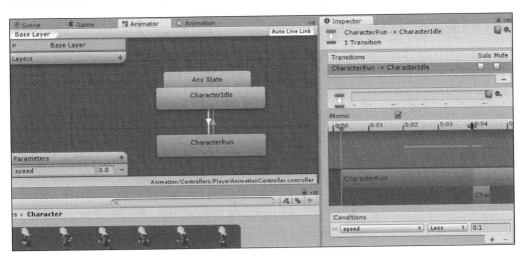

If you run the project at this point, the character still doesn't run when it moves.
For this, we need to update our **Character** movement script.

# Accessing controllers from a script

Like most things in Unity, to access another component, we just need a reference to
it. With the animation controllers, it is no different.

Update your `CharacterMovement.cs` script by performing the following steps:

- A new **Animator** reference to hold a link to our sprites animator is needed,
  as mentioned in the following code:

```
//Reference to the player's animator component.
private Animator anim;
```

- Discover the actual animator from the sprite object within the `Awake` function
  to ensure we capture it at startup using using the technique we highlighted
  earlier in *Chapter 2, Character Building, for accessing components*; in this case,
  the `Rigidbody2D` component:

```
void Awake()
{
  //Setting up references.
  playerRigidBody2D =
    (Rigidbody2D)GetComponent(typeof(Rigidbody2D));
}
```

- In the `Update` function, we update a `float` parameter we defined earlier in the animator with the value of the movement that we got from the user control. Refer to the following code:

```
void Update(){
    //Cache the horizontal input.
    movePlayerVector = Input.GetAxis("Horizontal");

    anim.SetFloat("speed", Mathf.Abs(movePlayerVector));
```

Now if you run the project, your hero will start running in the correct direction when you tell him to and then rest when you stop.

If you also arrange Windows in a way that you can see both the **Game** and **Animator** windows at the same time, you will see that each state will become active as and when it reacts to the input.

## Extra credit

We have a nice run and stand animation, but wouldn't it be better if our hero had a spring in his step? So let's extend our running animation, and also highlight one of the pitfalls of doing so and how to fix it by performing the following steps:

1. Select the **Player** game object, open the **Animation** window, and select the **CharacterRun** animation clip.

2. Click on the middle keyframe in the animation.

3. In the **Inspector** pane, change the **Y Transform** value to `0.1`.

This will update your animation as follows:

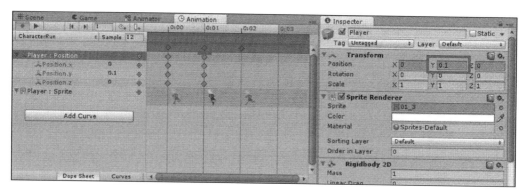

However, when you now run your project and make the hero run around, you will see the hero doing his new run animation and bobbing up and down as expected. However, it will soon stop moving; what the heck? The reason is simple; by setting the **Y** property of the game objects in the **Transform** pane, you also have to set the **X** and **Z** properties to 0 because they are all part of the **Transform** pane's **Vector3** property. This may be changed in future versions of Unity. However, currently, it isn't possible to just animate a single property of constructs, such as vectors or other complex types.

There is a workaround, which is more on the lines of how you should create complex game objects that have many parts. Just split **Character** from the rendering of its sprite by performing the following steps:

1. Rename our current **Player** game object to `PlayerSprite`.

2. Create a new game object named `Player`.

3. Click and drag the **PlayerSprite** game object to be a child of the **Player** game object.

4. Reset all the **Transform** pane's values of both the **Player** and **PlayerSprite** game objects (otherwise, everything will be an offset).

5. Remove the `CharacterMovement` script, `RigidBody 2D`, and `Box Collider 2D` components from the **PlayerSprite** game object and add them to the **Player** game object again.

 Also, be sure to update the options of the physics components and the bounds of the box collider. This is because they are not on the sprite object; they no longer automatically recognize the regions they need to work with but just tweak them until they are correct.

The **Player** (**Controller**) game object view will look like the following screenshot:

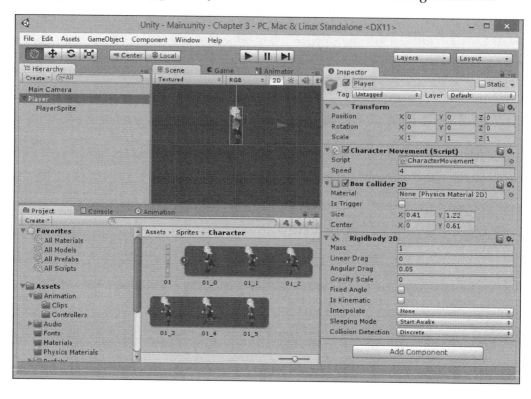

The **PlayerSprite (Animator/Sprite Renderer)** game object view is shown in the following screenshot:

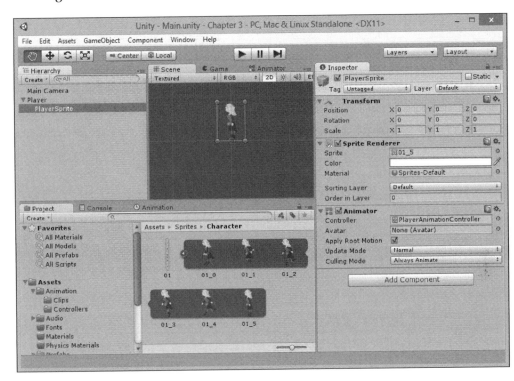

With our scene reordered, the player's movements and physics are controlled by the parent **Player** object, and the **Sprite Rendering** and **Animator** are controlled by the child **PlayerSprite** object. We just need to update our control script so it knows where to find everything. Perform the following step:

1. Edit the `CharacterMovement.cs` C# script and update it as follows:

   ° Add a reference to the point of the new **PlayerSprite** game object as follows:

   ```
   //Reference to the player's sprite GameObject.
   private GameObject playerSprite;
   ```

- ° Add discovery for the **PlayerSprite** game object and alter the discovery for the animation component based on the new `playerSprite` reference as follows:

```
void Awake()
{
    // Setting up references.
    playerRigidBody2D =
(Rigidbody2D)GetComponent(typeof(Rigidbody2D));
    playerSprite = transform.Find("PlayerSprite").
      gameObject;
    anim =
(Animator)playerSprite.GetComponent(typeof(Animator));
}
```

 Make sure you have renamed the GameObjects as shown in the previous screenshot or this will give an error when you run the project.

- ° Alter the `Flip()` logic to work with the **PlayerSprite** game object's rendering option as follows:

```
void Flip()
{
    //Switch the way the player is labelled as facing.
    facingRight = !facingRight;

    //Multiply the player's x local scale by -1.
    Vector3 theScale = playerSprite.transform.localScale;
    theScale.x *= -1;
    playerSprite.transform.localScale = theScale;
}
```

So, when we run the game now, the entire **Player** object is moved by the script and the animation runs independently.

# Getting curvy

As a nice last touch, let's clean up the running of the animation to be a bit smoother. At present, the hero jerks up and down with the frames it has, but we can improve this by using the **Curves** features of the **Animation** editor.

To do this, let's make some space in the **Animation** window's timeline to add a few extra frames by performing the following steps:

1. Move the last keyframe back from **0.02** to **0.04**.

2. Drag the **01_3** sprite again onto the timeline at **0.02** and **0.03**.

 You should now have five frames in the animation.

3. Set the **Position.y** property from 0.01 to 0.05.
4. Set the **Position.y** property from 0.02 to 0.1.
5. Set the **Position.y** property from 0.03 to 0.05.
6. Click on the **Curves** button at the bottom of the Animator window to switch between the views.

With extra frames and settings, you should now see the curve as shown in the following screenshot:

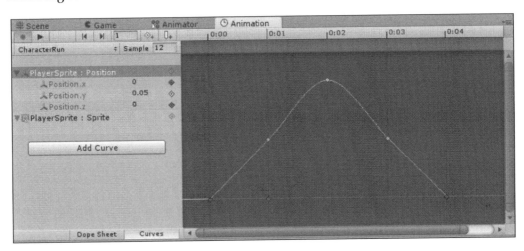

Now, while running the project, the slight hop in our hero's step should look a lot smoother.

# Going further

If you are of an adventurous sort, try expanding your project to add the following features:

- Try adding more animations from the hero's spritesheet, such as jumping.
- Expand the animation and curves for the hero. Try playing with some of the other options that were described in the overview.

# Summary

The updated **Animation** system provides a tremendous boost to the users with lots of hidden features. I've not covered everything as that would deserve another book entirely, so feel free to experiment further. The Mecanim system isn't just for animation either, and we will return to this later on.

We covered an overview of all the main Sprite animation components (**Animator, Controller, Clips, Keyframes**, and **Curves**), importing new sprites, animating sprites and controlling states, improving animations, and structuring renderers.

In the next chapter, we will build an environment for our character to walk around in, with environments, sprite layers, and scene navigation.

# 4
# The Game World

With our main character in hand, let's give him a home and a place to walk around. In this chapter, we will cover the basics of creating immersive areas where players can walk around and interact, as well as some of the techniques used to manage those areas.

This chapter will give you some practical tips and tricks of the spritesheet system introduced with Unity 4.3 and how to get it to work for you.

Lastly, we will also have a cursory look at how shaders work in the 2D world and the considerations you need to keep in mind when using them. However, we won't be implementing shaders as that could be another book in itself.

The following is the list of topics that will be covered in this chapter:

- Working with environments
- Looking at sprite layers
- Handling multiple resolutions
- An overview of parallaxing and effects
- Shaders in 2D – an overview

## Backgrounds and layers

Now that we have our hero in play, it would be nice to give him a place to live and walk around, so let's set up the home town and decorate it.

Firstly, we are going to need some more assets. So, from the asset pack you downloaded earlier, grab the following assets from the `Environments` pack, place them in `Assets\Sprites\Environment`, and name them as follows:

- Name the `ENVIRONMENTS\ STEAMPUNK\background01.png` file `Assets\ Sprites\Environment\background01`

- Name the `ENVIRONMENTS\STEAMPUNK\environmentalAssets.png` file `Assets\Sprites\Environment\environmentalAssets`

- Name the `ENVIRONMENTS\FANTASY\environmentalAssets.png` file `Assets\Sprites\Environment\environmentalAssets2`

# To slice or not to slice

As we progress through this book, you will notice that some assets are single textures, whereas others contain multiple images and you may wonder which method is best to create your assets and why it is best.

The answer (as it is in a lot of these situations) depends on the needs of your title.

It is always better to pack many of the same images on to a single asset/atlas and then use the Sprite Editor to define the regions on that texture for each sprite, as long as all the sprites on that sheet are going to get used in the same scene. The reason for this is when Unity tries to draw to the screen, it needs to send the images to draw to the graphics card; if there are many images to send, this can take some time. If, however, it is just one image, it is a lot simpler and more performant with only one file to send.

There needs to be a balance; too large an image and the upload to the graphics card can take up too many resources, too many individual images and you have the same problem.

The basic rule of thumb is as follows:

- If the background is a full screen background or large image, then keep it separate.

- If you have many images and all are for the same scene, then put them into a single spritesheet/atlas.

- If you have many images but all are for different scenes, then group them as best you can—common items on one sheet and scene-specific items on different sheets. You'll have several spritesheets to use.

You basically want to keep as much stuff together as makes sense and not send unnecessary images that won't get used to the graphics card. Find your balance.

# The town background

First, let's add a background for the town using the `Assets\Sprites\Environment\background01` texture. It is shown in the following screenshot:

With the background asset, we don't need to do anything else other than ensure that it has been imported as a sprite (in case your project is still in 3D mode), as shown in the following screenshot:

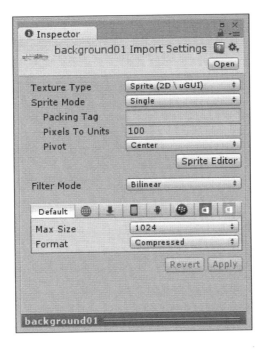

# The town buildings

For the steampunk environmental assets (Assets\Sprites\Environment\
environmentalAssets) that are shown in the following screenshot, we need a bit
more work; once these assets are imported, change the **Sprite Mode** to Multiple
and load up the Sprite Editor using the **Sprite Editor** button.

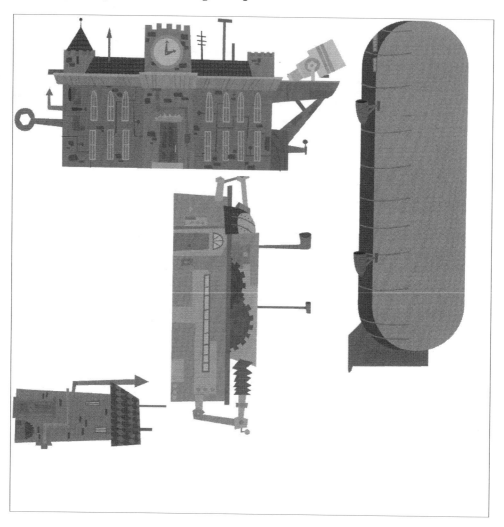

Next, click on the **Slice** button, leave the settings at their default options, and then click on the **Slice** button in the new window as shown in the following screenshot:

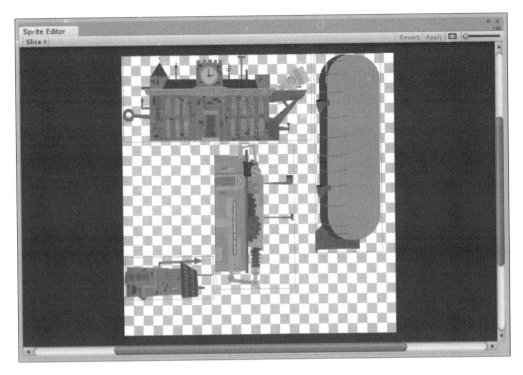

Click on **Apply** and close the Sprite Editor. You will have four new sprite textures available as seen in the following screenshot:

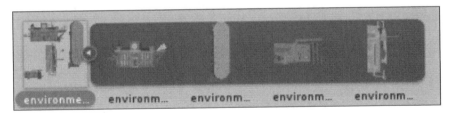

# The extra scenery

We saw what happens when you use a grid type split on a spritesheet and when the automatic split works well, so what about when it doesn't go so well? If we look at the `Fantasy` environment pack (`Assets\Sprites\Environment\environmentalAssets2`), we will see the following:

After you have imported it and run the **Split** in **Sprite Editor**, you will notice that one of the sprites does not get detected very well; altering the automatic split settings in this case doesn't help, so we need to do some manual manipulation as shown in the following screenshot:

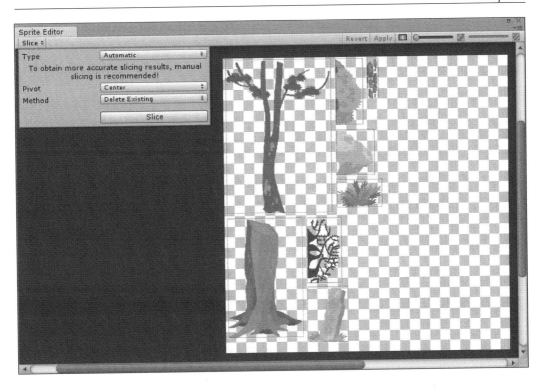

In the previous screenshot, you can see that just two of the rocks in the top-right sprite have been identified by the splicing routine. To fix this, just delete one of the selections and then expand the other manually using the selection points in the corner of the selection box (after clicking on the sprite box). Here's how it will look before the correction:

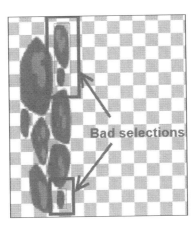

After correction, you should see something like the following screenshot:

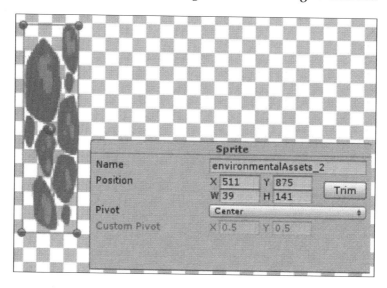

This gives us some nice additional assets to scatter around our towns and give it a more homely feel, as shown in the following screenshot:

# Building the scene

So, now that we have some nice assets to build with, we can start building our first town.

# Adding the town background

Returning to the scene view, you should see the following:

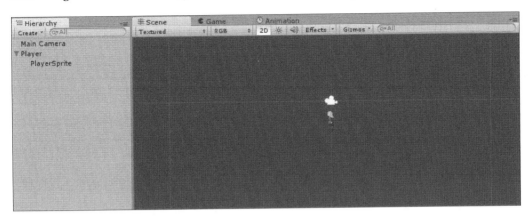

If, however, we add our town background texture (Assets\Sprites\Backgrounds\Background.png) to the scene by dragging it to either the project hierarchy or the scene view, you will end up with the following:

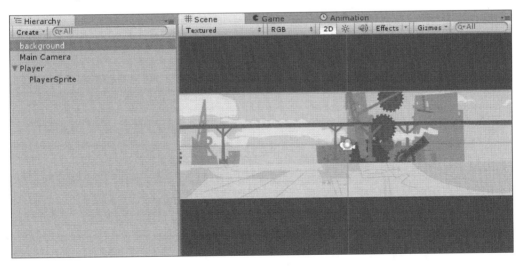

> Be sure to set the background texture position appropriately once you add it to the scene; in this case, be sure the position of the transform is centered in the view at **X** = 0, **Y** = 0, **Z** = 0.
>
> Unity does have a tendency to set the position relative to where your 3D view is at the time of adding it—almost never where you want it.

*Our player has vanished!*

The reason for this is simple: Unity's sprite system has an ordering system that comes in two parts.

# Sprite sorting layers

Sorting Layers (**Edit** | **Project Settings** | **Tags and Layers**) are a collection of sprites, which are bulked together to form a single group. Layers can be configured to be drawn in a specific order on the screen as shown in the following screenshot:

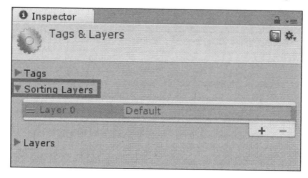

# Sprite sorting order

Sprites within an individual layer can be sorted, allowing you to control the draw order of sprites within that layer. The sprite **Inspector** is used for this purpose, as shown in the following screenshot:

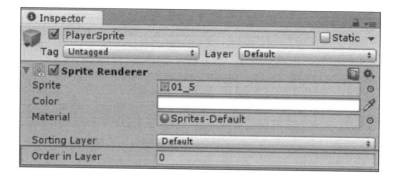

Sprite's **Sorting Layers** should not be confused with Unity's rendering layers. Layers are a separate functionality used to control whether groups of game objects are drawn or managed together, whereas **Sorting Layers** control the draw order of sprites in a scene.

So the reason our player is no longer seen is that it is behind the background. As they are both in the same layer and have the same sort order, they are simply drawn in the order that they are in the project hierarchy.

# Updating the scene Sorting Layers

To resolve the update of the scene's Sorting Layers, let's organize our sprite rendering by adding some sprite Sorting Layers. So, open up the **Tags and Layers** inspector pane as shown in the following screenshot (by navigating to **Edit | Project settings | Tags and Layers**), and add the following **Sorting Layers**:

- **Background**
- **Player**
- **Foreground**
- **GUI**

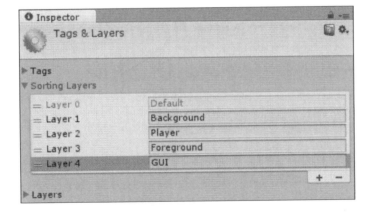

 You can reorder the layers underneath the default anytime by selecting a row and dragging it up and down the sprite's Sorting Layers list.

With the layers set up, we can now configure our game objects accordingly. So, set the **Sorting Layer** on our **background01** sprite to the **Background** layer as shown in the following screenshot:

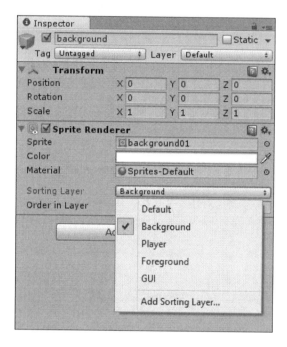

Then, update the **PlayerSprite** GameObject to the **Player** layer; our character will now be displayed in front of the background.

 You can just keep both objects on the same layer and set the **Sort Order** value appropriately, keeping the background to a **Sort Order** value of 0 and the player to 10, which will draw the player in front. However, as you add more items to the scene, things will get tricky quickly, so it is better to group them in a layer accordingly.

Now when we return to the scene, our hero is happily displayed but he is seen hovering in the middle of our village. So let's fix that next by simply changing its position transform in the **Inspector** window.

Setting the **Y** position transform to `-2` will place our hero nicely in the middle of the street (provided you have set the pivot for the player sprite to `bottom`), as shown in the following screenshot:

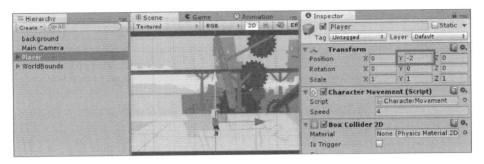

Feel free at this point to also add some more background elements such as trees and buildings to fill out the scene using the environment assets we imported earlier.

# Working with the camera

If you try and move the player left and right at the moment, our hero happily bobs along. However, you will quickly notice that we run into a problem: the hero soon disappears from the edge of the screen. To solve this, we need to make the camera follow the hero.

When creating new scripts to implement something, remember that just about every game that has been made with Unity has most likely implemented either the same thing or something similar. Most just get on with it, but others and the Unity team themselves are keen to share their scripts to solve these challenges. So in most cases, we will have something to work from. Don't just start a script from scratch (unless it is a very small one to solve a tiny issue) if you can help it; here's some resources to get you started:

- Unity sample projects: `http://unity3d.com/learn/tutorials/modules`
- Unity Patterns: `http://unitypatterns.com/`
- Unity wiki scripts section: `http://wiki.Unity3d.com/index.php/Scripts` (also check other stuff for detail)

Once you become more experienced, it is better to just use these scripts as a reference and try to create your own and improve on them, unless they are from a maintained library such as `https://github.com/nickgravelyn/UnityToolbag`.

To make the camera follow the players, we'll take the script from the Unity 2D sample and modify it to fit in our game. This script is nice because it also includes a Mario style buffer zone, which allows the players to move without moving the camera until they reach the edge of the screen.

Create a new script called `FollowCamera` in `Assets\Scripts`, remove the `Start` and `Update` functions, and then add the following properties:

```
using UnityEngine;

public class FollowCamera : MonoBehaviour {

    // Distance in the x axis the player can move before the
    // camera follows.
    public float xMargin = 1.5f;

    // Distance in the y axis the player can move before the
    // camera follows.
    public float yMargin = 1.5f;

    // How smoothly the camera catches up with its target
    // movement in the x axis.
    public float xSmooth = 1.5f;

    // How smoothly the camera catches up with its target
    // movement in the y axis.
    public float ySmooth = 1.5f;

    // The maximum x and y coordinates the camera can have.
    public Vector2 maxXAndY;

    // The minimum x and y coordinates the camera can have.
    public Vector2 minXAndY;

    // Reference to the player's transform.
    public Transform player;
}
```

The variables are all commented to explain their purpose, but we'll cover each as we use them.

First off, we need to get the player object's position so that we can track the camera to it by discovering it from the object it is attached to. This is done by adding the following code in the `Awake` function:

```
void Awake()
{
    // Setting up the reference.
```

```
        player = GameObject.Find("Player").transform;
if (player == null)
{
   Debug.LogError("Player object not found");
}


   }
```

> An alternative to discovering the player this way is to make the player property `public` and then assign it in the editor. There is no right or wrong way—just your preference.
>
> It is also a good practice to add some element of debugging to let you know if there is a problem in the scene with a missing reference, else all you will see are errors such as object not initialized or variable was null.

Next, we need a couple of helper methods to check whether the player has moved near the edge of the camera's bounds as defined by the **Max X and Y** variables. In the following code, we will use the settings defined in the preceding code to control how close you can get to the end result:

```
bool CheckXMargin()
{
    // Returns true if the distance between the camera and the
// player in the x axis is greater than the x margin.
    return Mathf.Abs
(transform.position.x - player.position.x) > xMargin;
}

bool CheckYMargin()
{
    // Returns true if the distance between the camera and the
// player in the y axis is greater than the y margin.
    return Mathf.Abs
(transform.position.y - player.position.y) > yMargin;
}
```

To finish this script, we need to check each frame when the scene is drawn to see whether the player is close to the edge and update the camera's position accordingly. Also, we need to check if the camera bounds have reached the edge of the screen and not move it beyond.

# Comparing Update, FixedUpdate, and LateUpdate

There is usually a lot of debate about which update method should be used within a Unity game. To put it simply, the FixedUpdate method is called on a regular basis throughout the lifetime of the game and is generally used for physics and time sensitive code. The Update method, however, is only called after the end of each frame that is drawn to the screen, as the time taken to draw the screen can vary (due to the number of objects to be drawn and so on). So, the Update call ends up being fairly irregular.

> For more detail on the difference between Update and FixedUpdate see the Unity Learn tutorial video at http://unity3d.com/learn/tutorials/modules/beginner/scripting/update-and-fixedupdate.

As the player is being moved by the physics system, it is better to update the camera in the FixedUpdate method:

```
void FixedUpdate()
    {
        // By default the target x and y coordinates of the camera
        // are it's current x and y coordinates.
        float targetX = transform.position.x;
        float targetY = transform.position.y;

        // If the player has moved beyond the x margin...
        if (CheckXMargin())
            // the target x coordinate should be a Lerp between
            // the camera's current x position and the player's
// current x position.
            targetX = Mathf.Lerp(transform.position.x,
player.position.x, xSmooth *
Time.fixedDeltaTime );
```

```
// If the player has moved beyond the y margin...
if (CheckYMargin())
       // the target y coordinate should be a Lerp between
       // the camera's current y position and the player's
       // current y position.
       targetY = Mathf.Lerp(transform.position.y,
          player.position.y, ySmooth *
             Time. fixedDeltaTime );

       // The target x and y coordinates should not be larger
       // than the maximum or smaller than the minimum.
       targetX = Mathf.Clamp(targetX, minXAndY.x, maxXAndY.x);
       targetY = Mathf.Clamp(targetY, minXAndY.y, maxXAndY.y);

       // Set the camera's position to the target position with
       // the same z component.
       transform.position =
        new Vector3(targetX, targetY, transform.position.z);
}
```

As they say, every game is different and how the camera acts can be different for every game. In a lot of cases, the camera should be updated in the LateUpdate method after all drawing, updating, and physics are complete. This, however, can be a double-edged sword if you rely on math calculations that are affected in the FixedUpdate method, such as Lerp. It all comes down to tweaking your camera system to work the way you need it to do.

Once the script is saved, just attach it to the **Main Camera** element by dragging the script to it or by adding a script component to the camera and selecting the script.

Finally, we just need to configure the script and the camera to fit our game size as follows:

Set the orthographic **Size** of the camera to 2.7 and the **Min X** and **Max X** sizes to 5 and -5 respectively.

# The perils of resolution

When dealing with cameras, there is always one thing that will trip us up as soon as we try to build for another platform — resolution.

By default, the Unity player in the editor runs in the **Free Aspect** mode as shown in the following screenshot:

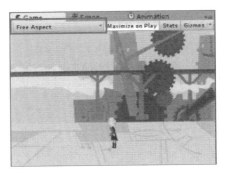

The **Aspect** mode (from the **Aspect** drop-down) can be changed to represent the resolutions supported by each platform you can target. The following is what you get when you switch your build target to each platform:

| Web Client | PC,Mac,Linux Standalone Windows / Windows 8 Google native client | iOS |
|---|---|---|
| ✓ Free Aspect<br>5:4<br>4:3<br>3:2<br>16:10<br>16:9<br>Web (960x600) | ✓ Free Aspect<br>5:4<br>4:3<br>3:2<br>16:10<br>16:9<br>Standalone (1024x768) | ✓ Free Aspect<br>iPhone Tall (320x480)<br>iPhone Wide (480x320)<br>iPhone 4 Tall (640x960)<br>iPhone 4 Wide (960x640)<br>iPad Tall (768x1024)<br>iPad Wide (1024x768)<br>iPhone 5 Tall (9:16)<br>iPhone 5 Wide (16:9)<br>iPhone Tall (2:3)<br>iPhone Wide (3:2)<br>iPad Tall (3:4)<br>iPad Wide (4:3) |
| **Android** | **Blackberry** | **Windows Phone** |
| ✓ Free Aspect<br>Remote (Not Connected) (10x10)<br>HVGA Portrait (320x480)<br>HVGA Landscape (480x320)<br>WVGA Portrait (480x800)<br>WVGA Landscape (800x480)<br>FWVGA Portrait (480x854)<br>FWVGA Landscape (854x480)<br>WSVGA Portrait (600x1024)<br>WSVGA Landscape (1024x600)<br>WXGA Portrait (800x1280)<br>WXGA Landscape (1280x800)<br>3:2 Portrait (2:3)<br>3:2 Landscape (3:2)<br>16:10 Portrait (10:16)<br>16:10 Landscape (16:10) | ✓ Free Aspect<br>Touch Phone Portrait (720x1280)<br>Touch Phone Landscape (1280x720)<br>Keyboard Phone (720x720)<br>Playbook Portrait (600x1024)<br>Playbook Landscape (1024x600)<br>9:16 Portrait (9:16)<br>16:9 Landscape (16:9)<br>1:1 (1:1) | ✓ Free Aspect<br>WVGA Portrait (480x800)<br>WVGA Portrait (9:15)<br>WVGA Landscape (800x480)<br>WVGA Landscape (15:9)<br>WXGA Portrait (768x1280)<br>WXGA Portrait (9:15)<br>WXGA Landscape (1280x768)<br>WXGA Landscape (15:9)<br>720p Portrait (720x1280)<br>720p Portrait (9:16)<br>720p Landscape (1280x720)<br>720p Landscape (16:9) |

To change the build target, go into your project's **Build Settings** by navigating to **File | Build Settings** or by pressing *Ctrl + Shift + B*, then select a platform and click on the **Switch Platform** button. This is shown in the following screenshot:

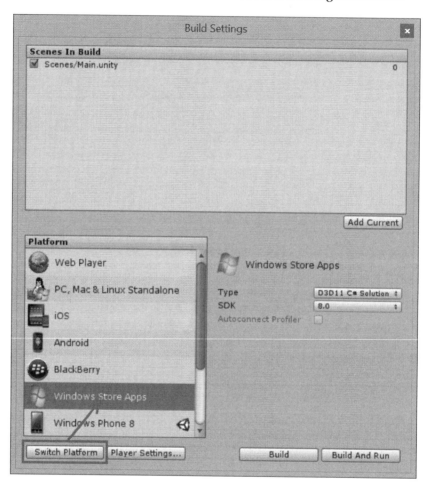

When you change the **Aspect** drop-down to view in one of these resolutions, you will notice how the aspect ratio for what is drawn to the screen changes by either stretching or compressing the visible area. If you run the editor player in full screen by clicking on the **Maximize on Play** button (Maximize on Play) and then clicking on the play icon, you will see this change more clearly. Alternatively, you can run your project on a target device to see the proper perspective output.

The reason I bring this up here is that if you used fixed bounds settings for your camera or game objects, then these values may not work for every resolution, thereby putting your settings out of range or (in most cases) too undersized. You can handle this by altering the settings for each build or using **compiler predirectives** such as #if UNITY_METRO to force the default depending on the build (in this example, Windows 8).

> You can read more about compiler predirectives in *Chapter 12, Deployment and Beyond*. Alternatively, check the Unity documentation at http://docs.unity3d.com/Manual/PlatformDependentCompilation.html.

# A better FollowCamera script

If you are only targeting one device/resolution or your background scrolls indefinitely, then the preceding manual approach works fine. However, if you want it to be a little more dynamic, then we need to know what resolution we are working in and how much space our character has to travel. We will perform the following steps to do this:

1.  We will change the min and max variables to private as we no longer need to configure them in the **Inspector** window. The code is as follows:

    ```
    // The maximum x and y coordinates the camera can have.
    private Vector2 maxXAndY;

    // The minimum x and y coordinates the camera can have.
    private Vector2 minXAndY;
    ```

2.  To work out how much space is available in our town, we need to interrogate the rendering size of our background sprite. So, in the Awake function, we add the following lines of code:

    ```
    // Get the bounds for the background texture - world
      size
    var backgroundBounds = GameObject.Find("background")
      .renderer.bounds;
    ```

3.  In the Awake function, we work out our resolution and viewable space by interrogating the ViewPort method on the camera and converting it to the same coordinate type as the sprite. This is done using the following code:

    ```
    // Get the viewable bounds of the camera in world
    // coordinates
    var camTopLeft = camera.ViewportToWorldPoint
      (new Vector3(0, 0, 0));
    var camBottomRight = camera.ViewportToWorldPoint
      (new Vector3(1, 1, 0));
    ```

4.  Finally, in the `Awake` function, we update the `min` and `max` values using the texture size and camera real-world bounds. This is done using the following lines of code:

```
// Automatically set the min and max values
minXAndY.x = backgroundBounds.min.x - camTopLeft.x;
maxXAndY.x = backgroundBounds.max.x - camBottomRight.x;
```

In the end, it is up to your specific implementation for the type of game you are making to decide which pattern works for your game.

# Transitioning and bounds

So our camera follows our player, but our hero can still walk off the screen and keep going forever, so let us stop that from happening.

## Towns with borders

As you saw in the preceding section, you can use Unity's camera logic to figure out where things are on the screen. You can also do more complex ray testing to check where things are, but I find these are overly complex unless you depend on that level of interaction.

The simpler answer is just to use the native Box2D physics system to keep things in the scene. This might seem like overkill, but the 2D physics system is very fast and fluid, and it is simple to use.

We already added the physics components, `Rigidbody` 2D (to apply physics) and a `Box Collider` 2D (to detect collisions) to the player in *Chapter 2, Character Building*. So, we can make use of these components straight away by adding some additional collision objects to stop the player running off.

To do this and to keep things organized, we will add three empty game objects (either by navigating to **GameObject | Create Empty**, or by pressing *Ctrl + Shift +N*) to the scene (one parent and two children) to manage these collision points, as shown in the following screenshot:

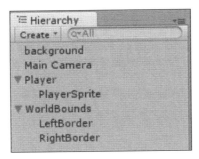

I've named them **WorldBounds** (parent) and **LeftBorder** and **RightBorder** (children) for reference. Next, we will position each of the child game objects to the left- and right-hand side of the screen, as shown in the following screenshot:

Next, we will add a **Box Collider 2D** to each border game object and increase its height just to ensure that it works for the entire height of the scene. I've set the **Y** value to 5 for effect, as shown in the following screenshot:

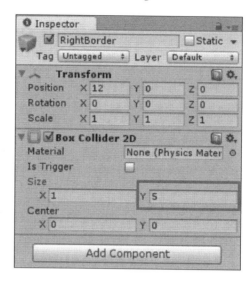

The end result should look like the following screenshot with the two new colliders highlighted in green:

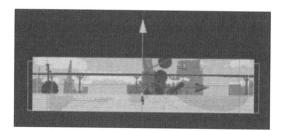

 Alternatively, you could have just created one of the children, added the box collider, duplicated it (by navigating to **Edit | Duplicate** or by pressing *Ctrl + D*), and moved it. If you have to create multiples of the same thing, this is a handy tip to remember.

If you run the project now, then our hero can no longer escape this town on his own. However, as we want to let him leave, we can add a script to the new Boundary game object so that when the hero reaches the end of the town, he can leave.

# Journeying onwards

Now that we have collision zones on our town's borders, we can hook into this by using a script to activate when the hero approaches.

Create a new C# script called `NavigationPrompt`, clear its contents, and populate it with the following code:

```
using UnityEngine;

public class NavigationPrompt : MonoBehaviour {

  bool showDialog;

  void OnCollisionEnter2D(Collision2D col)
  {
    showDialog = true;
  }

  void OnCollisionExit2D(Collision2D col)
  {
    showDialog = false;
  }
}
```

The preceding code gives us the framework of a collision detection script that sets a flag on and off if the character interacts with what the script is attached to, provided it has a physics collision component. Without it, this script would do nothing and it won't cause an error.

Next, we will do something with the flag and display some GUI when the flag is set. So, add the following extra function to the preceding script:

```
void OnGUI()
{
  if (showDialog)
  {
    //layout start
    GUI.BeginGroup(new Rect(Screen.width / 2 - 150, 50, 300,
      250));

    //the menu background box
    GUI.Box(new Rect(0, 0, 300, 250), "");
```

```
    // Information text
    GUI.Label(new Rect(15, 10, 300, 68), "Do you want to
      travel?");

    //Player wants to leave this location
    if (GUI.Button(new Rect(55, 100, 180, 40), "Travel"))
    {
      showDialog = false;

      // The following line is commented out for now
      // as we have nowhere to go :D
      //Application.LoadLevel(1);

    //Player wants to stay at this location
    if (GUI.Button(new Rect(55, 150, 180, 40), "Stay"))
    {
      showDialog = false;
    }

    //layout end
    GUI.EndGroup();
  }
}
```

The function itself is very simple and only activates if the showDialog flag is set to true by the collision detection. Then, we will perform the following steps:

1. In the OnGUI method, we set up a dialog window region with some text and two buttons.

2. One button asks if the player wants to travel, which would load the next area (commented out for now as we only have one scene), and close the dialog.

3. One button simply closes the dialog if the hero didn't actually want to leave. As we haven't stopped moving the player, the player can also do this by moving away.

If you now add the NavigationPrompt script to the two world border (LeftBorder and RightBorder) game objects, this will result in the following simple UI whenever the player collides with the edges of our world:

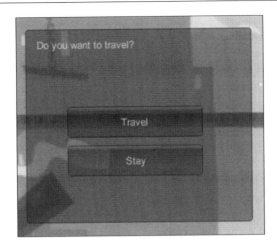

We can further enhance this by *tagging* or *naming* our borders to indicate a destination. I prefer tagging, as it does not interfere with how my scene looks in the project hierarchy; also, I can control what tags are available and prevent accidental mistyping.

To tag a game object, simply select a **Tag** using the drop-down list in the **Inspector** when you select the game object in the scene or project. This is shown in the following screenshot:

If you haven't set up your tags yet or just wish to add a new one, select **Add Tag** in the drop-down menu; this will open up the **Tags and Layers** window of **Inspector**. Alternatively, you can call up this window by navigating to **Edit** | **Project Settings** | **Tags and layers** in the menu. It is shown in the following screenshot:

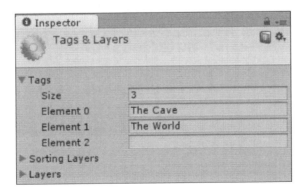

You can only edit or change user-defined tags. There are several other tags that are system defined. You can use these as well; you just cannot change, remove, or edit them. These include `Player`, `Respawn`, `Finish`, `Editor Only`, `Main Camera`, and `GameController`.

As you can see from the preceding screenshot, I have entered two new tags called **The Cave** and **The World**, which are the two main exit points from our town.

Unity also adds an extra item to the arrays in the editor. This helps you when you want to add more items; it's annoying when you want a fixed size but it is meant to help. When the project runs, however, the correct count of items will be exposed.

Once these are set up, just return to the **Inspector** for the two borders, and set the right one to **The World** and the left to **The Cave**.

Now, I was quite specific in how I named these tags, as you can now reuse these tags in the script to both aid navigation and also to notify the player where they are going. To do this, simply update the `Do you want to travel to` line to the following:

```
//Information text
GUI.Label(new Rect(15, 10, 300, 68), "Do you want to travel to " +
    this.tag + "?");
```

Here, we have simply appended the dialog as it is presented to the user with the name of the destination we set in the tag. Now, we'll get a more personal message, as shown in the following screenshot:

# Planning for the larger picture

Now for small games, the preceding implementation is fine; however, if you are planning a larger world with a large number of interactions, provide complex decisions to prevent the player continuing unless they are ready.

As the following diagram shows, there are several paths the player can take and in some cases, these is only one way. Now, we could just build up the logic for each of these individually as shown in the screenshot, but it is better if we build a separate navigation system so that we have everything in one place; it's just easier to manage that way.

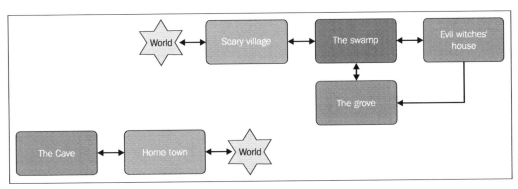

This separation is a fundamental part of any good game design. Keeping the logic and game functionality separate makes it easier to maintain in the future, especially when you need to take internationalization into account (but we will learn more about that later).

> Now, we'll change to using a manager to handle all the world/scene transitions, and simplify the tag names we use as they won't need to be displayed.
>
> So, **The Cave** will be renamed as just **Cave**, and we will get the text to display from the navigation manager instead of the tag.

So, by separating out the core decision making functionality out of the prompt script, we can build the core manager for navigation. Its primary job is to maintain where a character can travel and information about that destination.

First, we'll update the tags we created earlier to simpler identities that we can use in our navigation manager (update **The Cave** to `Cave` and **The World** to `World`).

Next, we'll create a new C# script called NavigationManager in Assets\Scripts, and then replace its contents with the following lines of code:

```
using System.Collections.Generic;
public static class NavigationManager
{


  public static Dictionary<string,string> RouteInformation =
    new Dictionary<string,string>()
  {
    { "World", "The big bad world"},
    { "Cave", "The deep dark cave"},
  };

  public static string GetRouteInfo(string destination)
  {
    return RouteInformation.ContainsKey(destination) ?
    RouteInformation[destination] : null;
  }

  public static bool CanNavigate(string destination)
  {
    return true;
  }

  public static void NavigateTo(string destination)
  {
    // The following line is commented out for now
    // as we have nowhere to go :D
    //Application.LoadLevel(destination);
  }
}
```

Notice the ? and : operators in the following statement:

```
RouteInformation.ContainsKey(destination) ?
    RouteInformation[destination] : null;
```

These operators are C# conditional operators. They are effectively the shorthand of the following:

```
if(RouteInformation.ContainsKey(destination))
{
    return RouteInformation[destination];
}
else
{
    return null;
}
```

Shorter, neater, and much nicer, don't you think?

For more information, see the MSDN C# page at `http://bit.ly/csharpconditionaloperator`.

The script is very basic for now, but contains several following key elements that can be expanded to meet the design goals of your game:

- `RouteInformation`: This is a list of all the possible destinations in the game in a dictionary.

  A static list of possible destinations in the game, and it is a core part of the manager as it knows everywhere you can travel in the game in one place.

- `GetRouteInfo`: This is a basic information extraction function.

  A simple controlled function to interrogate the destination list. In this example, we just return the text to be displayed in the prompt, which allows for more detailed descriptions that we could use in tags. You could use this to provide alternate prompts depending on what the player is carrying and whether they have a lit torch, for example.

- `CanNavigate`: This is a test to see if navigation is possible.

  If you are going to limit a player's travel, you need a way to test if they can move, allowing logic in your game to make alternate choices if the player cannot. You could use a different system for this by placing some sort of block in front of a destination to limit choice (as used in the likes of Zelda), such as an NPC or rock. As this is only an example, we can always travel and add logic to control it if you wish.

- `NavigateTo:` This is a function to instigate navigation.

  Once a player can travel, you can control exactly what happens in the game: does navigation cause the next scene to load straight away (as in the script currently), or does the current scene fade out and then a traveling screen is shown before fading the next level in? Granted, this does nothing at present as we have nowhere to travel to.

The script you will notice is different to the other scripts used so far, as it is a static class. This means it sits in the background, only exists once in the game, and is accessible from anywhere. This pattern is useful for fixed information that isn't attached to anything; it just sits in the background waiting to be queried.

 Later, we will cover more advanced types and classes to provide more complicated scenarios.

With this class in place, we just need to update our previous script (and the tags) to make use of this new manager. Update the `NavigationPrompt` script as follows:

1.  Update the `collision` function to only show the prompt if we can travel. The code is as follows:

```
void OnCollisionEnter2D(Collision2D col)
{
  //Only allow the player to travel if allowed
  if (NavigationManager.CanNavigate(this.tag))
  {
    showDialog = true;
  }
}
```

2.  When the dialog shows, display the more detailed destination text provided by the manager for the intended destination. The code is as follows:

```
//Dialog detail - updated to get better detail
GUI.Label(new Rect(15, 10, 300, 68), "Do you want to travel
  to " + NavigationManager.GetRouteInfo(this.tag) + "?");
```

3.  If the player wants to travel, let the manager start the travel process. The code is as follows:

```
//Player wants to leave this location
if (GUI.Button(new Rect(55, 100, 180, 40), "Travel"))
{
  showDialog = false;
  NavigationManager.NavigateTo(this.tag);
}
```

The functionality I've shown here is very basic and it is intended to make you think about how you would need to implement it for your game. With so many possibilities available, I could fill several chapters on this kind of subject alone.

# Backgrounds and active elements

A slightly more advanced option when building game worlds is to add a level of immersive depth to the scene. Having a static image to show the village looks good, especially when you start adding houses and NPCs to the mix; but to really make it shine, you should layer the background and add additional active elements to liven it up.

We won't add them to the sample project at this time, but it is worth experimenting with in your own projects (or try adding it to this one) — it is a worthwhile effect to look into.

# Parallaxing

If we look at the 2D sample provided by Unity, the background is split into several panes — each layered on top of one another and each moving at a different speed when the player moves around. There are also other elements such as clouds, birds, buses, and taxis driving/flying around, as shown in the following screenshot:

Implementing these effects is very easy technically. You just need to have the art assets available. There are several scripts in the wiki I described earlier, but the one in Unity's own 2D sample is the best I've seen.

 To see the script, just download the **Unity Projects: 2D Platformer** asset from `https://www.assetstore.unity3d.com/en/#!/content/11228`, and check out the `BackgroundParallax` script in `Assets\Scripts`.

The `BackgroundParallax` script in the platformer sample implements the following:

- An array of background images, which is layered correctly in the scene (which is why the script does not just discover the background sprites)

- A scaling factor to control how much the background moves in relation to the camera target, for example, the camera

- A reducing factor to offset how much each layer moves so that they all don't move as one (or else what is the point, might as well be a single image)

- A smoothing factor so that each background moves smoothly with the target and doesn't jump around

Implementing this same model in your game would be fairly simple provided you have texture assets that could support it. Just replicate the structure used in the platformer 2D sample and add the script. Remember to update the `FollowCamera` script to be able to update the base background, however, to ensure that it can still discover the size of the main area.

# Foreground objects

The other thing you can do to liven up your game is to add random foreground objects that *float* across your scene independently. These don't collide with anything and aren't anything to do with the game itself. They are just eye candy to make your game look awesome.

The process to add these is also fairly simple, but it requires some more advanced Unity features such as coroutines, which we are going to cover in another chapter. So, we will come back to these later.

In short, if you examine the `BackgroundPropSpawner.cs` script from the preceding Unity platformer 2D sample, you will have to perform the following steps:

1. Create/instantiate an object to spawn.
2. Set a random position and direction for the object to travel.
3. Update the object over its lifetime.
4. Once it's out of the scene, destroy or hide it.
5. Wait for a time, and then start again.

This allows them to run on their own without impacting the gameplay itself and just adds that extra bit of depth. In some cases, I've seen particle effects are also used to add effect, but they are used sparingly.

# Shaders and 2D

Believe it or not, all 2D elements (even in their default state) are drawn using a shader—albeit a specially written shader designed to light and draw the sprite in a very specific way. If you look at the player sprite in the inspector, you will see that it uses a special **Material** called **Sprites-Default**, as shown in the following screenshot:

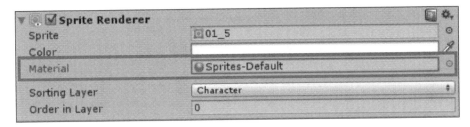

This section is purely meant to highlight all the shading options you have in the 2D system. Shaders have not changed much in this update except for the addition of some 2D global lighting found in the default sprite shader.

For more detail on shaders in general, I suggest a dedicated Unity shader book as it is more than I can cover here.

Clicking on the ⊙ button will bring up the material selector, which also shows the two other built-in default materials, as shown in the following screenshot:

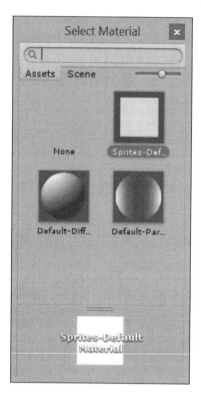

However, selecting either of these will render your sprite invisible as they require a texture and lighting to work; they won't inherit from the **Sprite Renderer** texture. You can override this by creating your own material and assigning alternate sprite style shaders.

To create a new material, just select Assets\Materials (this is not crucial, but it means we create the material in a sensible place in our project folder structure) and then right click on and select **Create | Material**. Alternatively, do the same using the project view's **Edit...** menu option, as shown in the following screenshot:

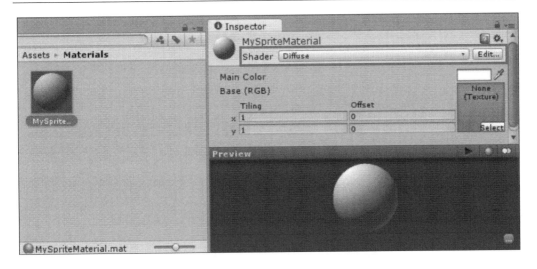

This gives us a basic default **Diffuse** shader, which is fine for basic 3D objects.
However, we also have two default sprite rendering shaders available. Selecting
the shader dropdown gives us the screen shown in the following screenshot:

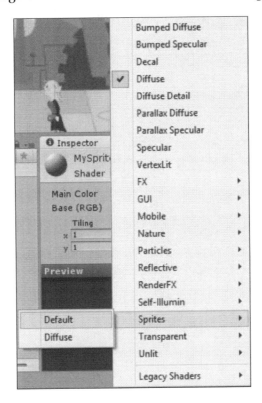

Now, these shaders have the following two very specific purposes:

- **Default**: This shader inherits its texture from the **Sprite Renderer** texture to draw the sprite as is. This is a very basic functionality—just enough to draw the sprite. (It contains its own static lighting.)

- **Diffuse**: This shader is the same as the **Default** shader; it inherits the texture of **Default**, but it requires an external light source as it does not contain any lighting—this has to be applied separately. It is a slightly more advanced shader, which includes offsets and other functions.

Creating one of these materials and applying it to the **Sprite Renderer** texture of a sprite will override its default constrained behavior. This opens up some additional shader options in the **Inspector**, as shown in the following screenshot:

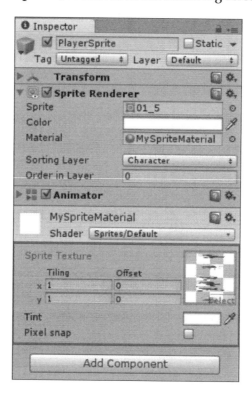

These options include the following:

- **Sprite Texture**: Although changing the **Tiling** and **Offset** values causes a warning to appear, they still display a function (even though the actual displayed value resets).

- **Tint**: This option allows changing the default light tint of the rendered sprite. It is useful to create different colored objects from the same sprite.

- **Pixel snap**: This option makes the rendered sprite crisper but narrows the drawn area. It is a trial and error feature (see the following sections for more information).

> Achieving pixel perfection in your game in Unity can be a challenge due to the number of factors that can affect it, such as the camera view size, whether the image texture is a **Power Of Two** (POT) size, and the import setting for the image. This is basically a trial and error game until you are happy with the intended result.

If you are feeling adventurous, you can extend these default shaders (although this is out of the scope of this book). The full code for these shaders can be found at `http://Unity3d.com/unity/download/archive`.

If you are writing your own shaders though, be sure to add some lighting to the scene; otherwise, they are just going to appear dark and unlit. Only the default sprite shader is automatically lit by Unity. Alternatively, you can use the default sprite shader as a base to create your new custom shader and retain the 2D basic lighting.

> Another worthy tip is to check out the latest version of the Unity samples (beta) pack. In it, they have added logic to have two sets of shaders in your project: one for mobile and one for desktop, and a script that will swap them out at runtime depending on the platform. This is very cool; check out on the asset store at `https://www.assetstore.unity3d.com/#/content/14474` and the full review of the pack at `http://darkgenesis.zenithmoon.com/unity3dsamplesbeta-anoverview/`.

# Going further

If you are the adventurous sort, try expanding your project to add the following:

- Add some buildings to the town
- Set up some entry points for a building and work that into your navigation system, for example, a shop
- Add some rocks to the scene and color each differently using a manual material, maybe even add a script to randomly set the pixel color in the shader instead of creating several materials
- Add a new scene for the cave using another environment background, and get the player to travel between them

# Summary

This certainly has been a very busy chapter just to add a background to our scene, but working out how each scene will work is a crucial design element for the entire game; you have to pick a pattern that works for you and your end result once as changing it can be very detrimental (and a lot of work) in the future.

In this chapter, we covered the following topics:

- Some more practice with the Sprite Editor and sprite slicer including some tips and tricks when it doesn't work (or you want to do it yourself)
- Some camera tips, tricks, and scripts
- An overview of sprite layers and sprite sorting
- Defining boundaries in scenes
- Scene navigation management and planning levels in your game
- Some basics of how shaders work for 2D

In the next chapter, we will build a conversation system. Be prepared for some heavy scripting!

# 5
# NPCs and Interactions

The world would be a lonely place if we were alone. So, in this chapter, we'll look to add in some more characters and give them something to say.

There are a few more fair technical solutions that Unity has under its belt; some are just programing-orientated, whereas some are specific to Unity. So, we'll go through each one of them and explain their pros and cons; plus, we'll look at some extensions that we can add to make them even better.

This is a heavy scripting chapter. All the techniques explained are not used in this chapter but are important to know, and what's more important is to know the difference between them and when to use them.

The list of topics that will be covered in this chapter are as follows:

- Advanced coding, delegates, events, and messaging
- Coroutines
- Scriptable objects and custom importers
- Building a conversation system
- Thinking beyond

## Considering an RPG

When making a role-playing-style game, there is a lot to consider. So far, we have just modeled our player using some standard statistics, but this could be done for any type of game. The thing that sets RPGs apart is their sheer depth and interaction with the living world.

If you are building an RPG game (or one with RPG elements), you need to get some research under your belt and construct your world, the places you can visit (and why), and the characters you will be talking to or fighting with. Some games even go so far as to construct an elaborate backstory that has nothing to do with the actual game.

RPGs have a rich history as they have been around for a long time, and they provide you with a wealth of information, examples, and resources to help you make a great game. One such site is called **DriveThruRPG** (`http://rpg.drivethrustuff.com/index.php`), which even today has an ever-growing catalogue of playbooks, magazines, and materials. As this site is constantly expanding, you have a perpetual resource to continue to build your game beyond the bounds of its first release. If you intend to make the best game out there, it'd be best to consider its long term future and additional content to add in later.

A lot of the content on DriveThruRPG is on a paid basis; however, there is also a great deal of free resources to get you started, and a lot of the magazines are free. Just be sure to check the license of whatever you buy to either use it as is in your game or as a base for your own content.

*Always check the license of anything you use.*

Breaking it down, the main parts of an RPG that this book will focus on are as follows:

- Interactive NPCs
- Noninteractive NPCs
- Enemy characters
- Conversations
- Experience
- Maps and places
- Battles

Other things you should consider (but are not covered) are as follows:

- Missions
- Backstory

- Supporting characters (team)
- Cutscenes (not essential, but really makes the game stand out)

The list might seem endless. However, if you focus on these main elements, you can always expand later.

A common mistake that a lot of new developers make is to design everything for their game from the beginning. Through experience though, you will learn that it is better to start small; first, you should build the main parts of your core game mechanics and then add more content or features over time. If you architect your game in the right way from the beginning, additional content can be added as expansions later on as extra revenue options.

# Advanced programming techniques

As part of this chapter, we start to go in depth with some advanced programming techniques. These enable us to structure our code better and add management to our game project instead of just adding game objects to the scene.

# Singletons and managers

Any project of a sufficient size and complexity is going to run into issues related to managing your game objects as and when they are added and removed from a scene. If you don't get your design right from the start, you are setting yourself up for a world of mess later. A common way to handle this is to use one of the three patterns, single instance managers, singletons, or a dependency system, to manage these controllers for you.

There are two main ways through which you can implement the singleton pattern in Unity. The first way is to use a public static parameter within a class to maintain the runtime class. This also allows any other script to access it from anywhere in the game and is useful if you want other events to cause the manager to do something, for example, things related to conversation systems or traps. You can also use an empty game object in the scene and attach a singleton pattern script to it. However, you could cause conflicts if you add more than one pattern.

Managers, on the other hand, are just central scripts that are particular to an individual scene to control and maintain the flow of the scene for one or many items.

# The manager approach – using empty game objects

Whereas singletons are game wide, there is often a cause for just a scene-based manager. Implementing this using an empty game object is very easy. Simply use **Create Empty** from the **GameObject** menu or the keyboard shortcut, as shown in the following screenshot. The placement of the new game object is up to you. If your controller's position is important (like with an enemy spawner), place it where you want the objects to spawn from. If not, it doesn't matter; it just needs to be in the scene somewhere. As it's an empty game object, it will not be drawn.

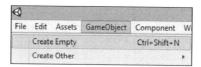

Then, create your manager script in the normal way. For example, the following script simply spawns the configurable enemy objects from a collection according to a simple repeating interval:

```
public class EnemySpawnManager : MonoBehaviour
{
  public float spawnTime = 5f;
  //The amount of time between each spawn.
  public float spawnDelay = 3f;
  //The amount of time before spawning starts.
  public GameObject[] enemies;
  //Array of enemy prefabs.

  void Start ()
  {
    //Start calling the Spawn function repeatedly after a delay.
    InvokeRepeating("Spawn", spawnDelay, spawnTime);
  }

  void Spawn ()
  {
    //Instantiate a random enemy.
    int enemyIndex = Random.Range(0, enemies.Length);
    Instantiate(enemies[enemyIndex],
    transform.position, transform.rotation);
  }
}
```

Then, simply attach your script to the new empty game object. For it to function, you will need to assign the prefabs of the types of enemies you want to appear in the scene by attaching them to the **Enemies** property, as shown in the following screenshot:

You could also extend the manager to keep track of the game objects it creates; additionally, instead of creating new objects each time, you can just allocate an object from a pool, thereby removing the need to create and destroy objects over time.

# The singleton approach – using the C# singleton pattern

The manager approach is fine in most cases, but you have to control each instance of the controller where it is placed. Moreover, you cannot interact with it or trigger it without more configurations added to the manager class, and then either binding the manager to other objects or using the dreaded Find function.

If you need a true manager, a better approach is to employ the singleton pattern for a manager class; refer to the following example:

```
public class MySingletonManager : MonoBehaviour {

  //Static singleton property
  public static MySingletonManager Instance {
    get; private set;
  }
}
```

```
//public property for manager
public string MyTestProperty = "Hello World";

void Awake()
{
  //Save our current singleton instance
  Instance = this;
}

//public method for manager
public void DoSomethingAwesome()
{ }
}
```

The preceding code is just a very basic singleton implementation, which you can attach to any game object in the scene.

Then, you can access the properties and functions within the singleton script by simply calling the following method from anywhere within your project:

```
//Set the public property of the singleton
MySingletonManager.Instance.MyTestProperty = "World Hello";

//Run the public method from the singleton
MySingletonManager.Instance.DoSomethingAwesome();
```

The class can run like any other class with updates, fixed updates, and so on. It can also be expanded very quickly.

One of the other common uses of this pattern is the use of global variables for your project. However, if you intend to use your singleton class across the scenes, you will also need to ensure that it is not destroyed when the scene unloads with a simple update. This is done by calling DontDestroyOnLoad when you initialize the class, as shown in the following code:

```
public class MySingletonManager : MonoBehaviour {

  //static singleton property
  public static MySingletonManager Instance { get; private set; }

  //public property for manager
  public string MyTestProperty = "Hello World";
```

```
void Awake()
{
  //First we check if there are any other instances conflicting
  if (Instance != null && Instance != this)
  {
    //Destroy other instances if they are not the same
    Destroy(gameObject);
  }

  //Save our current singleton instance
  Instance = this;

  //Make sure that the instance is not destroyed
  //between scenes (this is optional)
  DontDestroyOnLoad(gameObject);
}

//public method for manager
public void DoSomethingAwesome()
{    }
}
```

There are more complicated setups for singletons. If you so wish, you can read them at http://wiki.unity3d.com/index.php/Singleton.

There is another pattern named **Dependency Injection**. A more robust way to handle the need of manager- or factory-type requirements in any project is to implement an **Inversion of Control (IoC)** pattern, such as Dependency Injection.

Dependency Injection is a large subject, so we won't cover it in this book. The goal here is to make you aware of all the options when architecting your project. If you would like more detailed information on Dependency Injection, I'd recommend the post at http://blog.sebaslab.com/ ioc-container-for-unity3d-part-2/ to start with, and then you can work up from there.

Dependency Injection is a very powerful tool when employed correctly and can make your project a lot easier, so it is worth looking at it if you are serious. However, care is needed in its use, and it should not be used everywhere; it should only be used where it solves a particular problem.

A good Unity-based IoC framework is **StrangeIOC**, which can be found at http://strangeioc.github.io/strangeioc/ TheBigStrangeHowTo.html.

# Communicating between game objects

In any game, there are planned interactions between any components within the game. These could be as follows:

- Physics collision tests
- Reacting to being shot or shooting
- Opening and closing doors
- Triggers, switches, or traps
- Two or more characters talking

There are several ways in which you can achieve this, and each has their own particular traits. The selection of the implementations depends on what you need to achieve. The methods are as follows:

- Delegates
- Events
- Messaging

In this section, we will go through each method in detail and highlight the best uses of each.

# Delegates

We encounter delegates in our everyday lives. Sometimes they are managers, sometimes they are subordinates, and they could even be the barista at your local coffee shop. Delegates effectively are methods that accept pieces of work to do on behalf of someone else.

> Another form of delegates is to use the C# generics and the `Action` or `Action<T>` methods, which is a shorthand version of the implementations mentioned in the next section. For more information about generics and `Action`, refer to http://msdn.microsoft.com/en-us/library/018hxwa8(v=vs.110).aspx.

There are two main patterns in which delegates are used: the configurable method pattern and the delegation pattern.

 The scripts in this section can be found in `Assets\Scripts\Examples` under the `Delegates` script.

# The configurable method pattern

The configurable method pattern is used when a piece of work or function is passed to another method to be used to complete a task. This pattern is usually used where different pieces of code can perform a common task in unique ways, such as walking, running, or patrolling. All these tasks can be the default behaviors of a character. Refer to the following diagram:

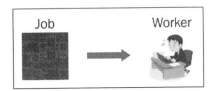

Here, you will have your code calling a `delegate` method, but the contents of this method can be different depending on what you have set it to.

For instance, refer to the following code:

```
using System;
using UnityEngine;
public class Delegates
{
    //Define delegate method signature
    delegate void RobotAction();
    //private property for delegate use
    RobotAction myRobotAction;

    void Start ()
    {
        //Set the default method for the delegate
        myRobotAction = RobotWalk;
    }
```

```
void Update()
{
  //Run the selected delegate method on update
  myRobotAction();
}

//public method to tell the robot to walk
public void DoRobotWalk()
{
  //set the delegate method to the walk function
  myRobotAction = RobotWalk;
}

void RobotWalk()
{
  Debug.Log("Robot walking");
}

//public method to tell the robot to run
public void DoRobotRun()
{
  //set the delegate method to the run function
  myRobotAction = RobotRun;
}

void RobotRun()
{
  Debug.Log("Robot running");
}
}
```

This means that when the DoRobotWalk method is called, it will set the delegate to the Walk method, and once updated, it will run the Walk behavior. If you call the DoRobotRun public method, it will change the delegate to the Run behavior, and once updated, it will run the Run behavior. This is a very simple kind of state machine with no conditions around.

# The delegation pattern

The delegation pattern is used where a method calls out to a helper library, and on completion of the required task, continues on back in the `main` function, as shown in the following diagram:

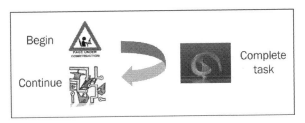

This is usually used with what you might download from the Web. When the download is finished, we do something with what we have downloaded.

For instance, refer to the following code:

```csharp
using System;
using System.Collections.Generic;
public class Delegates
{
  public class Worker
  {
    List<string> WorkCompletedfor = new List<string>();
    public void DoSomething(
      string ManagerName,
      Action myDelegate)
    {
      //Audits that work was done for which manager
      WorkCompletedfor.Add(ManagerName);

      //Begin work
      myDelegate();
    }
  }

  public class Manager
  {
    private Worker myWorker = new Worker();
```

```
public void PeiceOfWork1()
{
//A piece of very long tedious work
}

public void PeiceOfWork2()
{
  //You guessed it, yet more tedious work
}

public void DoWork()
{
  //Send worker to do job 1
  myWorker.DoSomething("Manager1",PeiceOfWork1);

  //Send worker to do job 2
  myWorker.DoSomething("Manager1", PeiceOfWork2);
}
}
}
```

Alternatively, you could just express it using the C# lamdas, which simply means you don't need to declare separate functions as follows:

```
public void DoWork2()
{
  private Worker myWorker = new Worker();

  //Send worker to do job 1
  myWorker.DoSomething("Manager1", () =>
  {
    //A piece of very long tedious work
  });

  //Send worker to do job 2
  myWorker.DoSomething("Manager2", () =>
  {
    //You guessed it, yet more tedious work
  });
}
```

If your delegate also uses a string as a parameter, the preceding example could be used as a download pattern where a helper library does the entire download and just returns the XML asset. This asset can then be unpacked and used in the game in your main function.

# Compound delegates

Both the configurable method pattern and delegation pattern are very powerful techniques when used correctly.

Another feature of delegates is that they can be compounded, meaning you can assign multiple functions to a single delegate. Also, when a delegate is called, all the methods assigned to the delegate will run, as shown in the following code. This feature is very handy when you want to chain several common functions together instead of one:

```
public class WorkerManager
{
  void DoWork()
  {
    DoJob1();
    DoJob2();
    DoJob3();
  }

  private void DoJob1()
  {
    //Do some filing
  }

  private void DoJob2()
  {
    //Make coffee for the office
  }

  private void DoJob3()
  {
    //Stick it to the man
  }
}
```

You can achieve the same output but with more flexibility by using the following code:

```
//A more intelligent WorkerManager
public class WorkerManager2
{
  //WorkerManager delegate
  delegate void MyDelegateHook();
  MyDelegateHook ActionsToDo;
```

```
public string WorkerType = "Peon";

//On Startup, assign jobs to the worker; note this is
//configurable instead of fixed
void Start()
{
  //Peons get lots of work to do
  if (WorkerType == "Peon")
  {
    ActionsToDo += DoJob1;
    ActionsToDo += DoJob2;
  }
  //Everyone else plays golf
  else
  {
    ActionsToDo += DoJob3;
  }
}

//With Update, do the actions set on ActionsToDo
void Update()
{
  ActionsToDo();
}

private void DoJob1()
{
  //Do some filing
}

private void DoJob2()
{
  //Make coffee for the office
}

private void DoJob3()
{
  //Play Golf
}
}
```

This also means it's dynamic and you can add additional functions to the delegate that will be called whenever the delegate is called.

 Word to the wise: only use chained delegates when you absolutely need the flexibility to do so as they are a more complex pattern to implement. They are also difficult to debug should something untoward happen.

# Events

We can describe events as "expected announcements". Imagine you have a bat phone at your desk; when it rings, you know it's "Batman" on the other end, usually telling you some trouble has been averted. Events are similar to this pattern where there is a hook; this is where you can listen for something to happen and then do something with that event. When it occurs, additionally, through events, you can pass this information to provide yourself with additional information about what has occurred, as depicted in the following image:

In the following code, events use delegates to describe how they are going to communicate. It defines the form that communication will take and what information will be passed when the event is fired:

```
//Delegate method definition
public delegate void ClickAction();

//Event hook using delegate method signature
public static event ClickAction OnClicked;
```

Now when an event needs to be initiated in your class, all it needs to do to notify any other code that is listening to the event is call the event like a method using `delegate` as the signature.

 However, what you must be careful about is that no one is listening to the event (no one has subscribed to it). To do this, you need to check that `delegate` is *not* null before you call it.

Refer to the following code:

```
void Update()
{
    //If the space bar is pressed, this item has been clicked
    if (Input.GetKeyDown(KeyCode.Space))
    {
        //Trigger the event delegate if there is a subscriber
        if (OnClicked != null)
        {
            OnClicked();
        }
    }
}
```

With the event exposed, any other class or game object that needs to be informed about the occurrence of the event just needs to subscribe to the event as follows using the += syntax:

```
void Start()
{
    //Hook on to the function's onClicked event and run the
    //Events_OnClicked method when it occurs
    OnClicked += Events_OnClicked;
}

    //Subordinate method
    void Events_OnClicked()
    {
        Debug.Log("The button was clicked");

    }

void OnDestroy()
{
    //Unsubscribe from the event to clean up
    OnClicked -= Events_OnClicked;
}
```

 It's always a good idea to clean up after yourself and unsubscribe from the events when you no longer need them, as shown in the preceding code, using the -= syntax.

This is a very simple example, but you could imagine exposing an event for when an enemy is destroyed and hooking your score system into it so that the score is incremented every time an enemy dies.

A better way is to write a separate method to call when you need to trigger the event; refer to the following code. In this way, you don't have the preceding code repeated throughout:

```
//Safe method for calling the event
void Clicked()
{
  //Trigger the event delegate if there is a subscriber
  if (OnClicked != null)
  {
    OnClicked();
  }
}
```

Now, all you have to do whenever the event needs to be fired is call the `Clicked` method that is shown in the preceding code, which is always safe and won't crash if there are no subscribers.

As a help, this code is the template I always use when creating an event. To simplify its creation, all you have to do to use it each time is change the name, and if necessary, the delegate signature if you need additional parameters; the following code will tell you how to do this:

```
//Logging template to send a string/report every time something //
happens
public delegate void LogMessage(string message);
public static event LogMessage Log;

void OnLog(string message)
{
  if (Log != null)
  {
    Log(message);
  }
}
```

# Messaging

Communication is a key factor in any game. A lot of times, we just use colliders or physics to notify two components that there is something to be aware of. This is a very basic form of communication. Other times, we use referencing or (in the case of Unity) trawl through the project's hierarchy to find another game object to communicate with or notify.

Unity has its own messaging-type functions, such as `SendMessage` and `BroadcastMessage`. Both functions actually implement event-style code (as in the preceding case) without actually declaring events, but they are *very* slow and shouldn't be used extensively.

The `SendMessage` function will call a named method on a game object (any method with the same name) with a *single* optional parameter as follows:

```
void OnCollisionEnter(Collision col)
{
  col.gameObject.SendMessage("IHitYou");
}
```

So, it will call the `IHitYou` method on whatever you will collide with. By default, this will not cause an error to be raised if whatever you collide with does not have the `IHitYou` method. However, if you wish, you can change this by adding `SendMessageOptions` when you call `SendMessage`, as follows:

```
void OnCollisionEnter(Collision col)
{
  col.gameObject.SendMessage("IHitYou",
    SendMessageOptions.RequireReceiver);
}
```

If you want to send a value (there can only be one) with the call, just add it after the method name and before `SendMessageOptions` (if set).

The `BroadcastMessage` method works in a similar way but will attempt to run your selected method on the selected `gameObject` and *all* its children as follows:

```
void OnCollisionEnter(Collision col)
{
  col.gameObject.BroadcastMessage("IHitYou");
}
```

Using either of the methods (as stated) is very slow. This is because it has to try and discover (under the hood) if the game object (and its children if using broadcast) has the method first; it will then attempt to run it. As Unity will not know until your game starts running and whether a game object will have that method, it has to perform this each and every time you try it.

# A better way

To break this dependency between the game objects and the need to keep references or the need to discover each other at the design or runtime stage, we need an intermediary that all objects know about, that is, a `Manager` class.

With this `manager` class, it will manage the list of game objects that want to listen to the messages and provide an easy way to notify anyone who's listening.

To implement this, we will use the singleton behavior described earlier by creating three simple, reusable components as a test case.

First, we create the `manager` class itself. So, create a `MessagingManager.cs` C# script and then replace its contents as follows:

```
using System;
using System.Collections.Generic;
using UnityEngine;

public class MessagingManager : MonoBehaviour
{
  //Static singleton property
  public static MessagingManager Instance { get; private set; }

  // public property for manager
  private List<Action> subscribers = new List<Action>();
}
```

The first property is the singleton instance for the `manager` class, while the second is a list of delegates that will be used to keep track of who needs to be notified.

Next, we add the `Awake` function to initialize the singleton approach:

```
void Awake()
{
  Debug.Log("Messaging Manager Started");
  //First, we check if there are any other instances conflicting
```

```
if (Instance != null && Instance != this)
{
  //Destroy other instances if it's not the same
  Destroy(gameObject);
}

//Save our current singleton instance
Instance = this;

//Make sure that the instance is not destroyed between scenes
//(this is optional)
DontDestroyOnLoad(gameObject);
}
```

This is the same as before but with a little extra debug information so you can see when it is initialized in the **Console** window.

Then, we add a method so we can register recipients or subscribers to the messages (with the associated UnSubscribe and ClearAllSubscribers methods), as follows:

```
//The Subscribe method for manager
public void Subscribe(Action subscriber)
{
  Debug.Log("Subscriber registered");
  subscribers.Add(subscriber);
}

//The Unsubscribe method for manager
public void UnSubscribe(Action subscriber)
{
  Debug.Log("Subscriber registered");
  subscribers.Remove(subscriber);
}

//Clear subscribers method for manager
public void ClearAllSubscribers()
{
  subscribers.Clear();
}
```

This method just adds the delegate you passed to the manager class to be added to the notification list.

Finally, we add a `Broadcast` method that tells the messaging system to let all the subscribers know that something has happened; the following code tells us how to do this:

```
public void Broadcast()
{
  Debug.Log("Broadcast requested, No of Subscribers = " +
    subscribers.Count);
  foreach (var subscriber in subscribers)
  {
    subscriber();
  }
}
```

Here, we simply loop through all the subscribers and notify them using their delegates; very simple!

As you can see, this is just a very basic messenger that when called will tell anyone who is listening that something has happened; there will be no extra information, no details, just an event. This is like the fire alarm in your building; when it goes off, you just run—you don't (usually) ask, you don't question—you just know that when that alarm goes off, you need to get out of the building!

To finish this `manager` class off, simply create an empty game object in your scene and add the script to it. There are ways to do that automatically, but I find this way is cleaner so that you always know what the active agents in the scene are. Later in *Chapter 10*, *The Battle Begins*, I'll show you a way to create an editor menu option to do this automatically for you.

Putting this to use is simple. As mentioned before, we need three scripts; we have the `manager` class, so now we need a client and a broadcast agent.

For the broadcast agent, create a C# script named `MessagingClientBroadcast` and replace its contents with the following code:

```
using UnityEngine;

public class MessagingClientBroadcast : MonoBehaviour {

  void OnCollisionEnter2D(Collision2D col)
  {
    MessagingManager.Instance.Broadcast();
  }
}
```

The preceding code is just a simple example so that when attached to an object with a 2D collider, it will trigger a broadcast. To test, just add it to one or both of the border objects in our game scene. In this way, if the player tries to leave the scene, it will ring the alarm bells.

At the moment though, no one is listening, so let's add a listener/receiver. Create another C# script and name it `MessagingClientReceiver`. This script will register for events and log in to the **Console** window with some information about the object it's attached to (obviously, there will be no information from the broadcast event as it has none); the following code will tell you how to do this:

```
using UnityEngine;

public class MessagingClientReceiver : MonoBehaviour
{
  void Start()
  {
    MessagingManager.Instance.Subscribe(ThePlayerIsTryingToLeave);
  }

  void ThePlayerIsTryingToLeave()
  {
    Debug.Log("Oi Don't Leave me!! - " + tag.ToString());
  }
}
```

In simple words, when the game object script is attached to a startup, it will register itself with the `MessagingManager` script, telling the `manager` class to run the second method in the script when the event occurs. As stated before, this just logs in to the **Console** window for now so that we have something to see.

Just for fun, also add this script to one or both of the borders in our scene; this is simply because we don't have anything else at the moment. You could add it to the player, making the event as an alarm that goes off and changing the `ThePlayerIsTryingToLeave` method to cause the player to run in the opposite direction if you wish.

If you run the project now, you should get the following results:

- One message to tell you that the `MessagingManager` script has started.
- One message per subscriber that has registered with the manager (although in the **Console** window, you may just see **2** next to the event because it is the same).

- When the event is triggered, you will get one message per subscriber to tell you that they have received it. Note that each message from the client is particular to the game object you attached it to as the message is different.

Now, you could have just executed the preceding code using the `Send` or `Broadcast` Unity methods, and it would have been much simpler. However, you should note that since we are using a single `manager` class, which is a static instance in the scene, at no point should any of the game objects involved need to know about each other. There is no need to search the hierarchy or add components to each other at editing time; it just works.

# Background tasks and Coroutines

Next up in the fabulous journey of scripting, we will cover the treacherous realm of background tasks. We use the background tasks to start something (in the background) so that it is runs independently of the normal game update and draw cycle.

> Coroutines, by default, run on the same thread as the normal game loop. If you are not careful, they can stop your game from running. (You can dispatch them on to separate threads in Unity Pro to offset the work in order to improve the performance.)
>
> For more information on Coroutines and the default execution order of methods, refer to the article in the Unity docs at `https://docs.unity3d.com/Documentation/Manual/ExecutionOrder.html`.

The following diagram shows that we can have a second process that runs alongside our main game:

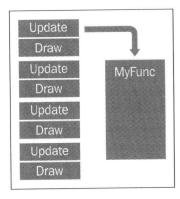

This is usually used for systems that are continually running and not for the main events on the screen, such as AI, a background trading system, or even a continual web-service-gathering data for the game.

Unity also has the ability to synchronize these background threads with a simple function that pauses the operation (or returns the control back to Unity) until the next frame of the game is drawn (`WaitForEndOfFrame` or `WaitForFixedUpdate`), which gives you a pattern like the following screenshot:

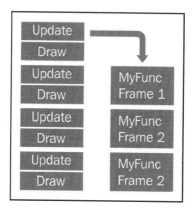

The benefit of this is that you can wait for the last update or draw cycle to finish before running your process. You might do this if you want to render what is drawn on the screen to an image and either save it to a disk or upload it to a web service or website.

The Unity documents provide a good example of using this behavior; you can find them at `https://docs.unity3d.com/Documentation/ScriptReference/WaitForEndOfFrame.html`.

# Enter Coroutines

The proper way to implement long-running tasks in Unity is through the use of a feature called Coroutines. In simple words, Coroutines are Unity's way of launching code in the background, but they do have a few caveats and features around them though.

Remember, Coroutines, run on the same thread as the normal game loop and use the same resources as the game loop (albeit at the same time). To enable threading (running processes on separate processors or pipelines, distributing the workload), you will need Unity Pro. Sorry to reiterate this, but it's a very important point to mention.

# IEnumerator

At their core, Coroutines are just normal methods, but they are implemented using a particular generic interface named IEnumerator as their return type. This enables Unity to track the method's state through several iterations (runs).

 Don't confuse IEnumerator with IEnumerable when defining your Coroutines; otherwise, you will find that they won't work.

To create a basic Coroutine, you simply need to set up the method as shown in the following code:

```
IEnumerator MyCoroutine()
{
    //Do something
    //Then return
    yield return null;

}
```

This would create a simple single-use Coroutine that would perform a single function, and when it's finished, it will die and go away.

A more common pattern is to have a loop of some kind within the function that will not finish until some condition is met; this is done by either using a while or for loop as follows:

```
IEnumerator MyCoroutine (){
    bool complete = false;
    while (!complete)
    {
        //Do some repetitive task
        //When done set complete to true

        //Then return control after each step
        yield return null;
    }
}
```

The preceding code will simply run in the background until the condition is met; for example, a timer that is counting down should stop when it reaches 0.

# Yielding

The Coroutines and IEnumerator feature are perfectly valid, but C# added a new operator in Version 2 (Unity now supports V4) called the `yield` operator. The `yield` operator suspends the current method on the current instruction line until the operation is complete; however, it also allows the CPU to continue in between each result that is returned by the called method or the instruction. The following example will pause the loop for two seconds in between the iterations while retuning the control back to the process.

Here's an example; say we have a function to print 10 lines:

```
IEnumerator Print10Lines()
{
  for (int i = 0; i < 10; i++)
  {
    print("Line" + i.ToString());
    yield return new WaitForSeconds(2);
  }
}
```

When the preceding code runs, it will simply loop 10 times, and each time it will print out the line number. However, before continuing, it will wait for 2 seconds.

 Do not confuse `IEnumerator` with `IEnumerable`. Coroutines and the `yield` keyword only work in a method that returns an `IEnumerator` feature. This is an easy mistake that can leave you scratching your head for hours.

# Starting Coroutines

There are actually two types of Coroutines (it is best to think of them in that way, even though they are actually the same thing): those that are just launched (`fire` and `forget`) and those that can be managed. The difference is just in the way they are called. The `fire` and `forget` Coroutine functions are simply called by using the following code:

```
StartCoroutine(MyCoroutine()); //or
StartCoroutine(MyCoroutine(MyParameter)); //to use parameters
```

In the preceding code, the `MyCoroutine` function is started using the `delegate` method. Once started, it will not finish until either the function ends or `StopAllCoroutines()` is called. Now, start the Coroutine using the following code:

```
StartCoroutine("MyCoroutine"); //or
StartCoroutine("MyCoroutine", myParameter); //to use parameters
```

In the preceding code, you specify the name of your Coroutine function and the method's name using a string. This enables you to stop the Coroutine from running anytime (and from anywhere) using the following code:

```
StopCoroutine("MyCoroutine");
```

> Currently, there are some enhancements being made in Unity that will enable you to stop the Coroutines that are called using the method's name. It is not clear yet whether this will be in the 4.x or 5.x timescales. Keep watching!

The invocation path is something to be kept in mind. You might ask why not just use the second method all the time. The answer is simple. Unity has to use slower methods to discover the method it needs to track when you provide the Coroutine's name as a string; just passing the method's name is quicker and smoother. The best advice would be to use each type according to its strengths. Only use the string launch method when you need to manage a background task and use the method names when it is a short-lived function that is solely aimed at accomplishing a single task. For everything else, just weigh up the pros and cons of each approach as you implement it.

Coroutines can be powerful additions to the arsenal of your game's framework, but they need to be implemented wisely; too many additions to your game (obviously) will just grind to a halt. If you only ever use the `fire` and `forget` Coroutines, you won't be able to stop them without shutting down all the rest as well (including those you started by naming them as a string).

# Closing the gap

So now that we understand how we call Coroutines, to make the `Print10Lines` method described earlier, we will call it as follows:

```
void Example1()
{
  StartCoroutine(Print10Lines());
  print("I started printing lines");
}
```

As explained, the preceding code will kick off the `Print10Lines` function and then continue forward while the routing to print the lines continues simultaneously. On the other hand, the following code will print 10 lines, and only after it is finished will it continue and notify you that printing has finished:

```
IEnumerator Example2()
{
  yield return StartCoroutine(Print10Lines());
  print("I have finished printing lines");
}
```

Any method that has a return type of `IEnumerator` has to be called using one of the `StartCoroutine` methods; just calling any method with `IEnumerator` on its own will do nothing. So, keep this in mind if you are wondering why something is not being called.

# Serialization and scripting

To finish with our theory for this chapter, we need to cover serialization in Unity. Now, Unity already serializes just about everything from the editor to your scene automatically (with a few exceptions) when it saves and loads the scene.

There are a few fringe cases where Unity will not serialize some data. These cases have to do with the current limitations of the Mono 2 framework that Unity uses under the hood. A full explanation of what doesn't work can be found in the following article; note that it is very technical and includes a link to the error report in Unity where it is recorded:

http://www.codingjargames.com/blog/2012/11/30/advanced-unity-serialization/

However, what if we want to actually use this serialization to our advantage within our game to save and load levels. We need bits of raw game data (or as we will continue with this later, saving conversations for our NPCs). To accomplish this, the best way is to use a Unity-inherited object named `ScriptableObject`.

The `ScriptableObject` entity allows you to save the data within the class that uses it for a `.asset` file in your project.

# Saving and managing asset data

To achieve this, we simply need to create a script (named `ScriptingObjects`) with some properties we want to serialize; then, we change its class inheritance from `MonoBehaviour` to `ScriptableObject` as follows:

```
using UnityEngine;

public class ScriptingObjects : ScriptableObject {

  public Vector2[] MyPositions;
}
```

Great! So we have some serializable data. However, to use it in the editor, we need to create an option in the editor to create and save these assets for us. Create a new script named `PositionManager` in the `Editor` folder under `Assets\Scripts` (create it if it does not exist yet), and replace its contents with the following code:

```
using UnityEngine;
using UnityEditor;

public class PositionManager : MonoBehaviour
{
  //Define a menu option in the editor to create the new asset
  [MenuItem("Assets/Create/PositionManager")]
  public static void CreateAsset()
  {
    //Create a new instance of our scriptable object
    ScriptingObjects positionManager =
      ScriptableObject.CreateInstance<ScriptingObjects>();

    //Create a .asset file for our new object and save it
    AssetDatabase.CreateAsset(positionManager,
      "Assets/newPositionManager.asset");
    AssetDatabase.SaveAssets();

    //Now switch the inspector to our new object
    EditorUtility.FocusProjectWindow();
    Selection.activeObject = positionManager;
  }
}
```

Any script that uses the `UnityEditor` namespace has to be placed in a special `Editor` folder. This ensures that it is only packaged with the editor solution and not used in the deployed game. Game projects are not deployed with the editor.

There is a lot to explain, but it is all commented very well in short, as follows:

- We define a menu option from where we will call our creation code
- We set up a new object that we want to serialize and create the file where it is to be stored
- We change the view of the editor to focus the inspector on the new object

 If you create custom classes to be used in serialization, you must tag those classes with the `[System.Serializable]` attribute. Otherwise, Unity will not know that they are for serialization. We will cover more on this later in the implemented example.

If you return to Unity now and right-click on the `Asset` folder (or click on the **Create** menu option in the **Project** view), you will see the new menu option you just created, as shown in the following screenshot:

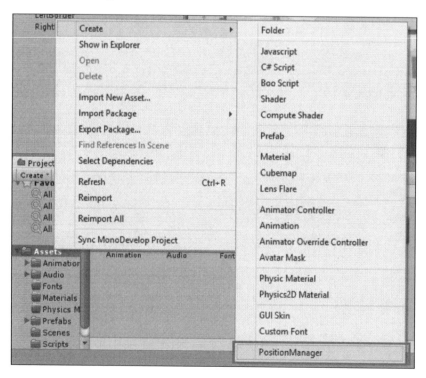

After clicking on it, you will see your new asset in the **Project** view (in the location you saved it to, in this case, the root of the `Asset` folder) and the **Inspector** view for your item, as shown in the following screenshot:

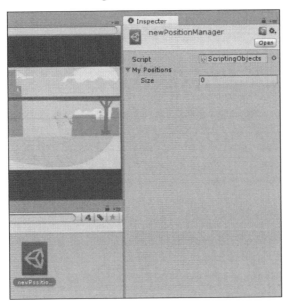

If we rename our new serialized object, give it some values, and save the scene or project, we will see the following screenshot:

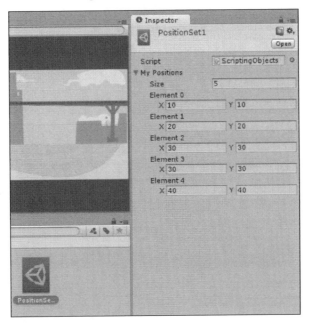

We go from the preceding screenshot to the following code stored in the .asset file (when opened from the .asset file generated in Unity from **File Explorer**):

```
%YAML 1.1
%TAG !u! tag:unity3d.com,2011:
--- !u!114 &11400000
MonoBehaviour:
  m_ObjectHideFlags: 0
  m_PrefabParentObject: {fileID: 0}
  m_PrefabInternal: {fileID: 0}
  m_GameObject: {fileID: 0}
  m_Enabled: 1
  m_EditorHideFlags: 0
  m_Script: {fileID: 11500000, guid:
    fa9c23f7a21df484a96802b68617f3b6, type: 3}
  m_Name: MyPositions1
  m_EditorClassIdentifier:
  MyPositions:
  - {x: 10, y: 10}
  - {x: 20, y: 20}
  - {x: 30, y: 30}
  - {x: 30, y: 30}
  - {x: 40, y: 40}
```

There is a fair amount of Unity information in the preceding code, but what is important is our serialized data at the bottom. So if we wish, we can edit this file outside of the editor and it will be reimported next time you open Unity.

# Using the serialized files in the editor

Using the files in the editor is a very simple task. Simply create a property in any script using the type of your serialized asset and then assign a project asset in the editor.

For example, edit the MessagingManager script and add the following property:

```
public ScriptingObjects MyWaypoints;
```

Then, the script will be exposed in the **Inspector** pane and you can assign it normally, as shown in the following screenshot:

You will also be able to access the contents of the serialized object from that script as well.

You cannot edit the contents of the serialized file in the assigned property by default. This is only achievable by using a custom property inspector, which will be covered in *Chapter 10, The Battle Begins*. However, it is still editable in the editor by opening the `Asset` folder itself.

# Accessing the .asset files in the code

Now, if you don't want to assign the asset through the editor, there is a way to just load the `.asset` file directly from the project.

Firstly, to do this, you will need to store your `.asset` files in a special folder named `Resources` in your `Asset` folder. You can read them there directly using Unity's own resource functions once.

As an example, open the `PositionManager` script and add the following function:

```
public static PositionManager ReadPositionsFromAsset(string Name)
{
    string path = "/";

    object o = Resources.Load(path + Name);
    PositionManager retrievedPositions = (PositionManager)o;
    return retrievedPositions;
}
```

This function, which is available from anywhere as it is static, will perform the following tasks:

- Using the Name parameter, it will read the .asset file from the root of the Resources folder
- It will convert the retrieved file to the correct object type
- It will return the deserialized object to the calling function

So now you can call up the data contained within your .asset file anywhere in your game project.

The same kind of pattern can also be used to download the .asset files from the Web for your project to add DLC or expand the levels of your game. A word to the wise though; if you do go down this route, be sure to compress and encrypt your assets that are meant for downloading to protect your IP.

Also, if you have any dependent files, such as images, be sure to download them separately.

However, to use the downloaded files as assets in your scene, you will require them to be packaged as asset bundles. This also requires Unity Pro.

# Putting it all together

Right, after all of that "brain input", let's start applying it to our game. In this chapter, we are aiming to add an NPC or two, give them something to talk about, and maybe add some special reactions.

If you haven't done so already, import the other character sprites and set up their animations as well. You can either add them to the scene or just create some prefabs in your **Project** view:

I've added the following characters (shown in the preceding screenshot):

- **Greandal** (left): This character is the local barkeeper and mayor of our lone village
- **Olaf** (right): This character is your hero's best friend and an all-round troublemaker
- **Greybeard** (center): This character is the strange wizard from the east

With these characters in place, we need to start adding some character to our NPCs as well as add our hero. In *Chapter 2, Character Building*, we outlined some classes to describe and manage the entities in the game, so let's bring them in now.

We could also do with a little tidying up of our `scripts` folder since we are generating a lot more content now. To do this, perform the following steps:

- Under `Assets\Scripts`, create four new folders: `Classes`, `Examples`, `Messaging`, and `Navigation` (the `Examples` folder isn't actually needed, but if you want to keep the code that is generated thus far in this chapter, we will place them here).
- Copy the `Entity` and `Player` scripts to the new `Classes` folder or create them if you haven't already.
- Copy the scripts from this chapter (`Delegates`, `Events`, `Coroutines`, `ScriptingObject`) to the `Examples` folder, or just delete them as they are not for the game itself. If you didn't create them, just ignore this step.
- Move the `Messaging` scripts to the `Messaging` folder, and likewise, the `Navigation` scripts to the `Navigation` folder.

Starting with Greybeard, add him on the left-hand side of the scene, next to the cave. This is because in the next section, he is going to stop our hero from entering the cave, as it is just too dangerous for such an impetuous youth.

To do this (using the lessons we have learned already), perform the following steps:

1. Create a new game object and name it `Greybeard`.
2. If you haven't done so already, import the `04.png` character spritesheet and use **Sprite Editor** to slice it up.
3. Give it a **Sprite Renderer** component using the **04_3** sprite from the **04** wizard's spritesheet.

4.  Create an idle animation for Greybeard using the **04_03** and **04_06** sprites so it appears that Greybeard is fidgeting (optional); then, add it to a new **Animator** component and add that to the Greybeard's game object.

5.  Finally, add a **Box Collider 2D** component with the settings shown in the following screenshot. This is so that the collider is of the same width as that of Greybeard himself but with a larger height so that the player can collide with it. Also, set the **Is Trigger** property to true/checked.

The final result should look something like the following screenshot:

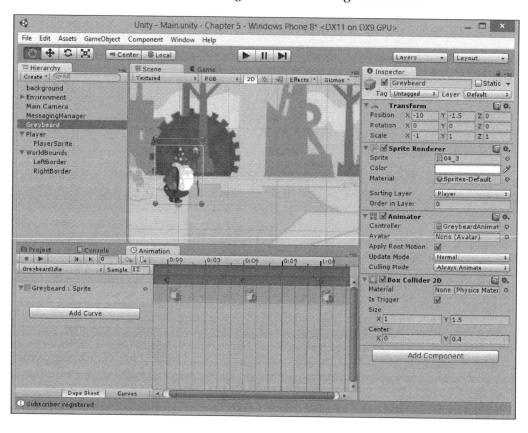

I added an animation that shows he is fidgeting on the spot. This is just because most old wizards are very crotchety, especially when they have to guard a cave full of dangerous monsters.

A few things to note while adding Greybeard are as follows:

- If you put Greybeard on the **Player** layer as I have done, the player will appear behind him. As this is not what we expect, set the sorting order for the **Player** to **10** so he appears in front.

- While running the game, if the hero bumps into Greybeard, he can fall backwards. If this happens, it is just because the **Player** object does not have the **Fixed Angle** parameter checked in the **Rigid Body 2D** component.

- NPC colliders should be set to **Triggers**. We want to be able to control whether the NPC should stop the player or not through the script instead of the physics system. So, on Greybeard's **Box Collider 2D**, check **Is Trigger**.

With this done, start building up the rest of your town using the skills you have learned so far. The following screenshot is what I came up with:

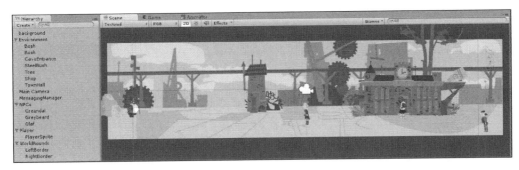

A few things to note are as follows:

- Organize your game hierarchy in a sensible manner so you can quickly find the things you need to manage. In the preceding screenshot, I created empty game objects for **Environment** items, such as houses and bushes. I also created an empty game object container for NPCs.

- Put the items on a layer that makes sense and then order the sprites on that layer appropriately.

Don't spend too long crafting the animation (unless you want to); all in all, the scene in the preceding screenshot took about 10 minutes to put together.

 If you check the sample project, I also added a pacing animation for Greandal using curves. We did this just to show how worried the mayor is about the state of affairs going on outside the town and all the rampaging beasts.

# Getting the NPC's talking

So far in this chapter, we have our populated town with characters, buildings, and so on. Therefore, let's give our hero something to talk about.

While building a conversation system for any game, there are many factors to consider, which are as follows:

- How long a conversation is going to be (we don't want the player to get bored with miles of text)?

- How many parties are likely to be involved in any discussion?

- Is this a flat one-sided conversation (such as a cutscene) or will the player be allowed to make decisions?

- Are there going to be branches in the conversation so that the conversation will change based on the player's response?

- How much content do you expect to be used in conversations (only text, video, cutscenes, animation, and so on)? All of this content will decide just how extensible your system needs to be.

- Will the conversation need to support any outbound triggers or states? Will the conclusion of a conversation unlock a door or grant the player with some experience or items?

There are lots of other factors that will affect both the design and implementation of a robust conversation for your game, so think about it carefully before touching the code.

 **A working example**

For this book, we are going to build a basic conversation system that is enough to meet the goals of the project at hand. However, I am explaining each part along the way, so if you want to expand on it, you can.

# The conversation object

When we want to start talking in the game, we first need to decide what you want to include in that conversation. You can include the following things:

- The name of the character who is speaking
- The text of the conversation
- An image of the character talking
- Choices
- The position of chat

The more you look at it, the more you can dream about what you want to include. You just need to remember the **KISS** principle (**Keep it simple, stupid**), that is, start small and then build on it.

So, create a new C# script, name it `ConversationEntry` in `Scripts\Classes`, and populate it with the following code:

```csharp
using UnityEngine;

[System.Serializable]
public class ConversationEntry {
    public string SpeakingCharacterName;
    public string ConversationText;
    public Sprite DisplayPic;
}
```

This gives us just the basics for our conversation system with regards to who's speaking, an optional picture that can be displayed in the conversation, and most importantly, the conversation text to be displayed.

We also tag this class with the `System.Serializable` code attribute so that the Unity serializer knows what to do with it.

# Saving and serializing the object for later

With our core conversation entry object generated, we can start to store the conversations in the `.asset` files for use in our game and also make it possible to create the conversations outside of Unity if you wish.

As a conversation is (usually) more than just an opening line, we need a management object that will support several lines/entries of the conversation and a couple of switches to denote whether the conversation has already been played. This way, if you have multiple conversations configured for a character, it will simply play the next conversation and not repeat itself. You could just track this on the object where you attach the conversations to, but this is cleaner.

As a rule of thumb, you should always keep flags, settings, or properties for a thing with another thing. If you start having variables to track the state of a thing elsewhere, it can get very messy. The only time this is not true is when a thing is meant to be shared across multiple objects.

Also note that the `ScriptableObject` entities are a fickle beast. They let us attach them to the game objects, and they can be automatically serialized and saved as part of the project. However, they are fixed assets that should only be edited in the editor. If you need to alter them as part of the game, you will need to save and store that change of state separately.

This is just a simple note to remember when architecting such things.

So, create another C# class in `Scripts\Classes` named `Conversation` and populate it with the following code:

```csharp
using UnityEngine;

public class Conversation : ScriptableObject {

    public ConversationEntry[] ConversationLines;
}
```

Now the first thing you will note is that this class is derived from a scriptable object class. As described earlier, this is what enables us to use Unity's serialization methods and store them as a `.asset` file.

We are not done yet as we need that final hook to enable us to create these (at least initially) in the editor.

Earlier, I showed you all of the code needed to create the asset for serialization, but this is rather a lot of code to be generated all the time. So, it's better to place that logic in a separate helper class that we can reuse rather than repeat ourselves all the time.

Earlier, with the `PositionManager` example, we created assets in the editor and reused them. You can reuse that code if you wish, but to simplify things, I added a little helper script to the example project in `Assets\Scripts\Classes`. The `CustomAssetUtility` class does all the work that the preceding code does. It also uses the C# generics so that it can be reused for any type of `SerializableObject` you want to throw at it. You don't have to use the class I provided; you can just use the code earlier instead if you wish, just replace the code where the helper function is used.

The C# generics is a fairly advanced C# topic, which we won't go into in this book. If you want to know more, check out `http://msdn.microsoft.com/en-us/library/ms379564(v=vs.80).aspx`; alternatively, it will be better to try *The C# Programming Yellow Book, Rob Miles, Department of Computer Science, The University of Hull*, which is a fantastic C# primer book available at `http://www.robmiles.com/c-yellow-book/`.

To show how we use this, let's create our editor script, which will create the conversation assets for us. Create a new folder in `Assets\Scripts` named `Editor`. In this folder, create a new script named `ConversationAssetCreator` in the `Editor` folder under `Assets\Scripts` and then replace its contents with the following code:

```
using UnityEditor;
using UnityEngine;

public class ConversationAssetCreator : MonoBehaviour {

    [MenuItem("Assets/Create/Conversation")]
    public static void CreateAsset()
    {
        CustomAssetUtility.CreateAsset<Conversation>();
    }
}
```

So, by using the helper function, instead of all the tangle of code to first generate our asset and then save it, we simply call our utility, tell it the type of asset we want to create (in angle brackets), and away it goes. I have crated the utility as well so that it can also take a string parameter if you want to force the folder you want to create the asset in; otherwise, it will take whatever is currently selected in the editor.

To test this out, create a new folder in the `Asset` folder named `Resources` (so we can call assets directly from the code if we so wish) and then create another folder in `Resources` named `Conversations`. This just keeps all our conversations in one place and doesn't clutter up the hierarchy. If you so wish, you could create further subfolders to identify characters, places, or whatever else you fancy. It won't have an impact on the running of the game; it will just keep it tidy.

With the `Conversation` folder under `Assets\Resources\` selected, click on **Create** in the **Project** menu and you should see a new option named **Conversation** (as you can see in the script earlier, this is what we named it as). When you click on it, a new **Conversation** asset should appear, as shown in the following screenshot, which is ready for you to start configuring:

Feel free to set up your new conversation in whichever way you like or check the sample in the project I've created for Greybeard. Name the conversation `GreybeardWarning` and give it the lines shown in the following screenshot:

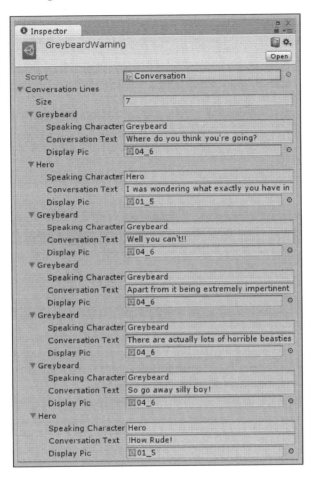

## The Conversation Component

The last thing we need is a simple component to be able to attach conversations to a character or other game object in keeping with the Unity-component-based way of building games.

So, create a new class in the `Classes` folder under `Assets\Scripts` named `ConversationComponent` and replace its contents with the following code:

```
using UnityEngine;

public class ConversationComponent : MonoBehaviour {

    public Conversation[] Conversations;

}
```

Nothing's complicated for now; the preceding code just holds an array of the possible conversations that the game object can have. Ideally, you would want to expand on this for a fuller conversation system, such as a pointer to the next conversation, or a way to track how many conversations have taken place, and so on.

# Building a basic conversation system

In order for our conversation assets to be of any use, we need a mechanism to play these conversations on the screen and have the user interact with them (if that's how your game rolls). For this, we need another manager that will take in conversations from characters and display them on the screen. If we had any logic, branching, or decisions in our conversations, it will handle those too.

Now, there are two basic approaches that we could take with the conversation system: one being reactive (where we use a messaging system to notify the manager that a conversation needs to take place) and one being just a utility (where scripts can request for a conversation to take place). Both are valid approaches, and it really comes down to personal preference as to which one you want to implement. To keep things simple, let's create the basic utility first and then point out where it can be enhanced.

## The manager

If we create our conversation manager as we did before with the messaging manager, we start with the simple singleton framework. However, we will lean on one of the great examples from **Unity Wiki** as our base.

In the sample project under `Assets\Scripts\Classes`, you will find a `Singleton` class that was sourced from `http://wiki.unity3d.com/index.php/Singleton`. This simply saves us time and code while creating singleton objects for use in our games and ensures they always have the same consistency.

With this in place, we can define our `Conversation` manager quite simply. Create a new C# script in `Assets\Scripts` named `ConversationManager` and replace its contents with the following code:

```
using System.Collections;
using UnityEngine;

public class ConversationManager : Singleton<ConversationManager >
{
  //Guarantee this will always be a singleton only -
  //can't use the constructor!
  protected ConversationManager () {}


}
```

Now that we have our manager, we can start adding functionalities to it.

## Starting a conversation

We want it to take a conversation item we have and do something with it because we have a manager. So, create a new function as follows:

```
public void StartConversation(Conversation conversation)
{}
```

This enables us to start a new conversation anywhere in the code by using the following code:

```
ConversationManager.Instance.StartConversation(conversation);
```

## Displaying the conversation

The manager is in place and we have a method to start a conversation, but it's not doing much right now. So, let's add some simple logic to display the text of the conversation on the screen. We will keep it simple since we are going to look into more complex GUI-related functionalities in *Chapter 8, Shopping for Weapons*.

Starting things off, we need some new properties in ConversationManager to control what needs to be displayed. So, open up the ConversationManager script and add the following properties to it:

```
//Is there a conversation going on
bool talking = false;

//The current line of text being displayed
ConversationEntry currentConversationLine;

//Estimated width of characters in the font
int fontSpacing = 7;

//How wide does the dialog window need to be
int conversationTextWidth;

//How high does the dialog window need to be
int dialogHeight = 70;
```

Each property explains its use, but everything will become clear as we add the rest of the functionality. Next, we'll add a Coroutine that will take a Conversation object and loop through all the lines to be displayed. Add the following function to the ConversationManager script:

```
IEnumerator DisplayConversation(Conversation conversation)
{
  talking = true;
  foreach (var conversationLine in conversation.ConversationLines)
  {
    currentConversationLine = conversationLine;
    conversationTextWidth =
      currentConversationLine.ConversationText.Length
        * fontSpacing;
    yield return new WaitForSeconds(3);
  }
  talking = false;
}
```

This simple Coroutine takes the conversation passed to it and loops through each of the individual lines of the conversation's text. Before we start, we set the `talking` flag to denote that a conversation is in progress; then, for each conversation line, we perform the following tasks:

- Set a pointer to the current conversation item in the list with the `currentConversationLine` property

- Figure out how long the text is to gauge how big our display area needs to be

- Wait for three seconds before moving on to the next conversation item

- When we run out of conversation lines, we set the `talking` flag to `false` to show that we have finished

So, we have a Coroutine looping through the text. The next thing to do is to use this information to display it on the screen. For this, we need an `OnGUI` method in our script as follows:

```
void OnGUI()
{
  if (talking)
  {
    //Layout start
    GUI.BeginGroup(new Rect(Screen.width / 2 -
        conversationTextWidth / 2, 50, conversationTextWidth + 10,
          dialogHeight));

    //The background box
    GUI.Box(new Rect(0, 0, conversationTextWidth + 10,
      dialogHeight), "");

    //The character name
    GUI.Label(new Rect(10, 10, conversationTextWidth + 30, 20),
        currentConversationLine.SpeakingCharacterName);

    //The conversation text
    GUI.Label(new Rect(10, 30, conversationTextWidth + 30, 20),
        currentConversationLine.ConversationText);

    //Layout end
    GUI.EndGroup();
  }
}
```

Like the navigation prompt in the previous chapter, we simply draw a GUI region, give it a background texture with the box using the default style, and then show two labels: one for the character who is speaking and one for the text of the conversation.

So, when the `talking` flag is set, Unity will know that it has to start drawing our conversation GUI on the screen.

To finish this off, we need to call the Coroutine from our `public` method, which other scripts can use to start a conversation:

```
public void StartConversation(Conversation conversation)
{
  //Start displaying the supplied conversation
  if (!talking)
  {
    StartCoroutine(DisplayConversation(conversation));
  }
}
```

# Adding more

There are two simple areas where we can take this further. We can use the sprite image and the style that we specified in the conversation item.

Adding the image is fairly simple; we just need to create enough space to display the image and then draw it.

Sadly, one of the areas that the new sprite system has not been merged with is the existing GUI system. It still relies on textures and not sprites. We can still work with it, but it means we have to select the sprite's texture from the spritesheet manually while drawing images. To do this, we use the `DrawTextureWithTexCoords` GUI function.

A word of warning though: the `DrawTextureWithTexCoords` function uses scaled coordinates while picking the section of the image you want to display. This usually trips up developers as it is not very well documented. The coordinates in the **Sprite** object are not scaled, so you have to convert them manually.

First, add a couple of properties to display the image using the following code:

```
//Offset space needed for character image
public int displayTextureOffset = 70;

//Scaled image rectangle for displaying character image
Rect scaledTextureRect;
```

The offset is to create space within our display region for the image, whereas the other property is to hold the scaling information to indicate that we need to pick our sprite from the spritesheet since the Unity system doesn't handle sprites.

Next, we need to calculate the scaling factor for the image for each conversation line, just in case we are using different sizes of textures for each character in the conversation. So, update the `DisplayConversation` Coroutine method with the following code:

```
IEnumerator DisplayConversation(Conversation conversation)
{
  talking = true;
  foreach (var conversationLine in conversation.ConversationLines)
  {
    currentConversationLine = conversationLine;
    conversationTextWidth =
      currentConversationLine.ConversationText.Length *
        fontSpacing;

    scaledTextureRect = new Rect(
      currentConversationLine.DisplayPic.textureRect.x /
        currentConversationLine.DisplayPic.texture.width,

      currentConversationLine.DisplayPic.textureRect.y /
        currentConversationLine.DisplayPic.texture.height,

      currentConversationLine.DisplayPic.textureRect.width /
        currentConversationLine.DisplayPic.texture.width,

      currentConversationLine.DisplayPic.textureRect.height /
        currentConversationLine.DisplayPic.texture.height);

    yield return new WaitForSeconds(3);
  }
  talking = false;
  yield return null;
}
```

Lastly, we just need to update the OnGUI method to make space for the image using the offset method and then add it to the draw list as follows:

```
void OnGUI()
{
  if (talking)
  {
    //Layout start
    GUI.BeginGroup(new Rect(Screen.width / 2 -
      conversationTextWidth / 2, 50, conversationTextWidth +
        displayTextureOffset + 10,dialogHeight));

    //The background box
    GUI.Box(new Rect(0, 0, conversationTextWidth +
      displayTextureOffset + 10,dialogHeight), "");

    //The character name
    GUI.Label(new Rect(displayTextureOffset, 10,
      conversationTextWidth + 30, 20),
        currentConversationLine.SpeakingCharacterName);

    //The conversation text
    GUI.Label(new Rect(displayTextureOffset, 30,
      conversationTextWidth + 30, 20),
        currentConversationLine.ConversationText);

    //The character image
    GUI.DrawTextureWithTexCoords(new Rect(10, 10, 50, 50),
      currentConversationLine.DisplayPic.texture,
        scaledTextureRect);

    //Layout end
    GUI.EndGroup();
  }
}
```

Note that the use of the DrawTextureWithTexCoords function and not the standard DrawTexture function is normally preferred in GUI drawing. This is because we are selecting the texture to be drawn from our spritesheet and we have to use scaled coordinates to pick the image as that is what the function uses. The Rect coordinates used in the Sprite object's textureRect property (the picking coordinates) are unscaled.

# Connecting the dots

So now that we have something to talk about, we just need to be able to attach it to the characters and then start displaying it on the screen for the player to interact with.

> This book will cover the GUI system in more depth in *Chapter 8, Shopping for Weapons*, so it will just include some basics here. You can come back and update your styles here later if you wish.

First, we need an empty class for our NPCs, which is derived from the `Entity` object. So, create a new C# script named `Npc` in the `Classes` folder under `Assets\Scripts` and replace its contents with the following code:

```
using UnityEngine;
public class Npc : MonoBehaviour
{
    public string Name;
    public int Age;
    public string Faction;
    public string Occupation;
    public int Level;
}
```

> As NPCs are things in the real world that we generate and place into the scene, we actually need to break the convention to inherit from the `Entity` class. This is actually a limitation in Unity because we can only use scripts that derive from `MonoBehaviour` can be attached to GameObjects in a scene. If you try to attach a class that uses or derives from `ScriptableObject`, the editor will throw an error. So as we are adding NPCs in our scene in the editor, we need to use a separate script.
>
> If you were generating the towns procedurally or loading them from a pre-built save file, then you could still use `ScriptableObject`-based classes. For more information on that, see *Chapter 7, Encountering Enemies and Running Away*.

With that created, add the script to our three NPCs in our scene. (Don't forget to name your characters in the **Inspector** pane as well.)

Next, add the **Conversation Component** to the Greybeard's **NPC** and then drag the conversation we just built to that character in the **Conversations** array.

The **Inspector** pane should now look like the following screenshot:

 To make the **Inspector** pane look a bit prettier, be sure to check out the editor extensions in *Chapter 10, The Battle Begins*.

So now that our character has a script and that we have the ConversationManager set up, we just need to trigger the conversation when the hero tries to enter the dark cave.

At the moment, the NavigationManager script that we used will let the player go anywhere. So first let's update that and add a bit more flexibility and configuration for the routes that the player can follow.

Open up the `NavigationManager` script in the `Navigation` folder under `Assets\ Scripts` and create a new `struct` method as follows:

```
public struct Route
{
  public string RouteDescription;
  public bool CanTravel;
}
```

The preceding code now enables us to have a simple mechanism to say whether a route is traversable or not. (In real scenarios, this should be serialized or it should have a manager for the player to remember where the player has traveled; otherwise, it is never going to get unlocked.)

Next, we need to update the `RouteInformation` variable to use this new `struct` method and update the information for the two destinations that we have already configured in our manager. This should enable us to state that you can travel to the big bad world but not to the cave as follows:

```
public static Dictionary<string, Route> RouteInformation = new
Dictionary<string, Route>() {
  { "World", new Route { RouteDescription = "The big bad world",
    CanTravel = true}
  },
  { "Cave01", new Route { RouteDescription = "The deep dark cave",
    CanTravel = false}
  },
};
```

As we are now using a `struct` method for our destination information, we also need to update the `GetRouteInfo` method to access the dictionary correctly and return the routes' description if found; we do this using the following code:

```
public static string GetRouteInfo(string destination)
{
  return RouteInformation.ContainsKey(destination) ?
    RouteInformation[destination].RouteDescription :
    null;
}
```

With that in place, all we need to do is check whether the `CanTravel` flag is true when the system requests, and if you're allowed to travel, update the `CanNavigate` method with the following code:

```
public static bool CanNavigate(string destination)
{
  return RouteInformation.ContainsKey(destination) ?
    RouteInformation[destination].CanTravel :
    false;
}
```

Here, we simply look at the destination from our route information and return with information on whether the player is allowed to travel there or not.

Now, when you try to go to the cave, you won't get the prompt from `NavigationManager` whether you want to travel to it or not.

To finish off, we just need to get the Greybeard NPC to listen for the message that the player will leave and then start his most troublesome conversation. So, remove the `MessagingClientReceiver` script (that was created in the *Messaging* section) from the left border (the cave) that you set up earlier and add it to the Greybeard NPC game object.

Now, Greybeard is subscribing to and receiving the messages for the player leaving. Next, update the `MessagingClientReceiver` script (in the `Messaging` folder under `Assets\Scripts`) and update the `ThePlayerIsTryingToLeave` method with the following code:

```
void ThePlayerIsTryingToLeave()
{
  var dialog = GetComponent<ConversationComponent>();
  if (dialog != null)
  {
    if (dialog.Conversations != null &&
      dialog.Conversations.Length > 0)
    {
      var conversation = dialog.Conversations[0];
      if (conversation != null)
      {
        ConversationManager.Instance.StartConversation
          (conversation);
      }
    }
  }
}
```

Here, we now look to see if a `ConversationComponent` script is on the game object it is attached to. If it is, we see if there are any conversations defined for this NPC; if yes, we call the `ConversationManager` script and ask it to start the first conversation.

> Granted, this is a simple example and should be extended in a full system to track conversations that are played or conditions that need to be met for a conversation to be played.
>
> At the moment, the conversation system will keep on going even after you have left the vicinity of the character you are talking with.

Now, if you run the project and try to enter the cave, the grumpy old Greybeard will pipe up and harass you, as shown in the following screenshot:

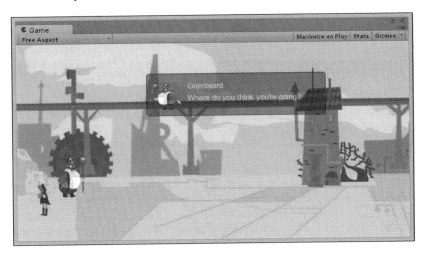

# Going further

If you are of the adventurous sort, try to expand your project to add the following features:

- Apply the scriptable object technique to other areas of the level
- Extend the Conversation manager to step the text letter by letter in the conversation text with another Coroutine
- Expand the event's messenger to support different types of events, passing text, or an object

- Add more conversations to the scene for Olaf and Greandal, either by using their collider or having more events (remember to use a grouping game object to keep the hierarchy tidy; I called my grouper, NPCs)

- Add some conversation logic to terminate the conversation if the player gets too far from the source

# Summary

What a marathon! This certainly has been the heaviest chapter so far, but there were a lot of advanced techniques to cover, and to do them justice, they needed a lot of explanation. Building a conversation system for any game needs a lot of planning to ensure you get the features you need for your game.

The lessons you learned in this chapter will set you in good stead for the future features.

We covered the ways to communicate between the game objects using events, delegates, and messaging solutions. We also covered working with background tasks and Coroutines, serialization and scriptable objects, constructing your own conversation system, and paid alternatives.

# 6
# The Big Wild World

As we start considering the wider bounds of our RPG world, we need to look at alternate views for the game. It's important to keep the player engaged and make them feel that they are entering a vast arena with lots of places to explore, especially when you initially release your game and you only have a few towns to visit.

Another thing to consider is whether you want fixed maps in your game or you want to venture down the rabbit hole of procedural generation. Both are valid routes and there's nothing to say that you only have to use one. In this chapter, we'll cover all the options and then implement a nice and simple system to walk through the basics.

The following is a list of topics that will be covered in this chapter:

- Resources to build a map
- Structuring and adding points of interest
- Working with prefabs
- Transitioning between views
- Marshaling input

## The larger view

Our budding hero is now ready to pack his bags and leave the shelter of his hometown for the wider world. So, we need to widen the scope of what the player can see and build a large map with places of interest to visit.

This usually opens the floodgates for just how big your game will be. Planning can decide whether your game will be a hit or feel just too short.

Maps in RPGs certainly aren't mandatory; several hit games just go from place to place with maybe an animation or cut scene to show movement. However, in the best cases, a map just opens up the scope of the game and gives the player an understanding of the world they are travelling in.

# Types of maps

When looking at what kind of map or world you are going to choose to connect the dots between places to visit or secret hideaways, there are a few paths you can take. Generally, there are two options:

- **Fixed**: In this option, images are usually drawn by an artist and have extensive detail of the world surrounding the player or are blank, exposing places as the player travels to or discovers them.

- **Generated**: In this option, each run of the game completely randomizes the places to go or events that will take place, with the focus being on unpredictability.

Both the preceding options are perfectly valid and there's nothing to say; you need to focus on just one or the other, mix it up if you wish. Generally, the better the variety, the better the chances of the player being engaged in your game—it will entice them to explore and play more.

Another keen element is that it should support repeatability and replayability—let players return to existing locations and discover new things, and reuse what you have to the fullest.

# Fixed maps

There are many resources to get maps for your title if you don't have a dedicated artist and, in some ways, these also provide insight or creative juice for how you want your maps to look. The following map image is a good example of a high-quality paid map:

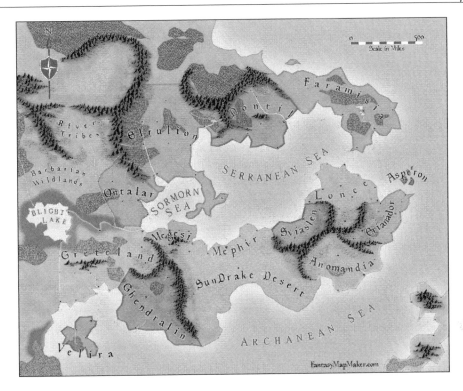

The first site to mention, primarily because it is also completely free, is `http://freefantasymaps.org/`. The preceding screenshot is a prime example of the level of quality you can get from the site. Although the images on the site are free to use for any purpose, I would recommend you to use their images to donate to the running of the site so that they remain free.

Another useful site is the **Cartographers' Guild** at `http://www.cartographersguild.com/`. This is a veritable map paradise with lots of content available for use in most projects. Unlike the preceding site, all works are protected and you will need to purchase them or gain rights to use them. However, they are of a very high quality.

When browsing maps and art, *always* be sure to check the license and usage policies of the images you download. This should be done whenever you acquire art, even from Google. Be safe, check, and get permission.

The same can be said for code and any other kinds of assets. If in doubt, check the license and even if it's free, just check with the author whether they feel it's ok to use in your project.

Always check the license on anything you download and use.

Another good feature of the Cartographers' Guild is that it allows you to request a map. They have an awesome request system and hundreds of artists are ready to commission anything your heart wants (see `http://www.cartographersguild.com/mapmaking-requests/`).

# Generated maps

There are also many other resources out there to get maps for your game. Another method is to use an online map generation system. Now, to be fair, most are aimed at tabletop gamers and most are of a low quality, but there are a few gems to be found.

The one I used for the game we are building is from `http://donjon.bin.sh/fantasy/world/`, because I like it and it provides fairly high-resolution generated images and includes world features and places. It looks like a nice place to have a holiday (if you are an Orc). The following image is the map I've used in the sample project with lots of interesting places to see and explore:

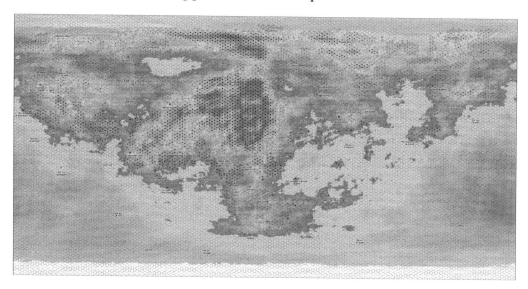

As you can see, there is a lot of detail here and a very large world for the player to explore.

DonJon's site also offers a vast array of other generators to build maps and other RPG elements. There are even name and game dialogue generators, so it really does meet most RPG needs.

## In-game generated maps

Now, if you want more control over what the player sees or will have in their game, you can go all the way and start building maps and more through either Unity's asset pipeline or in-code within the game.

External tools such as **Tiled** (`http://www.mapeditor.org/`), which is shown in the following image, can be used to build and design maps. It has many interesting features and can even output several layers. You can also use either top-down, 2D side scrolling, or even isometric maps.

Your free, easy to use and flexible tile map editor.

A great Unity example of this is a project called `uTiled` (`https://bitbucket.org/vinull/utiled`), which provides a Unity asset that can read maps from Tiled. Here, the author has customized a map generation system that uses an external tool to build maps according to a predefined set of map tiles, which are just small textures used when building the map.

The following image is a simple example of what can be achieved with Tiled editor that generates the maps:

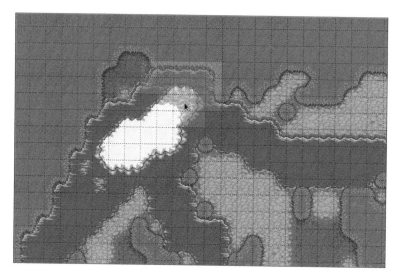

The project is a great example of not just how to import a 2D-based tile map system into Unity, but also how to construct and run these 2D maps in your game.

Using a system like uTiled, you can either build a selection of maps in Tiled for use as world maps in your game, or even full 2D scenes.

Alternatively, you could use procedural techniques (see the *Going procedural* section) to build the map while the game is running, using the framework to knit individual segments of your map together. We will discuss this more later.

# 2D doesn't mean you have to use only 2D

Just because the rest of your game is 2D, it doesn't mean you have to use 2D. Some of the best games I've seen use a mixture of 2D and 3D, and Unity will help you there because it's not limited.

Whether you have 2D play areas and 3D terrain for maps, or 3D villages and a 2D map, it doesn't really matter. Just go with whatever you are comfortable with or what fits with the aesthetic of your game.

Thanks to the way 2D is implemented in Unity, you can even mix it up by having 3D elements placed and animated in your 2D scene either as background elements or interactive components.

**A word to the wise**

Although you can mix the 2D and 3D rendering in a single scene, you cannot mix the 2D and 3D physics. This is simply because they are separate engines and have no connection to each other. Keep this in mind depending on what you are trying to build in your game.

# Going procedural

If you are the bold or adventurous sort, another route to flesh out your world is to procedurally generate it. What you usually see when you look for procedural generation in Unity are dungeon generators. In fact, some of the best examples I've seen out there involve randomly generated dungeons where every run of the game is different from the last. Other examples are usually found in endless running games where a style of procedural selection is done to choose the next running area or to put random scene items in.

When we try to apply this to RPG games, we want to balance the fixed part of the world/story we are looking to convey with a more random placement of towns/villages or places of interest. This will make the world we see different for every player but still convey the background of the theme.

Now, the whole subject of procedural generation is far too large to go into for this book, but I can give you a few points for where to look.

The best place to start is the **Procedural Content Generation Wiki** available at http://pcg.wikidot.com/; it's the go-to place to start learning the following general techniques:

- **Iterated function systems**: These are fractals to create land masses or structured areas
- **L-systems**: These are used for roads or path generation
- **Diamond-square and midpoint displacement algorithms**: These are used to create random height terrains
- **Perlin and simplex noise systems**: These are used to add further randomness to the generation

`Reddit.com` is also a great place for examples, questions, and queries on procedural generation. Two of the best reddits are as follows:

- `http://www.reddit.com/r/proceduralgeneration` (this is the main procedural generation reddit. Although it's mostly promotional these days, there are still a lot of older posts with samples and information. It's also a good place to start with questions.)
- `http://www.reddit.com/r/worldbuilding` (this is a good source of information for this section on maps for your game. It is mainly related to D&D, but it does contain a lot of useful information.)

**A word to the wise**

Procedural generation is not for the faint of heart, there is a lot of math involved and a lot of trial and error. However, if you can master small parts, you can achieve a truly wondrous game with lots of replayability.

Procedural generation is too large a subject for this book. Hopefully, I've given you a few tips and tidbits to get you going, so you know what to look for should you want to venture down this road.

# Screen space and world space

When dealing with either touch or mouse input, we have to recognize that coordinates managed by Unity are in **screen space** and not **world space**. Both of these terms are defined as follows:

- **Screen space**: This refers to coordinates relative to the screen / display area, starting at the top-left corner of the screen
- **World space**: This refers to the coordinates that are used inside the Unity engine

The starting position, (0, 0) 2D coordinate, for the mouse can be different depending on how you access it:

- If you use `Input.mousePosition`, then (0, 0) is in the top-left corner of the screen
- If, however, you use `Event.current.mousePosition`, then (0, 0) is in the bottom-left corner of the screen

For touch, however, it is always in the the top-left corner of the screen. This is something to keep in mind when you access input—always check.

When you poll for the mouse position (which can only be one mouse), use the following line of code:

```
Input.mousePosition
```

When we are looking at touch points (which can be many), we use the following line of code:

```
Input.GetTouch(<touch index>).position
```

However, because the position we get back is always in screen space, we need to convert it to world space when checking it against objects in the game world. Thankfully, this is very simple to do using the following built-in Unity function:

```
Camera.main.ScreenToWorldPoint(<screenCoordinate>)
```

> The preceding default function uses the main camera to translate the coordinate from screen space to world space. If you are taking input from an alternate view (like a mini-map), be sure to use the specific camera for that view to convert the value, or else you will get incorrect results.

> Remember that any coordinate you get back from the input system or used in world coordinates are always Vector3 coordinates. However, because this is a 2D game, we need coordinates in Vector2 coordinates, so you will need to convert the value you get back for any 2D functions such as colliders or 2D distance checking.

# Putting it together

Moving on from theory, we need to look at something to put on our map of the world, such as somewhere for our player to travel to and explore.

We not only need to provide graphical support in the game to open up areas on the map or just show the journey between two points, but we also need to connect these points with scenes in our game.

Now, we have already started the coding framework behind our places manager with the creation of the `NavigationManager` script, which keeps track of all the places available in the world for our player to travel to. Just add a few more routes for the manager to look after and that's up and running.

Then, there is the visual side. As we want a common way to create places/markers on the map, we can start to use prefabs in Unity so that we only have to design them once and then just reuse them on our map.

# Adding the map

Start off by copying your `world` texture into your project `Assets` folder in `Assets\Sprites\Environment`, and use any image you wish to use or generate one from `http://donjon.bin.sh/fantasy/world/` or `http://donjon.bin.sh/world/` like I have done.

> The following screenshot, which displays a map image, is included in the download associated with this title (`Sample_Assets\Worldmap.png`).

With that in place, create a new scene in `Assets\Scene` and call it `World` (this has to be the same as the name used in your `NavigationManager` script). In your scene, drag your `world` texture to the hierarchy and update your `MainCamera` GameObject to show the starting region for your world.

As the `world` texture I have used is rather large, I have set this to the top-left region of the map as shown in the following screenshot:

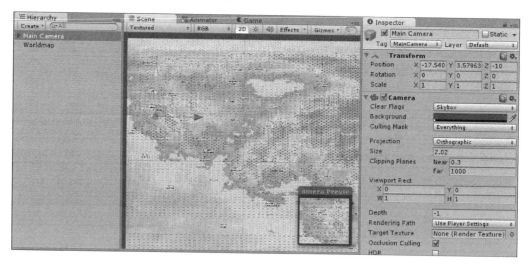

# Adding places of interest

With the world that the player can travel to in place, we need to add the player to the map and some places of interest.

Adding the player is simple; just create a new empty game object and call it `player`, then add the `Rigidbody2D` and `BoxCollider2D` components to it so that it will be able to interact with other points on the map. (You could use location testing, but it's simpler to use the physics system and it's not much overhead.)

Finally, it's best for the player to have something to see moving when traveling, so add a **Sprite Renderer** to the player game object and use a sprite image that suits it. I used the running hero sprite for effect but you could use whatever you wish.

You should end up with something like the following:

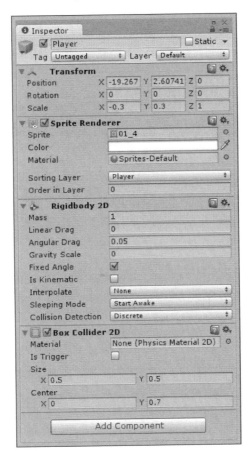

# Creating the MapPoint prefabs for reuse

Creating prefabs is very easy; just start creating a game object as you would do normally and once you are happy with the result, drag the whole object to the project view. The beauty is that just about anything can become a prefab for reuse in your game.

When you create a prefab and use it in your scene, any changes to the prefab will be automatically updated on all the objects you created with that prefab. However, changes to those objects themselves do not update the prefab or any other copies. All changes are one way from the prefab itself.

If you want to update the prefab, select the **Prefab** option in the editor and change it. Alternatively, select an instance in the scene, change the required properties, and then click on **Apply** to save the changes back to the prefab, as shown in the following screenshot:

This will only affect existing components and properties that were already on the prefab. To add new components or scripts to the prefab, you must edit the prefab itself.

The following screenshot shows a game object setup for a place of interest on our map as an empty game object with a simple BoxCollider2D component (set as a trigger). We can also see the NavigationPrompt script we used in earlier chapters to bring up the traveling GUI.

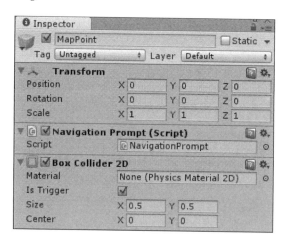

Finally, rename the new prefab to MapPoint so that we know what the prefab is for in our folder structure.

 With a collider set as a trigger, it will cause the OnTrigger functions (OnTriggerEnter2D and OnTriggerExit2D) to be called in scripts as opposed to the normal OnCollision functions (OnCollisionEnter2D and OnCollisionExit2D). Bear this in mind when applying scripts that rely on a collider. We will update our NavigationPrompt script accordingly.

With the prefab created, just drag it to the project's **Assets** window in Assets\ Prefabs\Environment. You will get a new Prefab asset for a map's place of interest, as shown in the following screenshot:

 Note that prefabs are always highlighted in blue, both in the project asset and hierarchy views. This makes them very easy to identify.

 Always reset the position transform for prefabs to 0; this makes it a whole lot easier when reusing them.

 For the sake of simplicity, I've kept the example simple, but you could expand on it to include a sprite renderer and use an additional image per place to identify it. Some great examples of map point icons can be found at http://calthyechild.deviantart.com/art/Fantasy-Map-TutorialxResources-258559867, which provides some great free resources and images.

Once the prefab is created, we can start to use it since this game object has now become the first instance of our `MapPoint` prefab. So, rename it to `Home` and place it over the town where the player starts, and then create a new tag for `Home` so that we can add it to our `NavigationManager` script.

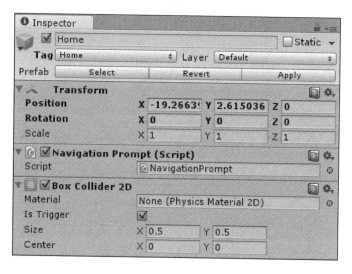

Next, create a new instance of our `MapPoint` prefab by dragging the prefab on to the scene and placing it over the town of Kirkidw (or any suitable place on the map near your start point; it's up to you to pick your own destination town). Rename it to `Kirkidw` and create/set a tag with the same name.

As highlighted earlier, if you wish, you can also add a sprite to the place's game object to highlight the town's position on the map. If you want, you can add the sprite renderer to the prefab and change the sprite image on each instance appropriately. If it's a common image, then just set the sprite on the prefab.

For the best results and to make the scene easy to read, add any new map points as children of the background texture (worldmap); this keeps the points of interest both anchored to the texture and neatly organized.

# Updating the NavigationPrompt script

The map points we have defined are set as triggers. We use triggers when we do not want any physics interactions between the collider and other rigid bodies; all we want is to be notified that one collider has moved over (in the case of 2D) or interacted with another collider.

As we are now using triggers, we need to swiftly update our NavigationPrompt script to work with triggers. So, open the NavigationPrompt script and add the following function in it:

```
void OnTriggerEnter2D(Collider2D col)
{
  //Only allow the player to travel if allowed
  if (NavigationManager.CanNavigate(this.tag))
  {
    showDialog = true;
  }
}
```

The function in the preceding code does exactly the same as the OnCollisionEnter2D function, which we already have, but this will now respond to the colliders that have been set as triggers using the is Trigger flag.

# Updating the NavigationManager script

As the player can now venture out of town, we need to update our NavigationManager script with additional places to visit, including our home town. We can do this simply by adding additional routes to our NavigationManager script as follows:

```
public static Dictionary<string, Route> RouteInformation = new
  Dictionary<string, Route>() {
  { "World", new Route {
    RouteDescription = "The big bad world", CanTravel = true}},
  { "Cave", new Route {
    RouteDescription = "The deep dark cave", CanTravel = false}},
  { "Home", new Route {
    RouteDescription = "Home sweet home", CanTravel = true}},
  { "Kirkidw", new Route {
    RouteDescription = "The grand city of Kirkidw",
      CanTravel = true}},
  };
```

Nice and easy; although you should note one small flaw. We use the scene name as a way to identify the area that we want to travel to and currently our home scene is called **Main**. So, rename the Main scene to Home, which should leave you with the following scenes in Assets\Scenes:

# Traveling by click or touch

With the map set up, we can head into the land of scripting to handle the players. Additionally (as highlighted earlier), we also need to ensure that the player doesn't move when the navigation GUI is displayed.

Before we begin, you should recall earlier that I mentioned about screen and world space conversion and the need to convert 3D (Vector3) coordinates to 2D (either a Vector2 or a Vector3 with the z value set to zero) else our calculations will be off. As our map will be controlled by click or touch (to spice things up a bit), we need to be able to access where the player has interacted on our map.

To this end, I added a set of extension methods to a new class called WorldExtensions in Assets\Scripts\Classes, replacing its contents with the following:

```
using UnityEngine;
public static class WorldExtensions
{
  public static Vector3 ToVector3_2D(this Vector3 coordinate)
  {
    return new Vector3(coordinate.x, coordinate.y, 0);
  }

  public static Vector2 GetScreenPositionIn2D(this
    Vector3 screenCoordinate)
  {
    Vector3 wp = Camera.main.ScreenToWorldPoint(screenCoordinate);
    return new Vector2(wp.x, wp.y);
  }

  public static Vector3 GetScreenPositionFor2D(this
    Vector3 screenCoordinate)
```

```
  {
    Vector3 wp = Camera.main.ScreenToWorldPoint(screenCoordinate);
    return wp.ToVector3_2D();
  }
}
```

The following extensions at the end of the current script are just for simplicity, but you could define them anywhere:

- Convert any Vector3 in to a 2D Vector3 with a zero z value
- Convert a screen space coordinate and return a Vector2 for 2D
- Convert a screen space coordinate and return a Vector3 with a zero z value for 2D

> The `this` keyword signifies that this is an extension method, allowing the function to be accessed by calling the function normally:
>
> ```
> var clickPoint = WorldExtensions.GetScreenPositionFor2D
>     (Input.mousePosition);
> ```
>
> Otherwise, you could directly access the function from the type identified by the `this` keyword:
>
> ```
> var clickPoint = Input.mousePosition
>     .GetScreenPositionFor2D();
> ```
>
> Extension methods are a very powerful and easy way to extend functions and methods on to existing object types. For more information on extension methods, visit `http://msdn.microsoft.com/en-gb/library/bb383977.aspx`.

## Managing input

With our helpers in place, next we'll create a new `MapMovement` script in the project under `Assets\Scripts` and replace its contents with the following:

```
using UnityEngine;

public class MapMovement : MonoBehaviour
{
    Vector3 StartLocation;
    Vector3 TargetLocation;
    float timer = 0;
    bool inputActive = true;
}
```

The properties are just there to track the progress of the player, and there is a flag to track when the GUI is active.

Next, we can add the input handling functions to the script in the `Update` method. Whenever you are giving an input, it's better to use `Input` as it gives more accurate results, as shown in the following script:

```
void Update () {

    if (inputActive && Input.GetMouseButtonUp(0))
    {
        StartLocation = transform.position.ToVector3_2D();
        timer = 0;
        TargetLocation = WorldExtensions.GetScreenPositionFor2D
            (Input.mousePosition);
    }
    else if (inputActive && Input.touchCount == 1)
    {
        StartLocation = transform.position.ToVector3_2D();
        timer = 0;
        TargetLocation = WorldExtensions.GetScreenPositionFor2D
            (Input.GetTouch(0).position);
    }
}
```

The process is very simple; test whether the user has clicked the mouse (`Input.GetMouseButtonUp(0)`) or touched the screen (`Input.touchCount == 1`). The value could be greater than 1, but we want just one touch in this case. When they do so, record the current position of the player as the start point, and where the user has touched or clicked as the end point (target).

 Input, as you will find in Unity, is not completely unified. You have to code and manage touch and mouse separately.

Now that we have a place to move the player to, we just need to add the ability to move the player once we have selected a target location and get the player moving on his merry way. So, add the following to the end of the previous `Update` function:

```
if (TargetLocation != Vector3.zero && TargetLocation !=
    transform.position && TargetLocation != StartLocation)
{
    transform.position = Vector3.Lerp(StartLocation,
        TargetLocation, timer);
    timer += Time.deltaTime;
}
```

In the preceding code, we simply check whether the user has selected a destination and check that we are not there already. If everything is fine, then we just keep updating the player's position using the `Lerp` function gradually over time.

With that done, simply add the script to the player game object we created in our scene earlier and run the project.

Although it works, you should instantly see one issue: when the players starts on the map, they are actually interacting with the place on the map they started from (`Home` in this case). Because it is interacting with that place already, this causes the navigation prompt to appear and asks them whether they want to go home.

As our player is not a scaredy cat and wants to venture further, let's fix that.

## Managing input priorities

When organizing your map navigation, input prioritization is an important point. When you have both GUI input and player input challenging for control, you should be able to manage which is currently active at any one time; otherwise, if both are active, you will get unexpected or duplicate results.

For instance, once you have your player moving using the mouse/touch, then the GUI to travel to that destination pops up and accepts input in both the GUI and the map movement at the same time. Hence, when you click on a button to travel or stay, then the map character will also move.

To combat this, the simplest and best way is to reuse our `MessagingManager` script with a new message to handle whether the GUI is taking input or the game is.

It may be advantageous to have both the GUI and game input working at the same time, for example, in situations where you have in-game buttons for actions. In these cases, you would test where on the screen the player interacted to decide which area gets the input. However, when the pause menu or alternate screen appears, you are still going to need to handle input priority.

So in the `MessagingManager` script, we add the following new handler to manage the GUI events. We also need to track whether the GUI is displayed or not, so we also need to manage a parameter for the event using a Boolean (`true` means GUI is displayed and `false` means GUI is hidden):

```
private List<Action<bool>> uiEventSubscribers = new List<Action
    <bool>>();
```

Then, like before, we need a subscribing and broadcasting function for the new event:

```
// Subscribe method for UI manager
public void SubscribeUIEvent(Action<bool> subscriber)
{
  uiEventSubscribers.Add(subscriber);
}

// Broadcast method for UI manager
public void BroadcastUIEvent(bool uIVisible)
{
  foreach (var subscriber in uiEventSubscribers.ToArray())
  {
    subscriber(uIVisible);
  }
}

// Unsubscribe method for UI manager
public void UnSubscribeUIEvent(Action<bool> subscriber)
{
  uiEventSubscribers.Remove(subscriber);
}

// Clear subscribers method for manager
public void ClearAllUIEventSubscribers()
{
  uiEventSubscribers.Clear();
}
```

You will note we only use a copy of the subscribers array. This is to ensure that the loop does not fall over when new subscriptions are added or existing ones are removed while it is progressing through the loop. It is unlikely in this scenario; however, it is a good practice to follow either this option or use locking methods to ensure that the array cannot be updated when the listis being traversed.

This ensures that when GUI events happen (if the game is paused and a pause menu is displayed or, as in this case, when the travel prompt appears), the GUI system just has one place to tell all scenes and objects that are listening through messaging when the GUI is in focus in the game (everyone else stop talking, GUI has the floor), and when it's finished

So, next we need to update our `NavigationPrompt` script to broadcast when the GUI is displayed and when it is hidden. First, let's refactor a bit and add a new method that controls what happens when the dialog state needs to change:

```
void DialogVisible(bool visibility)
{
   showDialog = visibility;
   MessagingManager.Instance.BroadcastUIEvent(visibility);
}
```

This just sets the `showDialog` flag we were using to the new state and then follows up by sending a broadcast of the new state (`true` means visible and `false` means not invisible). Next, wherever we previously changed the `showDialog` flag, we need to update it to use the new helper function. So, change the `showDialog` flag to the following:

```
showDialog = false -> DialogVisible(false);

showDialog = true -> DialogVisible(true);
```

Next, we need to update the `MapMovement` script to add in the messaging handlers so that the script knows when the GUI is displayed. So, add the following `Start` function to subscribe to the `MapMovement` script for the new UI events:

```
void Start()
{
   MessagingManager.Instance.SubscribeUIEvent(UpdateInputAction);
}
```

Then, add the corresponding function to toggle the `inputActive` flag we created earlier:

```
private void UpdateInputAction(bool uiVisible)
{
   inputActive = !uiVisible;
}
```

This just updates the `inputActive` property whenever the GUI informs us that it's onscreen.

If you haven't done it yet, update the `MessagingManager` script based on the example in the *Managing input* section to add the new UI event handler. Additionally, update the `NavigationPrompt` script to inform the message handler when the GUI is visible.

If you like Lamdas, you could actually write the preceding code to subscribe to the `MessagingManager` line as follows:

```
MessagingManager.Instance.SubscribeUIEvent(uiVisible =>
    inputActive = !uiVisible);
```

However, I've kept it simple in the project for all to read and it's a good practice to keep them separate in case you need to add more handling.

For more information on Lamdas, see the MSDN article at http://msdn.microsoft.com/en-gb/library/bb397687.aspx.

# Managing input order

If you run the code at this point, you will notice that all the changes we just made did not actually fix the problem. When we click on the play button, the player still moves to the click position. The reason for this is very simple: your machine is just too darn quick.

Basically, when you click on the GUI button, the UI event is fired. In the `MapMovement` script, however, it receives this straightaway and changes the `inputActive` flag. Then, when the `Update` method is called, the script thinks the UI has already gone away and receives the same click action and then proceeds to move the player.

We can handle this in one of two ways—either we can change the script execution order (visit http://docs.unity3d.com/Manual/class-ScriptExecution.html for more details, but this can become quite messy to manage), or we can simply update the `inputActive` flag at the end of the `Update` loop.

To keep things simple, let's do the latter. So, create the following new property at the top of the `MapMovement` script:

```
bool inputReady = true;
```

Then, instead of updating the `inputActive` flag directly, you would update the new flag instead. This allows us to delay the change in the input status for the script. So, update the `UpdateInputAction` method as follows:

```
private void UpdateInputAction(bool uiVisible)
{
    inputReady = !uiVisible;
}
```

Finally, at the end of the `Update` method, we would set the `inputActive` flag to the value of the new `inputReady` flag after checking all the user input and allowing the screen prompt to close first:

```
inputActive = inputReady;
```

Now when you run the project and the GUI is displayed, clicking on the play button no longer causes the player to move as well.

# Getting curvy

If you recall, back in *Chapter 3, Getting Animated*, I showed you the animation curves that can alter how a sprite or inspector value can be changed over time. You can also use these just about anywhere in Unity. So, we'll apply this to our `MapMovement` script to control how the player transits from his start position to his destination. To do this, simply add a new `public` parameter to the top of the `MapMovement` script (this can work on any script implementing `MonoBehaviour`) as follows:

```
public AnimationCurve MovementCurve;
```

When viewed from the editor, this will give you the custom inspector for an animation curve as shown in the following screenshot:

 You have to configure the curve initially from the editor for it to do anything; the default is simply a flat line with no movement.

When you click on the curve, you will get the animation curve editor, as shown in the following screenshot:

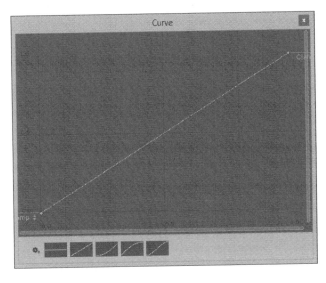

By default, no curve is defined and you have to configure a new curve. In the preceding screenshot, you can see a basic linear curve that grows over time. But this being an editor, you can apply just whatever kind of curve you want—either start with one of the presets at the bottom of the editor or start altering the curve by adding new animation keys (by right clicking on the curve and selecting **Add key**) and changing the curve characteristics. You can even create something as wacky as the one shown in the following screenshot:

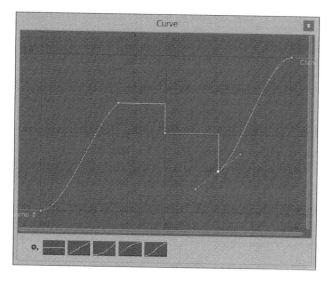

With your curve parameter available and configured, we can then alter our previous Lerp function in the MapMovement script to use the curve parameter as follows:

```
if (TargetLocation != Vector3.zero && TargetLocation !=
   transform.position && TargetLocation != StartLocation)
{
   transform.position = Vector3.Lerp(StartLocation, TargetLocation,
      MovementCurve.Evaluate(timer));
   timer += Time.deltaTime;
}
```

This, now gives us the ability to control how the Lerp function behaves at a very fine level.

This curve could be updated procedurally to alter the curve if there are mountains or other difficult terrain to maneuver over, or you could switch from doing a fixed input (as shown in the following code) and use more physics/forces to alter the interaction between the player and the terrain.

# Fixing the start location

To ensure that the hero doesn't actually run home on seeing the big bad wild world, we just need to simply stop him looking at home until he has actually gone far enough from home to actually miss it. To do this, we simply need to disable the collider on the player until he is not colliding with home anymore. We will perform the following steps to do this:

1. Achieving the start location is simple; just add a new property to the `MapMovement` script to track whether the player has actually started travelling yet. The code is as follows:

```
bool startedTravelling = false;
```

2. Next, we ensure that when the map scene starts, the player's `BoxCollider2D` component is actually turned off. We do this in the `Awake` function before anything is updated or checked. The code is as follows:

```
void Awake()
{
    this.collider2D.enabled = false;
}
```

3. Next, we change our `Update` function to take note of the new flag and also perform the check as follows:

```
void Update()
{
    if (TargetLocation != Vector3.zero && TargetLocation !=
        transform.position && TargetLocation != StartLocation)
    {
        transform.position = Vector3.Lerp(StartLocation,
            TargetLocation, MovementCurve.Evaluate(timer));
        timer += Time.deltaTime;
    }
    if (startedTravelling && Vector3.Distance(StartLocation,
        transform.position.ToVector3_2D()) > 0.5)
    {
        this.collider2D.enabled = true;
        startedTravelling = false;
    }
}
```

Here, we added another statement after the movement code to test whether the following conditions are satisfied:

- ○ Has the player has started travelling yet? If not, do nothing.
- ○ Is the distance between the place the player started at and the hero's current position far enough (in world space values)? If yes, then re-enable the player collider.

So once the player has moved a sufficient distance, the hero will then be able to interact with places on the map again.

4. Finishing off, we need to update the `StartTravelling` flag whenever the player taps or clicks a destination, or else the collider will never get enabled by the preceding code. So, update the `Update` function to set this appropriately by setting the following in both of the `if` statements:

```
if (inputActive && Input.GetMouseButtonUp(0))
{
    StartLocation = transform.position.ToVector3_2D();
    timer = 0;
    TargetLocation = WorldExtensions.GetScreenPositionFor2D
        (Input.mousePosition);
    startedTravelling = true;
}
else if (inputActive && Input.touchCount > 0)
{
    StartLocation = transform.position.ToVector3_2D();
    timer = 0;
    TargetLocation = WorldExtensions.GetScreenPositionFor2D
        (Input.GetTouch(0).position);
    startedTravelling = true;
}
```

# Traveling too far

The last snag to watch out for is when the player shoots straight through the town we are currently prompting them about and continues going. Thankfully, this one is very easy to handle.

We just need to check when our input has been disabled by the GUI by checking the new `inputReady` flag. If the input has only just been disabled, we do this by updating the end of the `Update` method in our `MapMovement` script as follows:

```
if (!inputReady && inputActive)
{
    TargetLocation = this.transform.position;
    Debug.Log("Stopping Player");
}
inputActive = inputReady;
}
```

So, when the UI event has turned off the `inputReady` flag but has not yet been synchronized with the `inputActive` flag, we simply stop the player in their tracks and fix their target position to their current position.

# Transitions

When you are transitioning between scenes/levels within Unity, it can appear a bit jarring to the player when a scene just freezes and then another one pops up. Even when you make the loading of the scene as fast as possible, there is still a flicker on the screen that is not smooth or fluid (as designers like to say).

Thankfully, we can easily fix this by adding some code to manage the transition between the towns and world in our game. We will do this by adding a `Fading` manager to our game.

To start off, in the same way as we did with the `Conversation` manager in the previous chapter, we will create a new class and apply our singleton framework to it. This is simply because there should only ever be one agent in our game managing the fading of a scene so it does not cause an issue if a player enters and then immediately exits a scene.

So, create a new `FadeInOutManager` C# script in the root of your project's `Assets\Scripts` folder and replace its contents with the following code to create a singleton manager that can be used by any scene:

```
using UnityEngine;
using System.Collections;
public class FadeInOutManager : Singleton<FadeInOutManager>{
// guarantee this will be always a singleton only -
// can't use the constructor!
  protected FadeInOutManager() { }
}
```

With this in place, we can start building the manager. First, start off with some properties as shown in the following code:

```
// The texture to display when fading
private Material fadeMaterial;
// Fading parameters
private float fadeOutTime, fadeInTime;
private Color fadeColor;

//Place holder for the level you will be navigating to
//(by name or index)
private string navigateToLevelName = "";
private int navigateToLevelIndex = 0;

//State to control if a level is fading or not,
//including public property if access through code
private bool fading = false;
public static bool Fading
{
   get { return Instance.fading; }
}
```

The properties are documented and used to control how long the fade should last when leaving the current scene into the next; there is an additional Material property so that you can use different textures to display on the screen when fading (maybe your game logo). Finally, there are some tracking properties if you are using the class to navigate scenes by index or scene name.

With the properties in place, we now need the following initialization code:

```
void Awake () {
   //Setup a default blank texture for fading if none is supplied
   fadeMaterial = new Material("Shader \"Plane/No zTest\" {" +
      "SubShader { Pass { " +
      "     Blend SrcAlpha OneMinusSrcAlpha " +
      "     ZWrite Off Cull Off Fog { Mode Off } " +
      "     BindChannels {" +
      "        Bind \"color\", color }" +
      "} } }");
}
```

In the previous code, we are simply setting up a default fading material in case you don't pass one as a parameter.

At the moment, this material would be overwritten the first time the manager is used to fade with a new material (defaults to the last material used). If you want to apply a material in the editor or use a prefab material, then remove or update this section of code.

Next, as we need to draw our fading image (the image is a part of the material, even if it's only a black color) to the whole screen, we are going to need a little helper function to do that using some of Unity's primitive drawing functions.

Primitives, in graphics terms, refers to when you manually draw lines, quads, or shapes using manually-created vertexes, vertices, and indexes. For more information about the editor, visit https://docs.Unity3D.com/Documentation/Manual/PrimitiveObjects.html. For more information on using the low-level graphics library in scripting, visit https://docs.Unity3D.com/Documentation/ScriptReference/GL.html.

Now, you can create a new C# class to hold the following drawing function if you wish, but I have simply appended it to the FadeInOutManager script. Use whichever method suits you; I kept it in FadeInOutManager because it's integral to the operation of that function. It's still static, so it is still reusable wherever I need it. The code of the required class is as follows:

```
public static class DrawingUtilities
{
  //Helper utility to draw a full screen texture
  public static void DrawQuad(
    Material aMaterial,
    Color aColor,
    float aAlpha)
  {
    aColor.a = aAlpha;
    aMaterial.SetPass(0);
    GL.PushMatrix();
    GL.LoadOrtho();
    GL.Begin(GL.QUADS);
    GL.Color(aColor);
    GL.Vertex3(0, 0, -1);
    GL.Vertex3(0, 1, -1);
```

```
      GL.Vertex3(1, 1, -1);
      GL.Vertex3(1, 0, -1);
      GL.End();
      GL.PopMatrix();
  }
}
```

This is just a very basic function using the low-level graphics library (the GL library, more information about this library can be found at `http://docs.unity3d.com/ScriptReference/GL.html`) to define a simple 2D plane that will be displayed in front of the camera. On that plane, I set the material/texture that will be drawn with it and then adjust the alpha (transparency) of the plane. To see how this is used, let's add the following core fading coroutine to the manager:

```
      private IEnumerator Fade()
      {
        float t = 0.0f;
        while (t < 1.0f)
        {
          yield return new WaitForEndOfFrame();
          t = Mathf.Clamp01(
            t + Time.deltaTime / fadeOutTime);
              DrawingUtilities.DrawQuad(
                fadeMaterial,
                fadeColor,
                t);
        }
        if (navigateToLevelName != "")
          Application.LoadLevel(navigateToLevelName);
        else
          Application.LoadLevel(navigateToLevelIndex);
        while (t > 0.0f)
        {
          yield return new WaitForEndOfFrame();
          t = Mathf.Clamp01(t -                    Time.deltaTime /
            fadeInTime);
          DrawingUtilities.DrawQuad(
            fadeMaterial,
            fadeColor,
            t);
        }
        fading = false;
      }
```

This coroutine is very simple and yet so powerful; walking through it, what happens is as follows:

1. When the fade starts, we define a fading value and set it to zero.

2. Then, we run a while loop that runs until our fade value is 1 (full fade). In this loop, we perform the following actions:
   - Wait for the last frame to be drawn (keeps it smooth)
   - Update our fade value based on how much time has passed against how long the fade should last
   - We use the `Mathf.Clamp01` function to ensure the value does not go above a certain range, limiting it to a maximum value
   - Then, we use the drawing function we created earlier to draw a plane/quad to the screen using our fading value as the alpha value

3. When fading out has completed, we load the next level as normal. However, we check whether we have used an index or a name for the scene selection.

4. Finally, we repeat step 2, but this time fading in instead of out by looping our fading value to 0.

5. When finished, we set the fading flag to `false` to indicate that the script execution is complete.

Now, it is very important how we launch this coroutine because it could be interrupted at any time, either by exiting the game or by another fade being requested before the last fade finished. To be able to stop it from anywhere in the game, we need to ensure it is only launched using its string name. This allows us to use the `StopAllCoroutines` function to kill it.

 As stated in the previous chapter, if you have long running coroutines, always ensure they can be started using their string names. Use method/delegate names only for short-lived coroutines.

All that's left to complete our `FadeInOutManager` script is the public function that scenes will be able to use to kick off the process. The code for this script is as follows:

```
private void StartFade(
    float aFadeOutTime,
    float aFadeInTime,
    Color aColor)
{
    fading = true;
    Instance.fadeOutTime = aFadeOutTime;
    Instance.fadeInTime = aFadeInTime;
    Instance.fadeColor = aColor;
    StopAllCoroutines();
    StartCoroutine("Fade");
}
```

As you can see, when fading starts, we set the flag to denote fading has started, capture the values for the manager used to control the fading motion, stop any existing coroutines from running that might be from the existing scene or a previous fading action, and kick off the `Fade` coroutine.

Then, we need the following public static (available anywhere) function that you can use to start the level fading process:

```
public static void FadeToLevel(
    string aLevelName,
    float aFadeOutTime,
    float aFadeInTime,
    Color aColor)
{
    if (Fading) return;
    Instance.navigateToLevelName = aLevelName;
    Instance.StartFade(aFadeOutTime, aFadeInTime, aColor);
}
```

I've included many more overloads for the manager in the sample project. So, it is as flexible as it needs to be for the game, including the ability to pass a material to change the fading image, specify alternate fading values, or fade to another level by index instead of name.

# Updating level loading to use fading

Next, in order to actually navigate to the world, we need to enable our
`NavigationManager` script to actually load our next scene and use the new
`FadeInOutManager` to transition smoothly.

So, open up the `NavigationManager` script in `Assets\Scripts\Navigation` and
look for the following lines:

```
public static void NavigateTo(string destination)
{
    //Application.LoadLevel(destination); <- commented out for
        now as we have nowhere to go :D
}
```

Update the previous lines with the following lines:

```
public static void NavigateTo(string destination)
{
    FadeInOutManager.FadeToLevel(
        destination,
        2f,
        2f,
        Color.black);
}
```

Now, if you return to the town scene and run it and try to leave the town for the
Big Bad world, it will fail—but in a nice way.

If you still have the messaging scripts attached to the `RightBorder`
game object (the right-most bounds of the town), you'll notice a
Greybeards conversation will start. This is because of the simplistic
nature of the messaging system. Just remove the scripts from that
object for now to stop that.

The reason is simple, because we haven't told Unity we have any scenes in our
game yet. You have only been effectively testing whatever scene you have been
in at the moment.

# Updating build settings to include new scenes

To add new scenes, we need to set up the Build Settings options for our project to tell it we have some additional scenes to choose from. Open **Build Settings** by navigating to **File | Build Settings** from the main menu or use *Ctrl + Shift + B* on the keyboard. The **Build Settings** window looks as shown in the following screenshot:

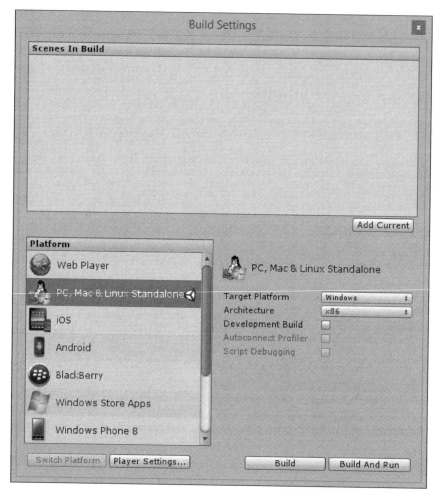

From here, you control how each platform will be built and what is contained within the build. It's also used to change the default editor settings and screen aspects (as described in *Chapter 4, The Game World*) that are available. We will cover more on this later in *Chapter 12, Deployment and Beyond*, when we start building for platforms such as Windows, Windows Phone, iOS, or Android.

As you can see in the following screenshot, the **Scenes In Build** list is currently empty. So when we run the game, it will just run the current scene in the editor. To update this list, either drag the scenes from the project hierarchy or use the **Add Current** button to add the scene you are currently viewing. So, add the two current scenes into the **Scenes In Build** list as shown here:

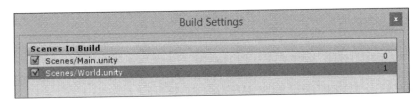

Now, one important thing to note is the order of the scenes. As you may expect, Unity will always start the project with scene **0**, so be sure that the town is the first scene in the list. You can do this by simply dragging the scenes up or down.

Now, when you start the game from the town and run screaming from the town, you will nicely fade out from the town into the Big Bad world.

> This ordering of scenes is very useful and powerful. Some developers like to put levels in order so that they can use the index to progress through.
>
> However, another trick if you are having trouble with a particular scene in your game when running on a device is to reorder the scenes in the build so that the troublesome one is the starting scene. This saves you from having to keep playing through till you get to that scene or writing code to accelerate you. Granted, you need to ensure whatever settings required for the scene are set on load if you debug this way.

# Going further

If you are the adventurous sort, try expanding your project to add the following:

- Add sprites for each of the towns; maybe even animate those sprites when the place is new to draw attention to them.
- Add a camera-tracking script similar to the one used in the Home scene so that the player can move further around the map.
- Create new scenes for the places to visit and get some more characters and conversations going.

- Add a `LineRenderer` component to the `MapMovement` script (visit `http://cgcookie.com/unity/2013/05/03/animate-a-line-draw-using-line-renderer-component/`) to show a line as the player moves.

- Animate the player and flip the image when the hero moves in the opposite direction as we did in the town.

- Add a keyboard input to move the player instead of just touch and click.

- Return to the `CharacterMovement` script and add touch/mouse input.

- Update the `Fading` manager to use curves and/or more images, and try to add a middle image/scene between loading levels. This is commonly used for ads or to hide long loading times.

# Summary

Hopefully, you can appreciate by the end of this chapter how even a simple map-like interface has its own flavors and complexities, but there is so much more you could do to enhance this area. Depending on your style of game, the player could spend quite a lot of time on the map exploring (such as Zelda) or they could just be zipping through. So, plan time accordingly to decide how much you want to invest.

If you target mobile platforms, then other input strategies are very important. On handheld devices, if players use the keyboard, they generally lose over half the screen. So, all they have is touch input. Similarly, on consoles and PCs, they don't have touch input, only keyboards or mice and gamepads. Input is a big area, but we will revisit this area in *Chapter 12, Deployment and Beyond*.

In this chapter, we covered the following topics:

- Building the wider world using textures, texture generation tools, map tools, and some hints at procedural generation

- The different UI interactions and marshaling input priority between GUI and game

- Adding smoothing techniques to scene transitions and how to use animated curves in places other than animation

- Adding some smooth transitions between scenes

# 7
# Encountering Enemies and Running Away

The world is full of big and scary things, or so at least our budding hero is about to find out; you'd think someone would have warned him.

At the heart of most RPG-style games are the bad guys. How they think and how they confront and challenge you will mark your game as either too hard or too easy. Sadly, there isn't any real middle ground (you can't please everyone all the time). However, we can ensure a fair system all round and engage the players with systems that will surprise and entertain them as they move around in the big bad world.

The following topics will be covered in this chapter:

- Planning for event systems
- State machines
- Basic AI techniques

## Event systems

When you're looking to engage the player roaming around in your game, it is best to throw them off guard and challenge them when they least expect it; this ensures that the player is paying attention while playing, and it also serves to keep them on their toes at all times.

The following methods help to achieve this:

- **Fixed systems**: This is where the places and interactions are actually planned in advance by forcing the player to be drawn in to an event at prescribed times/places

- **Random generation**: This involves using random systems to challenge the player within a given time frame or occurrence, giving the player a chance of an event but not a certainty of one

There are merits and demerits with either approach for the player as they interact with your game. Fixed systems are easy to implement but limit replayability (game becomes dull in the second or subsequent runs), whereas random systems can be trickier to get the balance right but it also mean the player will likely keep playing longer or get irritated very quickly.

Finding the balance between implementing events is a tricky process, which you will have to find the right sweet spot for in your particular game, and inevitably all games implement this differently.

Also, remember that there is no silver bullet and no reason not to use both systems together, using fixed systems to tell a story and random events to keep it interesting.

# Exploring randomness

Now one strange thing to keep in mind is that there is no such thing as a completely random system, especially in gaming and computing. You can get close with some really complex mathematical systems but nothing is truly random. The best we can do is make it random enough to fool the player making them believe it is random.

The reason for this is simple: computers are not random and don't think in random terms. When they generate a random number, they are using a seed (a unique number to base their random generation on) to work out what number to give you. But every time you generate a number based on that same seed, it will always be the same sequence; this is known as **pseudo-random**.

So, if I generate a random number from a seed of 1234, every number generated from that seed will always follow the same pattern (1, 5, 3, 7, 2, 4, 10, and so on). Most basic systems try to balance this out by also randomly generating the seed number, but this again falls under the same pattern. However, it does make the random pattern a little more random. A lot of systems use the date or current clock tick as the seed. It's important to know and remember this when you are planning to use random systems.

There is also a drawback to trying to make your random system even more random: you end up spending more time computing the random number in your game and stealing resources from other systems such as physics, AI, and so on. It's always a balancing game to ensure you plan where your precious system resources are going to be spent. For instance, if you use a triple-pass-random system using several levels of Perlin noise generated for each frame, it is a heavy burden on the CPU (although, this is a rather extreme example, you should never generate it for every frame unless there is a very good reason to do so!).

In most cases, developers use other effects to try to create randomness by using noise generating systems (Perlin/fractals/Gaussian drift) and other techniques to try to make the best use of low-cost generation systems with as few passes needed to get the desired result. By combining two or more systems, you can create an approximate and fairly complex random system.

 If you want to read up more on random and pseudo-random systems, you can get a full history on RANDOM.ORG at `http://www.random.org/randomness/`, which also features some examples of free and paid random systems.

There is another side to this predictability of basic random number generation systems: these can be used in various procedural techniques to build game items. If you can predict a sequence of numbers based on a particular seed, you can use that sequence to always build the same thing each and every time.

So, if you want a set of events to always occur in a particular order, you can actually use the basic random system to create a fixed event system; just use the seed you need to generate the sequence you need to use.

# Planning for random code/generation

A key point of any good game design when you even start to think about adding random code/generation to your game is to stop/look and listen. Never rush into using random systems in your game, else you will end up rewriting it at least three times before you're done, and even then you won't be absolutely happy with the result.

Start working from a simple base and ask yourself:

- Do I actually need it to be random or will it get configured?

  This is the first and most important question: are you trying to add random code/generation because it's easier to throw in, and will a fixed configuration be more suitable (is it really random you're after)?

Never use randomization lightly, even when it is just a range of numbers you want to pick from; always question whether it is the right tool for the job. Inevitably, using randomization is always going to be more expensive in terms of processing (especially with more complex systems with deepening levels of recursion or noise generation) than a simple mathematical equation to approximate the values you are after. Do your research.

- Where in your design do you see the need for randomization?

  Be specific! What do you actually need to be randomized or sampled?

  For example, in this RPG project for the random battle events on the map, we need to figure out the following:

  - The chance of an event occurring on a journey
  - Where on the journey the event will occur
  - What will be the starting condition of the battle, number of enemies, their strength, and who fights first

- In each area, how frequently will you need a random sample?

  Because of the cost of random selection, you need to decide when and where the generation will take place. If you need a single random for each frame, that might be okay (depending on what else is happening in each frame); but if you have many, then it may be better to prefill an array of random numbers at the start of the scene and perform a predictive selection of numbers in that array (either stepping through or selection based on other factors).

- What level of complexity does the random sampling/generation need?

  So once you've decided where you need randomization and how often you need it, only then do you decide on how complex that generation needs to be. Is it simply picking a random number or do you need a more accurate random number predication by using one of the aforementioned complex techniques such as Perlin noise or fractal sampling?

  This is arguably a much trickier question as how random do you need to be, in a lot of cases only testing will tell; does your current random technique let you down and the pattern always seems obvious? Does it hamper your gameplay?

For the purposes of this book, I will keep the use simple; this section is mainly to highlight all the complexities of using random systems in games. This might sound like a nice idea to begin with, but beware, here be dragons, even if it's just as simple as a single random number picked in a range in each frame.

Another important consideration is that random generation is not free. Depending on the system you use it could also generate garbage and hamper the performance of your game that may not seem obvious at first glance.

# True randomness

There is another course of logic in random generation systems called **True Random Number Generators (TRNGs)**. They go to great lengths to guarantee the randomness of a generated number with greater and greater precision, but these also come at a heavy cost (if you really need them, however, they are worthy of study).

In games, however, it is usually sufficient to rely on pseudorandom systems, both for their efficiency as well as their predictability. They can be used for bug reproduction or being able to do lock-step games over the net with only player input, for example, in RTS games, or level-generation systems based on seeds, for example, Worms. Another reason is that you often don't want 100 percent randomness, you want something like a shuffle bag or similar to ensure that the event happens "randomly enough" within a time frame.

# Basic Artificial Intelligence

Artificial Intelligence(AI) is a term banded around most game systems and is a general bucket for several techniques for machine-based learning systems. Its sole aim is to fool the user/player into believing that the system is behaving like any living being, mainly to challenge the player in head-to-head battles or helpful supporting characters.

Some systems used to achieve this are as follows:

- **Path-finding**: This helps AI-controlled entities navigate through levels to a specific destination
- **Flocking**: This orders how multiple AI entities will relate to each other within a given area
- **State machines**: These are fixed and basic sensor-driven intelligence to drive AI actions.
- **Rule-based expert systems**: These are the defined logic systems for an AI entity to derive action from and aid decision making

- **Neural networks**: These are advanced learning networks for AI entities, typically used to predict the performance of the AI and also understand the predictable behavior of opponents
- **AI algorithms** (reinforced learning / simulated annealing / genetic calculations): These are many different ways to reinforce neural networks and decision engines for better predictable behavior

The area of AI can be a very complicated minefield. It is often seen by some as a "nice thing to have"; however, getting it right is a very long and drawn out task no matter the size of the project.

My advice, especially if you are just starting out, is to lean on existing implementations either through the asset store or the Unity wiki to begin with and learn from there. The whole subject of AI has spawned numerous books and entire sites such as `http://aigamedev.com/` (a fantastic general resource).

Start simple and move from there. For the purposes of this book and the RPG game, we will focus on a simple state machine implementation using basic sensors to help drive the AI.

# State machines

In life, as well as game development, state machines (or **Finite State Machines (FSM)** as they are more commonly called) are a core component for day-to-day running. At a basic level, they tell us exactly what we are doing right now, what we were doing previously, and what we can do next.

They are commonly used for:

- Menu systems
- Game-level transitions
- AI/Behaviors

We can implement these within games in various ways, from the very basic (and generally hard to manage) to a more ordered system and beyond with full state managers.

A basic state machine is like a flowchart and looks something like the following diagram:

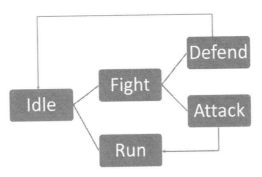

# Defining states

In all implementations, we start with a collection of states: these define both what conditions/states are in the game and what we do when that state changes.

These states describe both what can happen when that state is active and what other potential states could result in an action from the current state. If we take the example from UnityGems, which describes a simple case using a television(TV), we would end up with the states listed in the following table:

| State | Description | Actions |
|---|---|---|
| TV off | No activity is present and nothing is displayed. | The power button turns the TV on. |
| TV on | The TV displays images and plays sound. | The power button turns the TV off. |
| | | The up button selects the previous channel. |
| | | The down button selects the next channel. |
| | | The menu button displays the menu. |
| Menu displayed | The TV displays the menu, overlaying the normal display. | The power button turns the TV off. |
| | | The menu button turns the TV on (menu hidden). |
| | | The up button highlights the previous menu item. |
| | | The down button highlights the next menu item. |
| | | The ok button activates the menu item. |

So from each individual state, there are a number of options; in some cases, the same action will lead to the same result (such as the power button), some actions will do different things based on what the current state is (such as the up and down buttons).

It's important to note that in any game, you will likely use many state systems, from menus to in-game controls and AI.

So once you have your collection ready, the next step is to define an enumeration in C# as follows, for example, using the previous states:

```
enum TvState
{
  Off,
  On,
  Menu
}
```

# Simple singular choice

The simplest way to implement a state system is using the C# switch statement; the benefit here is that there can only be a single result:

```
if (Input.GetButtonDown("Up"))
{
    switch (currentTvState)
    {
        case TvState.Off:
            //Nothing, tv is off
            break;
        case TvState.On:
            //Channel Up
            break;
        case TvState.Menu:
            //Menu selection up
            break;
    }
}
```

So as you can see in the previous example, we have simply implemented the pattern for the Up button on the remote, and depending on what the television is doing currently, it will act appropriately.

This is good for menus, but is limiting in situations where based on the state, we might want to do multiple things.

# Planning for multiple cases

The alternate simple approach to state machines is to use the `if` blocks to test what a state is: the only downside is that this can become very cumbersome to manage very quickly. Consider a slightly more complex scenario (related to the game) where a group of thugs are battling with you, but they are only confident when they are in a group and will run if their health is good. Such a system wouldn't be possible using the previous `switch` style (or at least will be difficult to do so), so by using several `if` blocks as shown in the following code, we can achieve something like this:

```
if (EnemyState == State.Idle)
{
    //Check for player
    // If player found EnemyState == State.Attacking
    //Check for fellow enemies
}

if (EnemyState == State.Attacking && PlayerState == State.Idle)
{
    //Enemy Sneak attack
}

if (EnemyState == State.Attacking)
{
    //Play Attacking Music
}

if (EnemyState == State.Attacking && Health < 5)
{
    //Run away
}

if (EnemyState == State.Attacking && PlayerState ==
  State.RunningAway)
{
    //Give Chase
}
```

Now, although the previous code can be nested or transformed into `switch` statements, writing it this way gives us other advantages: for one, we control when and under what conditions certain things will happen, for example:

* Battle music will always be played when the battle begins

- Enemies will chase the player unless they have low health
- At any point that the player is idle, the enemies will have a sneaking advantage

However, with either system, you are going to end up with a lot of code-making decisions around your game, such as the player, enemies, NPCs, and so on. This will make it hard to manage, and even worse to try debug; perhaps Unity offers us another way?

# State managers

Following on from the Animation tutorial in *Chapter 3, Getting Animated*, we have seen that Unity has a very powerful state machine system built in it already using Mecanim. We have only used it for animation so far, but like AnimationCurves, we can use this to build a nice graphical system that is easier to maintain.

 Although the state machine is very powerful for controlling what states are available and how they transition between states, it can't actually implement actions (other than animation). There are triggers built into the state system, but these are not fully supported on all platforms. So if you use them, keep it limited.

To achieve this properly, you need to separate out the responsibilities for what does what within the state system into the following parameters:

- **Inputs**: What factors will be fed into the state system to affect change
- **The decision engine**: The core logic that drives the state machine
- **Outputs**: What the game will do based on the current state

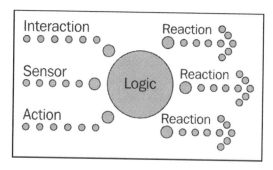

The previous diagram shows an example of how you would componentize your state machine; this pattern is very extensible because it means you can apply separate scripts for each of the inputs, which also means many areas of the game can have an input to the state system. The outputs/reactions to states or state changes can also be componentized (but don't have to be) so that you can swap and change AI behaviors to the different states based on what you are implementing them on. Enemy 1 may be very brave and just act, and Enemy 2 might be a bit more cautious and require other enemies close by before attacking.

Implementing this in Mecanim Animation controllers is very simple since at its heart it is a state machine itself, as shown in the following screenshot:

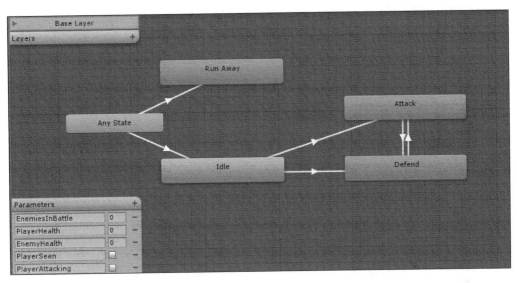

In the previous screenshot, we can see a simple example of this: there are no animations connected to any of the states. We are just using them to track and control what drives our state machine. Using the parameters, it's easy to configure the following settings:

- If the player is seen, the enemy attacks
- If the player is seen and is attacking, the enemy should defend
- If the player attacks when the enemy is attacking, the enemy should defend
- If the player stops attacking, then the enemy should attack back
- If at any time the enemy health is less than 2 and the player's health is greater than 2, the enemy should run away
- If at any time the enemy loses sight of the player, then go back to idle

So by controlling the input, we know how the enemy will behave, and this is completely configurable within the controller without any complex scripting.

# Sensors

Using the Mecanim state machine in this way is very powerful and just having scripts update the parameters of the state machine through input (user taps a key, or scene loads) is simple enough. However, if you want reactive AI, you might want to think about sensors.

Sensors are effectively the AI's eyes and ears and whatever else it wants to use to detect action within a scene (even if it's an alarm or trip wire). Generally, they are self-contained components that look after themselves and inform whatever they are attached to. They can be as complex or as simple as you need them to be.

A basic sensor might be an empty game object with a trigger collider (the trip wire), which tells the enemy state machine that the player has come into view. Alternatively, you could use ray casting (yes, even in 2D) to check whether the target is in view.

One of the best examples of a sensor I've seen is a wandering game object with a sphere trigger that wanders round the screen to represent the point where the enemy was looking at. If it falls on the player or an object that has been moved in the scene, then all hell breaks loose.

# Putting it together

As you would expect, we need to create a new scene for our battles. There is a choice to make whether you want to create several scenes for different battle areas or define one generic scene and randomize the contents of that scene to add variation. Obviously there are pros and cons to each approach, but ultimately the choice is up to you.

# Building the new scene

For now, we will keep things simple and just create a new scene and then configure it as our battle area. So, add a new scene called **Battle** to the project and make it look pretty with some additional background scene elements.

For this example, I have used the Fantasy background (`Environments\Fantasy\Background01.png`) with some of the environmental assets from our asset pack to create the following screenshot:

The Fantasy background from the free assets pack with the sprite's X scale set to 1.5 to better fit the camera

 Remember to group your additional environmental assets under a single empty game object to keep them tidy in the **Project** hierarchy, and also set the sprite layer and order appropriately for all elements, including the background texture.

# Adding the first enemy

We need to create a prefab for our first enemy. Doing so is simple. First, let's start with the goblin character in the asset pack (`Fantasy_Pack\01_Characters\05.png`), split its sprite up using **Sprite Editor**, drag sprite image `05_03` on to the scene, and then rename the new game object to `Goblin`. The enemy would look as the following diagram:

With the character in place, it's time to give the nasty little fellow some logic; we won't use this just yet in this chapter but it's good to have it from the beginning (see *Chapter 10*, *The Battle Begins*, for the applied AI).

So create a new animator controller called `GoblinAI.controller` and place it in `Assets\Animation\Controllers`, which gives us the basic Animator view, as shown in the following screenshot:

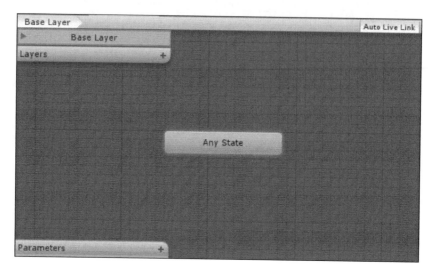

Next, we need some parameters to control the state machine, so add the following parameters to the controller by clicking on the + symbol on the parameters bar and selecting the correct data type, as shown in the following screenshot:

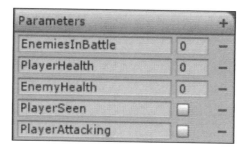

The parameters to be added and their data types are as follows:

- `EnemiesInBattle`: Int
- `PlayerHealth`: Int

- `EnemyHealth`: Int
- `PlayerSeen`: Bool
- `PlayerAttacking`: Bool

Now that we have some input parameters, next up we need our states. So, create the states shown in the following screenshot on the current animation layer by right-clicking and navigating to **Create State | Empty**:

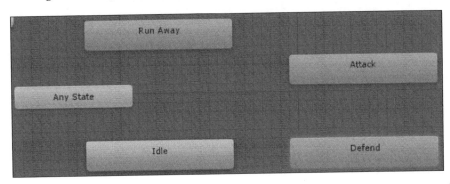

The states to be added are as follows:

- Idle
- Run Away
- Attack
- Defend

 You should note that the first state will be colored orange, whereas the rest are colored grey. This is simply because the first one you create becomes the default state (the state the state machine will start with). You can change the default state at any time by right-clicking on it and selecting **Set As Default**.

So with the parameters and states in place, all that is left is to connect everything up and finalize the state machine. So as we did in *Chapter 3, Getting Animated*, we need to create some transitions between the states along with the conditions for those transitions, as shown in the following screenshot:

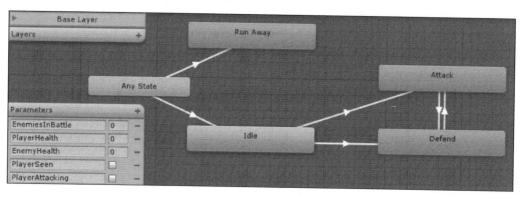

As seen in the previous screenshot, the states and their transitions are as follows:

- `Idle -> Attack - PlayerSeen = true`

  Goblin attacks player when he sees him

- `Idle -> Defend - PlayerSeen = true and PlayerAttacking = true`

  If the player attacks first when they are seen by the Goblin, then defend

- `Attack -> Defend - PlayerAttacking = true`

  Switch to defend if the player attacks

- `Defend -> Attack - PlayerAttacking = false`

  As soon as the player stops attacking, switch back to attack

- `Any State -> Idle - PlayerSeen = false`

  If the Goblin loses sight of the player at any time, go back to idle

- `Any State -> Run Away - EnemyHealth < 2 and PlayerHealth > 2`

  The Goblin is basically a coward; if at any time its health drops too low and the player is a lot healthier, then it will run away as fast as its little legs will take it

Now that we have our AI state machine for our Goblin, select the **Goblin** game object in the **Scene** hierarchy and add a new **Animator** Component in the **Inspector** menu and drag the newly created animator to it, which should now look like the following screenshot:

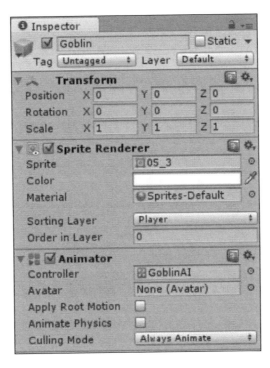

Now that we have our Goblin set up, we just need to create a prefab from it. So drag the **Goblin** game object from the **Scene** hierarchy and place it in Assets\Prefabs\ Characters. You can now delete the original in the scene as we don't need it anymore.

> If you ever need to change or add to a prefab, you can do this at any time by selecting the prefab and updating it in the **Inspector** menu. This will automatically update any scene object created from the prefab. However, if you add the prefab to the scene and then change it, the changes you make will only be for that instance in the scene and will not update the prefab.
>
> As noted in the previous chapter, you can also update the prefab from the instance by clicking on the **Apply** button.

# Spawning the horde

Now that we have our Goblin enemy, we need to be able to randomly drop some into the battle. For this, we need to set up some spawning points (because we don't want them to appear just anywhere) and a script to manage them.

So first create a new empty game object in the scene and call it SpawnPoints. This is just a container to keep the spawn points all together. Next, create nine more empty game objects, make them children of the SpawnPoints game object, and then name them Spawn1, Spawn2, and so on, as shown in the following screenshot:

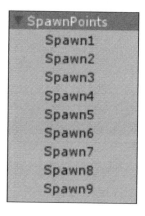

Now, position each Goblin in the scene where you want it to appear.

While doing this, I find that adding the prefab manually to each spawn point and then positioning it makes it a lot easier to find the right spot. However, remember that the order in which you add them to the scene is important as it affects what order they are drawn in.

You can also alternatively add an editor script to the object to make it easy to use in an editor. See *Chapter 11, Onward Wary Traveller*, for more information on editor scripts.

After a bit of tinkering, I ended up with the following (I also added a hero character for effect):

An example scene where 8 Goblins (out of the possible 9) have spawned in

Now we know where the Goblins are going to appear; we just need to get them there, so we'll manage this with a `BattleManager` script.

The purpose of this script is to manage the life cycle of the battle scene, from setting up the battle scene to taking turns to attack and finalizing the battle once complete.

We start off by creating a new `BattleManager` C# script and placing it at the top of the project `Assets` folder along with the other managers (if you wish, you can create a separate `Managers` folder and organize them there). As this script only works when we are in a battle, there is no need to make it a singleton. Battles come and go and they should only last for the length of the current battle.

 For now, we will just set up the framework for the battle scene and get it populated. Our poor hero has no chance to defend himself yet, so we'll just let him run away with his tail firmly between his legs.

First, we'll add some variables that we can configure from the scene using the following code:

```
public GameObject[] EnemySpawnPoints;
public GameObject[] EnemyPrefabs;
public AnimationCurve SpawnAnimationCurve;
```

These lines maintain the spawn points the battle manager knows about, the possible enemy prefabs it can spawn into the scene, and a curve that we can use later to control how we animate the Goblins. More on this later.

Next, we have some control variables to manage the battle as it ensues. This is done using the following code:

```
private int enemyCount;

enum BattlePhase
{
    PlayerAttack,
    EnemyAttack
}
private BattlePhase phase;
```

These states are only temporary. In *Chapter 9, Getting Ready to Fight*, and *Chapter 10, The Battle Begins*, we will build on this for a more full-fledged system using Mecanim.

We keep a count of how many enemies are active in the scene as well as what phase the battle is in at the moment (along with our own enumeration of the states the battle can be in; you can always add more). Finally, we have a flag to monitor whether the enemy characters have actually started fighting.

Now when the script is run, it needs to initialize the battle arena; so add the following code to the `Start` method:

```
void Start () {
    // Calculate how many enemies
    enemyCount = Random.Range(1, EnemySpawnPoints.Length);
    // Spawn the enemies in
    StartCoroutine(SpawnEnemies());
    // Set the beginning battle phase
    phase = BattlePhase.PlayerAttack;
}
```

As this is a one-time coroutine, we are just initializing it with the method definition instead of the string name of the method. There is no need to stop it since it only runs till all the Goblins are in the scene and then stops.

Keeping things simple for now, we generate a random number of Goblins who will attack (or be found wandering round the wood waiting to be chopped). Then, we spawn them in using a coroutine and start battle with the player going first.

 Since we simply need a fixed random number and we are only doing it at the beginning of the scene, we are just using the Unity Random function. If we needed a more complex random selection or more frequent selection, we would change this to something more complex or preloaded.

Now that we know how many Goblins we need in the battle, we can spawn them in. I've used a coroutine here so we can animate them one by one as follows:

```
IEnumerator SpawnEnemies()
{
    // Spawn enemies in over time
    for (int i = 0; i < enemyCount; i++)
    {
        var newEnemy =
            (GameObject)Instantiate(EnemyPrefabs[0]);
        newEnemy.transform.position = new Vector3(10, -1, 0);

        yield return StartCoroutine(
            MoveCharacterToPoint(
                EnemySpawnPoints[i], newEnemy));

        newEnemy.transform.parent =
            EnemySpawnPoints[i].transform;
    }
}
```

Here, we loop through how many Goblins we'll need, create a new instance using the prefab we created earlier, set its position off screen, and then animate it on to the screen using yet another coroutine (shown in the following code). When the coroutine finishes animating, we anchor it to the spawn point it was meant for.

 I made the Enemy prefabs into an array, so we can support multiple types of enemies in the battle.

So that the Goblins don't appear, we use the `AnimationCurve` parameter we added to the script and a coroutine to move the Goblin from off screen to its intended spawn point, as follows:

```
IEnumerator MoveCharacterToPoint(GameObject destination,
GameObject character)
{
    float timer = 0f;
    var StartPosition = character.transform.position;
    if (SpawnAnimationCurve.length > 0)
    {
        while (timer < SpawnAnimationCurve.keys[
            SpawnAnimationCurve.length - 1].time)
        {
            character.transform.position =
                Vector3.Lerp(StartPosition,
                    destination.transform.position,
                        SpawnAnimationCurve.Evaluate(timer));

            timer += Time.deltaTime;
            yield return new WaitForEndOfFrame();
        }
    }
    else
    {
        character.transform.position =
            destination.transform.position;
    }
}
```

Using the same logic we used in the previous chapter when moving the character on the map, we work out where the game object is starting from and then use a `while` loop to keep the game object moving until it finally reaches its destination. However, to improve things, this time we base the loop on the length of the `AnimationCurve` parameter we have defined for this transition.

This allows greater flexibility and allows us to have more complex and longer animations.

- First we check whether there are animation steps (keys) within AnimationCurve (if you want something to just pop in to place, then don't configure a curve)

- If there are keys in the animation, then we keep iterating until we reach the last key in the animation based on the time of that step and our current iteration time

Then within the loop, we use Lerp for the position of the object from start to finish using the animation curve to control its time and rate.

We only go to the next animation step when the next frame is ready (using the WaitForEndOfFrame function) else the animation would happen all at once; so we do it gradually each frame.

You could use yield return null; however, this happens indeterminately and could cause the coroutine to be called several times per frame depending on how long the last render/draw took. Since this is a smooth animation, we need to process it for each frame. If it is another operation that just needs controlled cycles/iterations, returning null may be preferred.

Next, we need to give the player a way to interact with the battle scene, so we'll add some GUI buttons that only appear if we are in the player's battle phase. We need the following code to do this:

```
void OnGUI()
{
    if (phase == BattlePhase.PlayerAttack)
    {
        if (GUI.Button(new Rect(10, 10, 100, 50), "Run Away"))
        {
            NavigationManager.NavigateTo("World");
        }
    }
}
```

Now, add a new empty game object to the battle scene, name it `BattleManager`, and then attach the new script to it. Once there, we can configure it by adding the spawn points we created earlier to `EnemySpawnPoints` and the Goblin prefab to the `EnemyPrefabs` parameter along with the Spawn Animation Curve, as shown in the following screenshot:

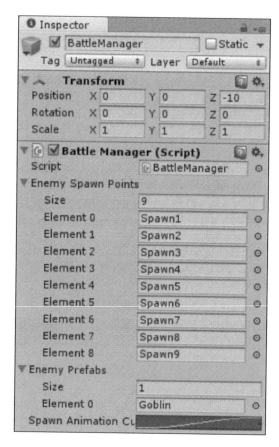

# Getting back home

Now, as the player hits the yellow streaked button to run away (obviously skipped his ninja skill training back home), we see a very obvious problem: the map scene is starting afresh back at home. This is simply because we are not tracking where the player left the previous scene.

There are two ways to handle this: either we record where exactly everything is in every scene and where the player enters and exits, or we can simply track the last known position (or possibly a mixture of the two?).

For now, let us simply implement the last known position method. To do this, we are going to need a central place to remember everything about our game world (well, at least the important bits we want to track), such as the player's stats, options and preferences they have set, and where they have been in the world. Some of these will need saving for the next time the player runs the game and some are just for the current instantiation, but we will cover saving and loading later in *Chapter 11, Onward Wary Traveller*.

The settings we need don't have to be part of any scene, actively tracked in the scene, or even interact with other game components. So we don't need a class that implements MonoBehaviour or ScriptableObject; we do, however, need it to be around all the time and not be reloaded in every scene. For this, we need a very simple static class (we implemented one of these earlier in *Chapter 6, The Big Wild World*, with NavigationManager).

Create a new C# script in Assets\Scripts\Classes called GameState and populate it with the following code:

```
using System.Collections.Generic;
using UnityEngine;

public static class GameState {

    public static Player CurrentPlayer =
        ScriptableObject.CreateInstance<Player>();
    public static bool PlayerReturningHome;
    public static Dictionary<string, Vector3> LastScenePositions =
        new Dictionary<string, Vector3>();
}
```

Here, we have some simple static properties to:

- Track the player's stats
- A flag to note whether the player is running home away from a battle
- A dictionary to record the scenes the player has been to and the last position they were in that scene

Simple enough, but to avoid unnecessary code duplication I have also added some helper methods to the GameState class to manage and simplify the use of the LastScenePositions dictionary (to save time later).

So add the following code to the end of the GameState class:

```
public static Vector3 GetLastScenePosition(string sceneName)
{
    if (GameState.LastScenePositions.ContainsKey(sceneName))
    {
        var lastPos = GameState.LastScenePositions[sceneName];
        return lastPos;
    }
    else
    {
        return Vector3.zero;
    }
}

public static void SetLastScenePosition(
    string sceneName, Vector3 position)
{
    if (GameState.LastScenePositions.ContainsKey(sceneName))
    {
        GameState.LastScenePositions[sceneName] = position;
    }
    else
    {
        GameState.LastScenePositions.Add(sceneName, position);
    }
}
```

The preceding code is fairly similar but it ensures simple and effective use of any dictionary class, checking the following:

- When you request a value from the dictionary, it checks whether it exists first and then returns it
- If the value doesn't exist in the dictionary yet, it returns a default value
- When you add a new value to the dictionary, it checks whether it already exists, and if it does, then it updates the existing value
- If the value does not exist when you try to add it, it just adds it to the dictionary

Dictionaries are powerful when used correctly: you can find values by index (in this case a string) or you can find them by ID (like in arrays). You can even loop over dictionaries with for or foreach loops.

However, depending on how you use them, they may not perform well and can also generate garbage, so use them carefully.

For more details, see the C# article at `http://blogs.msdn.com/b/ shawnhar/archive/2007/07/02/twin-paths-to-garbage- collector-nirvana.aspx`. The article is based on XNA but rings true for any C# platform.

There are also considerations when you need to serialize the values from a dictionary since they are handled differently on some platforms, and in some cases not even supported for serialization.

With the `GameState` class in place, we just need to update the `MapMovement` script for the map to load the last position if one exists, and save the last position when exiting the scene (and in any other scene that will need the logic).

So, update the `MapMovement` script's `Awake` method with the following code:

```
void Awake()
{
    this.collider2D.enabled = false;
    var lastPosition =
        GameState.GetLastScenePosition(Application.loadedLevelName);

    if (lastPosition != Vector3.zero)
    {
        transform.position = lastPosition;
    }
}
```

The previous code simply looks for a last position for the current scene, and if there is one, it moves the player to it.

Similarly, when closing the scene, we just need to store the last position. To do this, we add an `OnDestroy` method as follows and save the player's current position:

```
void OnDestroy()
{
    GameState.SetLastScenePosition(
        Application.loadedLevelName, transform.position);
}
```

# The missing random piece

We have our battle scene up and running, and when the player runs away he/she will still be at the place on the map where the battle occurred. Wouldn't it be nice to also enter the battle scene? So let's add that.

To keep things simple (you can always extend it later), we will just use a simple probability to work out whether the player is likely to enter a battle while travelling. If a battle is going to occur, we just figure out then where on the player's journey the battle will take place. This way it looks random and catches the player off guard when it happens (if it does, there's always a chance it won't).

Alternatively, you could place empty game objects on the scene with colliders to change the probability of an event occurring and have a script to start a battle if one happens. Similar techniques are used in the Pokemon style games where deep grassy areas always have a higher probability of a random battle occurring.

So to start off, we will add a couple of extra parameters to control the battle event probability in the MapMovement script, as follows:

```
int EncounterChance = 100;
float EncounterDistance = 0;
```

Ideally, the EncounterChance parameter should be controlled by some logic based on the player's level and how dangerous the area of the world they are currently in, but you can extend that later if you wish.

It is set to 100 for now to ensure the player will always hit the first battle to send him home.

Next, in the `Update` method where we track when a player taps or clicks on the map to move, we check the probability of an event occurring. If that event occurs, then set the `EncounterDistance` property as follows to denote when the event will occur along the player's journey:

```
if (inputActive && Input.GetMouseButtonUp(0))
{
    StartLocation = transform.position.ToVector3_2D();
    timer = 0;
    TargetLocation =
     WorldExtensions.GetScreenPositionFor2D(Input.mousePosition);

    startedTravelling = true;

    //Work out if a battle is going to happen and if it's likely
    //then set the distance the player will travel before it
    //happens
    var EncounterProbability = Random.Range(1, 100);
    if (EncounterProbability < EncounterChance &&
        !GameState.PlayerReturningHome)
    {
        EncounterDistance = (Vector3.Distance(StartLocation,
        TargetLocation) / 100) * Random.Range(10, 100);
    }
    else
    {
        EncounterDistance = 0;
    }
}
```

 At this point, you will notice that the code between touch and click is becoming duplicated; try to refactor this (clean it up) so less code is duplicated. There is no spoon.

We know that if an event occurs and when it does, all that is left is to act on it. So, in the Update method where we animate the player across the screen, we simply need an additional check to see whether we have travelled to the event and if so, stop and enter the battle. We can do so using the following code:

```
if (TargetLocation != Vector3.zero && TargetLocation !=
transform.position && TargetLocation != StartLocation)
{
    transform.position =
        Vector3.Lerp(StartLocation,
            TargetLocation,
    MovementCurve.Evaluate(timer));
    timer += Time.deltaTime;
}
if (startedTravelling && Vector3.Distance(StartLocation,
    transform.position.ToVector3_2D()) > 0.5)
{
    this.collider2D.enabled = true;
    startedTravelling = false;
}


//If there is an encounter distance, then a battle must occur.
//So when the player has travelled far enough,
//stop and enter the battle scene
if (EncounterDistance > 0)
{
    if (Vector3.Distance(StartLocation,
        transform.position) > EncounterDistance)
    {
        TargetLocation = Vector3.zero;
        NavigationManager.NavigateTo("Battle");
    }
}
```

# One last thing

Now that the player has left home, found some nasty goblins, and run away, it would be nice if he didn't encounter anymore until he next leaves home.

So using the additional flag `PlayerReturningHome` we set in the `GameState` class, we can set this in the battle manager when the player hits the button. We also then need to unset this when the player leaves home again. So, update the `OnGUI` method in the battle manager to set the `PlayerReturningHome` flag to `true`.

Then for the home scene, set the flag to `false` when the player leaves. This can be achieved by either editing an existing script in the home scene or adding a new one to change the flag state in the `OnDestroy` method mentioned earlier, or update the `NavigationManager` script to set the flag when the player travels home. It is your choice. In the sample code, I have added this to the `NavigationManager` script, as shown in the updated `NavigateTo` method here:

```
public static void NavigateTo(string destination)
{
if (destination == "Home")
{
GameState.PlayerReturningHome = false;
}
FadeInOutManager.FadeToLevel(destination);
}
```

Then when the `NavigationManager` script detects that the destination is the Home scene, it will update the flag to `false` in the `GameState` class.

It is up to you and your game's design whether this is true for all battles or just for the first; it all depends on the style of the game you are building.

 Don't forget to add the new Battle scene to the **Build** settings if you want to see it in the final project!

# Going further

If you are the adventurous sort, try expanding your project to add the following:

- Add a coroutine to take the player home when he runs from the battle
- Plan and add further logic to determine the probability that a player will enter the battle, either using the described zones or based on player stats
- Add a few more enemy types and integrate the enemy class into the prefab (we will do this later but you can have a go yourself now)

- Try putting together another battle scene and update the battle logic to pick a random scene

- Separate the random logic into its own manager class and try a few different patterns

# Summary

Picking when and how often a player will enter battles is a tricky balance between fun and engagement. Do it too often and they will get annoyed, too few and they will get bored. Also, the battles need to be achievable and stretch the player at the same time. It is a complex paradox that if planned wrong, can ruin your hardwork. The best solution when all is said and done is to get your game play tested by as many people as possible and genuinely accept feedback no matter how harsh.

Alongside random generation of course is predictive planning: if you have a story to tell, you also need to have a framework to replay that story over a period of time, balancing when you need a random event or picking up the next page in your book.

In this chapter, we covered random generation, what it means, and when to use it effectively; some very simple uses of random; built a battle scene and planned for expansion; basic AI concepts and State Engines; enabled the player to run away and fight another day; and built on our use of the `AnimationCurve` system.

# 8

# Shopping for Weapons

Arguably, the inventory system in any good RPG game is one of the most important components. Depending on the style or background of your design, it may be even more important than the story or battle system. The reason I say this is because the way in which you'd design and implement your shopping and inventory system will alter how your game is played and how quickly the player will progress through your creation.

Another factor that we will cover in this chapter is **monetization**. Every title needs to have a monetization story so that the player will eventually be able to make money through his or her hard work. There always has to be some kickback in the end to help you pay the bills or keep tabs on your sanity. It doesn't have to be money; it could just be recognition or an aid to your portfolio. However, in most cases, it's about money.

The list of topics that will be covered in this chapter is as follows:

- Looking at the inventory and items
- Building a shop and an inventory UI layer
- Looking at monetization options
- Handling back navigation

## Why do we shop?

People have been asking this question since caveman times probably (although granted that Walmart wasn't yet open). What things do you need to help you become contented in the world; let me pose that eternal question as an example, "Do these shoes make me look fat?". Such questions have no real answer other than our appetite as humans to collect things, and if they help us feel good about our lives, all the better.

The same is true in the gaming world. Adventures need things to help the budding adventurer along, to make them better, and look better in a lot of modern games.

The motivation to buy things is strong, and we have come to expect this in almost any game. From a simple adventure game where we just pick things up off the street that may come in useful later, fashion games where you have to be as pretty as possible, to full-fledged RPG games where inventory is everything, this motivation is indispensable. If you haven't got that level 20 sword of ultimate banishing, you just aren't going to make it in the world. Even FPS games aren't immune to this phenomenon. If you can't upgrade and tweak your weapons, you are seen as old and out of touch.

One of the biggest rises in consumerization these days has happened in the casual market; just about every casual game has coins that you can collect to unlock power-ups, extra levels, or even skins for your character to change their appearance (they serve no actual value but just add further depth to the game). It is astounding how simple tap-and-flick games have become some of the biggest marketing machines.

It is important to keep all of this in mind and look at the real world when designing any shopping/inventory system for your RPG game. The more it feels like something that someone would do in real life, the more at home they will feel with it, and the easier they will find using it.

You should always be asking the following questions to yourself while designing such a system:

- How does an item add value?
- Does it seem affordable?
- Is it going to improve the play? (Doesn't actually have to?)
- Is it desirable?
- Is it better to know what the player will already have and why?
- Is it for single use (consumable) or fixed (durable/nonconsumable)?
- Will it break or wear out over time?

A lot of this leads us beyond just what is good for the game; it leads us to what is good for the player. Another factor that can lend weight to this is whether we are going to monetize certain powerful items. However, we will cover more on this later.

# The power of an item

At the core of any inventory/shopping system are the individual items themselves. They need to be designed in a way that will not only set each item apart from every other item, but will also ensure that they work together to benefit the player as they travel through your world.

Items generally have their individual properties. Refer to the following table:

| Item/property | Description |
|---|---|
| Slot | Can this only be used in a certain slot for the player or in general? |
| Stackable | Can items, such as ammo or potions, be stacked on top of each other? |
| Health | Yes, items should have health and they shouldn't degrade. |
| Strength or damage | What is the effect on the player's health (can it be negative to add health)? |
| Defense | Does the item protect the player at all, even if only a little bit? |
| Power | Does the item have its own source of power/ammunition? Is it limited? |
| Recharge rate | Does the item recharge itself or not? Can it be recharged? |
| Size | Is the item bulky and cumbersome? |
| Weight | Is it light or heavy? Will it encumber the player or slow them down? |
| Storage | Similar to a backpack, does it enable the player to carry more? Negative would mean that they will carry less. |
| Cost | What is the in-game or real currency value of an item? |
| Trade-in value | In some systems, the item's health will impact this. |
| Perks | Does the item have bonuses that will also enhance the player? |
| Abilities | Similar to perks, does the item grant a special action to the player? |
| Use/type | Is it a weapon, armor, potion, and so on? |
| Category | Does it have a specific category within its type? |
| Level | Can the item be leveled up, making it stronger, or is it a fixed level? |
| Durable or consumable | Is the item nonconsumable, durable, purchasable, or one-time consumable? |
| Rarity | Is the item one of a kind, simply hard to find, or a commonplace object? |

A lot of the preceding items will just depend on the style of the game you are making; not all will fit, but you should review each of them in turn as you design the shopping/inventory system.

# Building your shop

Using the items, we are going to design our game. Now we need to start thinking about how the player can be provided with these items. Do they need to be bought from a shop, are they found somewhere, and can they be sold later, or does the player simply throw them away once done with them and move on to the next shiny thing? In some games, the previous item becomes fused with the new one to highlight a progression.

The next thing that should come to mind once you have settled on some sort of shopping system is how the player will access it. In most RPG games, it is the traditional roadside shop or wandering peddler. The player has to travel to a certain location in order to buy items. In the case of some of the rarer items, they have to travel to a specific shop or a mystic sear guarding the item in order to acquire it.

Laying out the shop's design is fairly easy, simply because it is a shop. You don't have to worry about loads or size; it is just a storefront.

Some examples of different shop layouts are as follows:

| | |
|---|---|
| 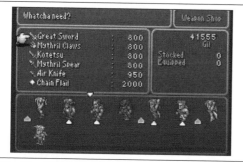 | Final Fantasy has a very basic text layout where each shop or shop owner only stocks a single type of item. |
| World of Warcraft employs a much more graphically rich but still a very basic system with few categories to choose from. |  |

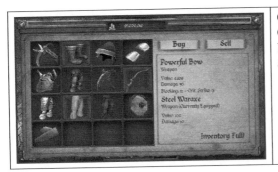

Other titles, such as DaggerVale from Concept Softworks, use a simple grid-based approach showing all the wares that a shop stocks.

The pattern you choose will entirely depend on the style of your game.

Some games, however, take a different approach. They make the storefront available from anywhere in the game, which can be simply accessed through the player's inventory; items can be bought and sold anywhere in such games.

# Laying out your inventory

Your character's layout is usually a lot more restricted as compared to that of a storefront. However, the character's layout needs to follow the same design pattern you are using in your game.

These systems usually fall into a couple of patterns.

# Rule of '99

Players are limited to a certain number of each item. The number can vary based on the item (for instance, you can have only one weapon) or its effect on the player's load. As a rule of thumb, 99 should be the maximum number. However, it's up to how your game will use the item to denote its maximum number.

In the Final Fantasy series of games, Rule of '99 was used throughout its inventory system, allowing the player to carry no more than 99 potions at a time or anything else for that matter, as shown in the following screenshot:

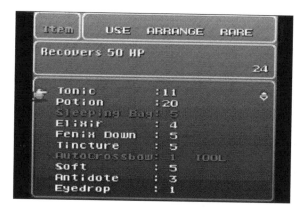

# Encumbrance system

A system based on the strength, endurance, and energy of a player is a faux-style system. It ensures that the player cannot carry more than he or she is able to; generally though, it doesn't take into account the size of the item, just its weight. This provides a more taxing system for the player, forcing them to only carry what they need.

Skyrim implements this system very well; it not only forces the player to manage their load when looting but also focuses on leveling up the player to increase what they can carry, as shown in the following screenshot:

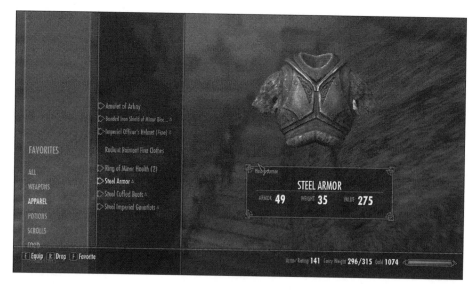

# Slot-based system

A slot-based system is a variation of the preceding encumbrance system. Instead of weight, it uses a grid system for the player's inventory and assigns a certain number of those grid points to an item. These points relate to how bulky or awkward a particular item is going to be. This generally limits the player more than other systems because it forces the user to reserve enough space to carry the items they really need.

The Fallout series and the upcoming Wasteland 2 games implement a very effective slot-based system.

It gets tricky for the player when large mission items require a lot of slots. Refer to the following screenshot:

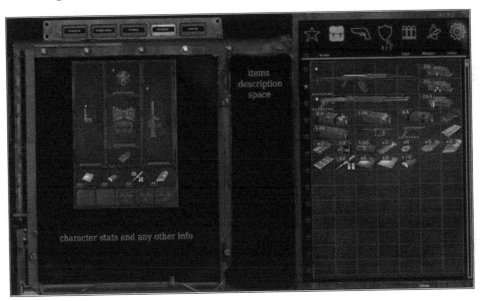

# A mini game

Another approach is to go a step further with an inventory system and evolve it into a mini game in itself. Generally, players don't just move things around or sort them; instead, they start combining items within the inventory to create or craft new items or just upgrade them. A crazy idea I saw that was going around was to turn the inventory screen into a game of Tetris with new items being dropped; if you could place them, you would be successful.

It certainly brings a new challenge. Moreover, if the bandwidth of your game can allow it, it's certainly another opportunity to make use of.

# Real world

The most complex system to implement is a real world or a simulated kind of inventory pattern to use. Attempting to make a player carry things around needs to be as real as possible. It embodies all of the preceding systems and adds rules around the need for special belts to carry axes/swords. Hooks and backpacks have to be carefully packed. In some games, the player carries lots of items on their belt or back; this generates noise, making them less stealthy.

# Getting paid

One of the hardest decisions we have to make with our creations is how to get paid. It is sure that we love our creations and they are a part of us, but there should always be some sort of reimbursement for our effort.

Some of the most common patterns for monetization in games are paid, paid with trial, ad supported, in-app purchase, and in-game currency.

# Paid

Games are usually sold at a fixed price. For big game studios, this is generally the only option, especially with disk-based delivery and some marketplaces.

The emphasis on a paid-only pattern means that you need a high-quality sales portfolio for your game and outstanding game-marketing assets (logos, screenshots, videos, and so on).

What is also just as important is the blurb about your game. It really has to stand out and draw the player in to make them part of their hard-earned cash.

# Paid with trial

Offering a trial with your game is a great way to entice the players in. Obviously, it gives them a taste of your game before they commit to pay for it.

 Be honest about the trial though; there have been many cases of annoyed players where games were published for free but were actually limited trials. Do not upset your potential buyers; be upfront about it.

You still need a good presence with your marketing and storefront, but the trial is also another great option to draw them in.

When going down the trial route, be sure to pick a single path and stick to it, either by limiting the game, offering so many levels, or even having a time-limited play. Just don't mix them!

Another factor in offering trials is that each platform you deploy to may have a different way of providing it, either directly from the marketplace or through marketplace APIs. It's best to design how your game will behave in a trial and link that to a flag or option. You can then control the game separately from the menu or check the game on startup.

# Ad supported

Often, the ad-supported option is the route for a lot of free-to-play mobile titles. This is one option that can be difficult to get right. If there are too many ads, the player will just get annoyed and uninstall it. Alternatively, if there are few ads, you are not going to get much back from it.

A key thing to remember about ads is that it's all about presentation and numbers. You need thousands of ads presented through your titles to make any kind of money back from the ad providers. It will be better if the player also clicks on the ad, as this generates better revenue; however, you cannot bet that the player will do this.

**Warning**

Do not attempt to fake or force the player to click on ads. It's a very bad experience and will most likely force the player to uninstall your game quickly. Also, the ad providers are clever enough to work out whether you are faking the clicks; if yes, they'll simply not pay for you.

I have seen cases where developers have layered ads on top of each other to maximize the ad's presentation or use the GUI controls in close proximity to the ads, tricking the player to click on them. These are very bad practices and should be avoided. At best, you won't get paid for your ads; at worst, it will significantly get you bad reviews and lower down your number of players.

A few actions that generally work are as follows:

- Displaying a non-UI blocking portion of the screen in the gameplay
- Just displaying the menu or non-game screens (for example, the inventory and the pause screen)
- Displaying ads only in the loading screens
- Pop-up ads that appear when an event occurs
- Ads on the purchase screens

You can mix and match the preceding patterns, but remember there is a fine line between background annoyances that the player can just ignore if they don't want to look and screens that are too intrusive and overbearing. Test with a selected audience and alter your implementation based on their feedback **before** you publish it.

The terms used by the ad providers aren't meant to befuddle you, but they do take some getting used to. Some of the terms and their meanings are described as follows:

- **Fill rate**: This term is the percentage rate at which the ads will be sent to your game. If the provider has run out of ads or has none for your ad settings (age, region, language, and so on), this can drop to zero, meaning no ads.

- **Impressions**: This term is a figure to denote the number of successfully shown ads in your game. Beware of the same ad shown several times; some ad providers count this as the same impression. Just check against your own experience.

- **Click through rate (CTR)**: This term is the higher paid option with ads to denote that the players are actually clicking on the ads to look into them.

- **eCPM**: This term is basically a unit of measurement of how much you will be paid per click or impression. Usually, you just need to multiply this figure by the number of impressions to see how much you will get. Note that this figure will go up and down based on just about anything, including the weather.

- **AdTypes**: There are various ad types and sizes supported by each provider with different capabilities. Banners are the simplest. Being of a screen area size, they take up the entire screen while displaying the ad. Others such as interspatial are interactive and generally take up the entire screen. Check each provider to know what they support and which you want to use.

Another factor to keep in mind is publishers. They will all perform differently in different markets and languages. Generally, ad publishers focus on a few selected markets or only take advertisements in certain languages, and so on.

Some of the publishers are as follows:

- **Microsoft PubCenter**: This publisher is strong in the US but is weak elsewhere

- **Smaato**: This publisher is strong in central Europe and the US but poor in non-English countries

- **Inneractive**: This publisher provides a good mix of support and ads across the globe but suffers from low or poor fill rates in practice (something they are working on)

- **Google AdMob**: This publisher is strong across the globe, but you need millions of impressions to make any real money

There are many more publishers out there, such as InMobi, VServe, Leadbolt, and others, that have their strengths and weaknesses. You will be able to determine which publisher works best for you in which countries by personally testing them.

When using advertising, it is very important to add your own instrumentation to your title to track how the adverts are doing. Don't just use the ad publisher's figures from their respective dashboards. This way, you can manage yourself with what works best for you and alter your plans accordingly. Don't just publish and let go; manage effectively to improve your returns.

While implementing ads, there is no rule that says you have to use only one provider. Always hedge your bets with the ad providers and implement as many as you are comfortable with, structure your ad presentation in a framework so that you always show the best-performing adverts first, and use another ad network if the current one isn't delivering.

If this seems a bit much to do by yourself, there are several frameworks out there that will do this for you. The ad-rotating solutions are fully featured to work with a number of ad providers and ensure that you always display ads.

One such framework is a solution named **AdRotator**, which is open source and works with most platforms. You can check it out at `http://getadrotator.com`. There are others on the Unity asset store as well; just be sure to check what platforms they support (iOS, Android, Windows Phone, and so on). So, you might have to use a few different ones for all the platforms you deploy to. For example, **Vserv. mobi** (`www.vserve.com`) can also display ads from other providers and not just its own.

# In-app purchase

A common feature being implemented in most of the games these days is in-app purchases. This feature is simply your paid shopfront within the game to unlock levels, purchase rare items, or remove unwanted features such as ads.

In some cases, in-app purchases have been used to implement the trial functionality; publishing the title as free, and then offering an in-game unlock option. On consoles such as Ouya, this is a standard practice.

Note that with the trial system, be upfront if your game is sold as a trial. Players do not like this and will aggressively mark down and slam titles that appear free until they are forced to pay to play!

In-app purchases on most of the platforms come in the following two forms:

- **Durable/nonconsumable**: These are in-game items that the player can purchase, and have real-world value (such as a sword, an unlockable area, or even the ability to turn off advertising if your game is ad-supported). These are generally single-use items, and you can verify with the marketplace of the platform to check whether the player has purchased them or not. It is advised that you also manage the information locally to ensure that you don't slow the game down on startup while checking. You can also keep this information on a backend service, just in case the user resets their device or transfers to a new one; this is not mandatory however.

  These can only be purchased once

- **Consumable**: Effectively, consumables are in-game currency, items that are meant to be recharged and replenished over time.

  The big difference between consumables and durables is that consumables are not tracked on the server (other than in the payment history, but the payment history is not available in apps/games)

  These can be purchased many times over

Besides the store/marketplace for each platform, there are some online services that will create payment systems for you, saving you from recreating everything for each platform you support. One such service is called **Lotaris** (http://www.lotaris. com/), which offers many different ways for players to purchase items and apps. You still, however, have to publish your app to each platforms' store.

**Warning**

If you are using in-app purchases, beware that the big brother is watching. Employing unethical or illegal practices when implementing these systems could bring about a whole heap of trouble.

For more information, check out the article at http://webarchive. nationalarchives.gov.uk/20140402142426/http://www. oft.gov.uk/news-and-updates/press/2014/05-14.

*Read this now* if you plan to or are already using in-app purchases.

# In-game currency

Virtual currency, as a practice in games, has been rising steadily. The basic premise being that the game is generally free to play and uses some kind of in-game currency, which the players can earn in the game. This currency usually takes two forms; the basic coin, which can be earned in-game, and the premium coin, which can only be bought with cash (or for completing rare and special events).

The idea is simple; play through the game slowly and normally. However, if you want to advance quicker or get ultra-rare items, you need to buy and spend the premium coin for those items. In some cases, you can also convert the premium coin to the basic coin to get the in-game currency quicker.

Although this makes a steady profit in single player or offline games, it really comes into its own with the multiplayer option online. It seems there is a growing market for people to advance quicker than others or just to beat their friends quicker.

Implementing coin systems is generally harder than just implementing in-app purchases but makes for an easier-to-manage ecosystem.

Also, see the warning about in-app purchases, as this applies heavily to in-game currency/bitcoin systems as well, if not more.

# Putting it together

As with other areas in this book, we will just keep things simple when implementing the sample project. You can always extend or replace it later if you wish.

We will also look at two slightly different approaches: using a scene for the shop and a layer system for the inventory.

# Gathering the shop assets

For the shop, we'll just create a new scene to keep things simple as we expect to enter a shop and leave it when we are done.

As I couldn't find anything I liked, I created a simple shop interface for use in the scene, as shown in the following screenshot:

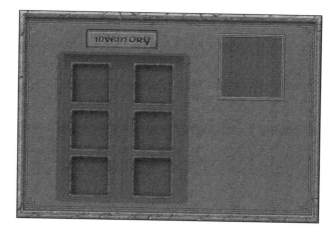

These are just enough features for what we need to implement in the shop. For items to show in the shop, I turned back to the Web and found a fantastic site, `http://ccrgeek.wordpress.com/`, where there are an astounding amount of free icon spritesheets to choose from. I picked one of the `Weapon Icons 1.png` weapon spritesheet from the amazing **Icons to Characters RTP** set found at `http://ccrgeek.wordpress.com/2012/05/29/more-converted-graphics/`.

 You can also find the image following in the supporting assets' `.zip` file that accompanies this title.

Here is what it looks like:

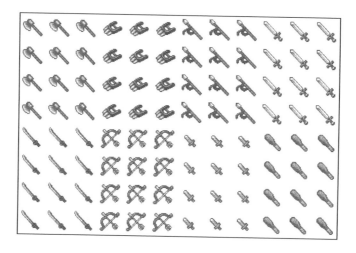

This gives us a nice array of weapons to choose from. For our character, you can always use the other icon sets for equipments, tools, food, and so on, if you wish.

Lastly, on the image front, we also need some buttons (included in the supporting assets with this title), so I created a **Back** button, as shown in the following screenshot:

I also created a **Buy** button as shown here:

Nothing too fancy, just enough to get the job done.

# Building the shop scene

To make the best use of the new 2D system, we can create a new scene to place the shopping interface for the player to use; so we'll create a new scene named Shop.

With this in place, just copy the assets from the sample assets pack accompanying this title for the shop interface into your project's Assets folder (ShopScreen images for the environment and BackButton, BuyButton, and Weapon Icons 1 images for props). Then, drag the ShopScreen image on to the new scene and check that the new game object is called **ShopScreen**. Additionally, ensure that the sprite-sorting layer for each of the sprite renderers is appropriate so that they get drawn in front; to do this, set all of them to the foreground layer.

 The Weapon Icons 1 image is a spritesheet, so remember you'll need to set its **SpriteMode** option to multiple and splice it with **Sprite Editor**. Each image is of 32 x 32 pixels.

As we are using the 2D system for the shop screen, we have greater flexibility to design the screen without using Unity's native GUI system.

 Unity is soon going to release a new GUI system in Version 4.6, which could be used to replace what we are building here; however, currently it is not available. Nevertheless, this section is written so that it will be easily translatable and you'd not need to replace the code of the current GUI framework.

So first, we need to create some empty game objects to place all the UI elements we need on the screen, adding the following assets as children of the **ShopScreen** game object:

- **BackButton**: An object that will capture when the user wants to exit the screen
- **OwnerSlot**: A place to display the sprite of the shop's owner
- **Slot01** and **Slot06**: The available shop inventory slots
- **Purchasing section**: An empty grouping game object; this is used so that we will be able to enable/disable all the purchasing options together
- **BuyButton**: An object to capture the user wanting to purchase an item; it is attached to the **PurchasingSection** object
- **PurchasingItem**: A place to display the object that the user has currently selected to buy; it is attached to the **PurchasingSection** object

 Remember that as this is 2D, check whether each of the game object's transform has only **X** and **Y** position values. Reset the **Z** value to zero if it is not that already!

When you have put all the game objects into the scene, you should have something like the following screenshot:

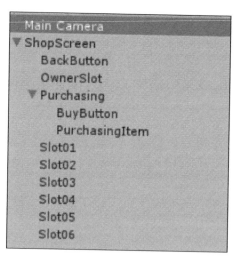

You can just assign appropriate sprites to the **Buy** and **Back** buttons. The rest of the object images are dynamic and are assigned at runtime. They will also need to be able to render sprites, so add a **Sprite Renderer** component to each of them.

Next, arrange each of the items appropriately on the screen according to what the item is. You should end up with something like the following screenshot:

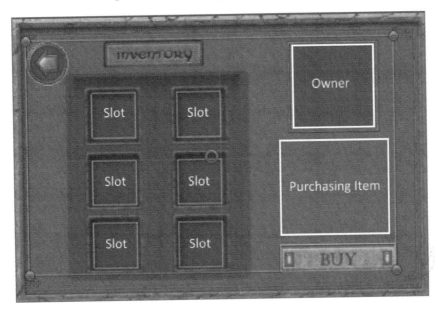

 Note that I find it useful when I have dynamic items that can display different items to temporarily assign a sample sprite to the object while placing it and then remove the sprite later.

Lastly, for the layout, we need to add 2D colliders to all the objects that we intend the user to be able to click on; so, add an appropriate 2D collider to the following objects:

- **Slots**: Add a **Box Collider 2D** component, scaling the collider's size to fit the graphics on the screen. For example, for a 32 x 32 image, scale the collider by `0.32` for both the **X** and **Y** position.
- **Buy button**: Add a **Box Collider 2D** component. It should scale automatically, but it's good practice to check.
- **Back button**: Add a circle collider 2D component.

With the layout in place, we need something for the screen to use. So, let's add some items.

# Creating inventory items

Like with conversation items we created in *Chapter 4, The Game World*, we want to be able to simply manage items that can be used or bought in our game.

First, we need a scriptable object to describe our inventory items. So, create a new script in `Assets\Scripts\Classes` named `InventoryItem` and populate it with the following structure:

```
using UnityEngine;

public class InventoryItem : ScriptableObject
{
  public Sprite Sprite;
  public Vector3 Scale;
  public string ItemName;
  public int Cost;
  public int Strength;
  public int Defense;
}
```

 Note that we haven't implemented all of the properties we described earlier, just a subset as an example. You can add more if you wish.

Now that we have our scriptable object, we need an editor script to create our inventory items. So, create another script in `Assets\Scripts\Editor` named `InventoryItemAssetCreator` and populate it with the following structure (note that we are again using our generic utility class to make this very easy to implement):

```
using UnityEngine;
using UnityEditor;

public class InventoryItemAssetCreator : MonoBehaviour {

  [MenuItem("Assets/Create/Inventory Item")]
  public static void CreateAsset()
  {
    CustomAssetUtility.CreateAsset<InventoryItem>();
  }
}
```

With this in place, we can now create some inventory items. Create a new folder in `Assets\Resources` named `Inventory Items`, navigate to that folder, and create a new `InventoryItem` class from the **Create** menu (right-click on **Create** or use the `Project` folder window's **Create** menu option).

With the new `InventoryItem` asset created, we can configure our first weapon. Rename the asset to `Lv0_Sword` and then configure its properties as shown in the following screenshot:

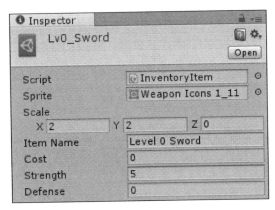

You can configure the properties using the following settings:

- Set the **Sprite** property to a sword sprite image from the weapon icons spritesheet (**Weapon Icons 1_11**)
- Scale the image up as by default it is quite small (**X 2, Y 2, Z 0**)
- Give it a name via the **Item Name** field
- Set **Cost** to 0 to denote it's a free item
- Set **Strength** to 5 and **Defense** to 0 so the weapon at least has some effect

Save the sword Inventory Item and then create another weapon or two in the same manner. I also created an axe with the same values.

# Managing the shop

Now that we have our shop interface and some stock we can put in it, it's time to bring them together.

First, we need to set up a shop manager who looks after the day-to-day running of the shop, then we will add the shelves to the shop to manage where we can put the stock.

 As the ShopSlot and ShopManager folder depend on each other, we need to create them together. Until both are complete, you will most likely see errors; just keep this in mind as we progress.

It is always the same when you are creating codependent classes.

First, we need the shop manager itself. To keep things neat, create a new folder in the project's Assets\Scripts folder named Shop, then create a new script in the Shop folder named ShopManager. This just ensures that any script related to shopping is stored here if you want to expand it later. The manager is only used in this one scene, so we don't need to make it a singleton.

To start off, we will just add some parameters so we can control the shop we are creating and set it up as follows:

```
using UnityEngine;

public class ShopManager : MonoBehaviour {

    public Sprite ShopOwnerSprite;
    public Vector3 ShopOwnerScale;
    public GameObject ShopOwnerLocation;
    public GameObject PurchasingSection;
    public SpriteRenderer PurchaseItemDisplay;
    public ShopSlot[] ItemSlots;
    public InventoryItem[] ShopItems;
    private static ShopSlot SelectedShopSlot;

    private int nextSlotIndex = 0;
}
```

When the player enters the shop's screen, we want to be able to display the current shop owner and a selection of their wares. So, when ShopManager starts, we need to configure those items as follows:

```
void Start () {
  var OwnerSpriteRenderer =
    ShopOwnerLocation.GetComponent<SpriteRenderer>();
```

```
OwnerSpriteRenderer.sprite = ShopOwnerSprite;
OwnerSpriteRenderer.transform.localScale = ShopOwnerScale;

if (ItemSlots.Length > 0 && ShopItems.Length > 0)
{
  for (int i = 0; i < ShopItems.Length; i++)
  {
    if (nextSlotIndex > ItemSlots.Length) break;
    ItemSlots[nextSlotIndex].AddShopItem(ShopItems[i]);
    ItemSlots[nextSlotIndex].Manager = this;
    nextSlotIndex++;
  }
}
}
```

Here, we just took the configured sprite for the shop owner and assigned it to `SpriteRenderer` then scaled for the relevant game object, and then looped through all the available slots in the shop and picked out items from its inventory to place in them, ensuring we only stock as many items as the shop can handle.

You will notice that the last function actually has an error. This is because we did not add the actions/behaviors for the `ShopSlot` folder. We will fix that shortly.

Next, we need some helper functions that represent the actions/behaviors that the shop is capable of performing; first, we add the ability to select an item for purchase using the following function:

```
public void SetShopSelectedItem(ShopSlot slot)
{
  SelectedShopSlot = slot;
  PurchaseItemDisplay.sprite = slot.Item.Sprite;
  PurchasingSection.SetActive(true);
}
```

Then, we add the ability to clear the selected item from the shop using the following function:

```
public void ClearSelectedItem()
{
  SelectedShopSlot = null;
  PurchaseItemDisplay.sprite = null;
  PurchasingSection.SetActive(false);
}
```

Finally, we add the ability to purchase the currently selected shop item using the following function:

```
public static void PurchaseSelectedItem()
{
  SelectedShopSlot.PurchaseItem();
}
```

Each of the preceding functions are self-contained and controls each of the steps necessary to perform each action. They do so by enabling or disabling the screen elements, such as `PurchasingSection`, to perform actions on dependent objects such as the shop slots.

You will note that this last function is also set as `static`. This is to enable it to be accessed from anywhere in the code without referencing it or performing `GetComponent` for the `ShopManager` script.

As stated in the previous sections, it might seem like you could make everything static and avoid using `GetComponent` altogether. However, using statics has certain overheads and can lead to a messy and hard-to-diagnose code; it should not be overly used. If in doubt, don't use it, unless necessary.

 If you wish, you can define `ShopManager` as a singleton. However, unlike the singletons used so far, this shop will need to be destroyed when the scene is unloaded. Otherwise, you will always get the same shop. This is unless you also change how we load the shop.

With the `ShopManager` set up, we can now create the missing definition for `ShopSlot`. This will define the slots in the shop that remember what is being stored on the shelf. Create a new script in `Assets\Scripts\Shop` and name it `ShopSlot` replacing its contents with the following code:

```
using UnityEngine;

public class ShopSlot : MonoBehaviour {

  public InventoryItem Item;
  public ShopManager Manager;
}
```

Now, to add other functions for the shop slots that will be used by the manager, add the following functions to the `ShopSlot` script:

```
public void AddShopItem(InventoryItem item)
{
  var spriteRenderer = GetComponent<SpriteRenderer>();
```

```
    spriteRenderer.sprite = item.Sprite;
    spriteRenderer.transform.localScale = item.Scale;
    Item = item;
}
public void PurchaseItem()
{
    GameState.CurrentPlayer.Inventory.Add(Item);
    Item = null;
    var spriteRenderer = GetComponent<SpriteRenderer>();
    spriteRenderer.sprite = null;
    Manager.ClearSelectedItem();
}
```

 The previous line in the `PurchaseItem` method where we add an `InventoryItem` to a players inventory will give an error until we update the player definition in the upcoming *Updating the player inventory definition* section.

The first function enables the ability to add an inventory item to the current slot and display it, and the second function controls how an item is purchased. Again, each function is distinct, and is just related to the task that it is to perform. Wherever possible, you should follow this pattern as it will make maintaining or extending your game much easier later.

Finally, we need to add one last piece of code in order to enable the player to click on the items in the shop slots; so, add the following function to the `ShopSlots` script:

```
void OnMouseDown()
{
    if (Item != null)
    {
        Manager.SetShopSelectedItem(this);
    }
}
```

 In these examples, I used `OnMouseDown` to capture the mouse click/ touch tap from the user. However, this doesn't seem to work on all platforms. If your intended platform doesn't support it, you just need to add some **input raycasting** to test whether the GameObject has been hit.

Check the following Unity forum post for a discussion on the subject: `http://forum.unity3d.com/threads/unity-2d-raycast-from-mouse-to-screen.211708/`

The preceding code simply uses the interaction between the **Box Collider 2D** on the input `OnMouseDown` event, and as long as there is an item in the slot, it tells the `ShopManager` script that you have selected it.

# Adding 2D button behaviors

Now that we can stock our shop and purchase items from it, we just need the ability for users to buy items when selected, so create a new script named `BuyButton` and place it in `Assets\Scripts\Shop` with the following contents:

```
using UnityEngine;

public class BuyButton : MonoBehaviour {

  void OnMouseDown()
  {
    ShopManager.PurchaseSelectedItem();
  }
}
```

The preceding code simply calls the static `Purchasing` function we created in the `ShopManager` script earlier to buy an item on any game object that has a 2D collider placed on it, as we did with the `ShopSlot` script.

# Updating the player inventory definition

Now that we have a definition for `InventoryItem` folders, we can update the `Player` class so that the player can carry the correct item. So, open the `Player` class under `Assets\Scripts\Classes` and update the script to use the new `InventoryItem` class instead of a string:

```
using System.Collections.Generic;
public class Player : Entity
{
  public List<InventoryItem> Inventory = new
    System.Collections.Generic.List<InventoryItem>();
  public string[] Skills;
  public int Money;
}
```

# Stocking the shop

With all our scripts in place, let us return to the shop scene, start applying them, and finally get some stock displayed on the shelves.

So first, let's attach the following scripts:

- Attach the `ShopManager` script to the `ShopScreen` game object

- Attach the `BuyButton` script to the `BuyButton` game object
- Attach the `ShopSlot` script to each of the slots in the shop

Now, our shop is ready to receive its owner and some inventory items to stock. So, select the `ShopScreen` game object; once you do this, you should see the following configuration options in the **Inspector** pane:

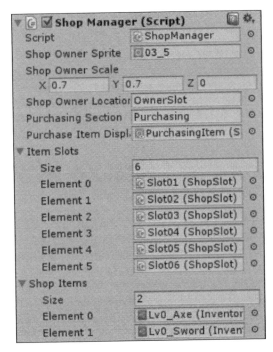

I've preconfigured **Shop Manager** as an example. So, let us walk through what is available:

- We have the sprite and scale for the shop owner. I selected one of Greandal's poses and scaled him appropriately. (The mayor is multitalented and also owns almost everything in town, including the shop.)
- I then attached the **Purchasing Section** and **Purchase Item Display** item to the scene. We could have discovered these in the scene by the name or tag if you so wished. There are often many ways of doing the same thing.
- Next, I set the **Item Slots** pane's **Size** to 6 and attached each of the available slots in the shop by dragging them from the **Project** hierarchy on to the **Inspector** pane. You can also achieve this by using the dot icon next to each element and finding the slots in the scene.

- Finally, I set the **Shop Items** pane's **Size** to 2 and dragged the two `Inventory Items` we created earlier in `Assets\Resources\InventoryItems` on to each element of the **Shop Items** array.

If you now run the scene at this point, you should see the following output:

- The owner along with your shop items are displayed.

- Clicking on an item connects the mouse or touches the box collider on the slot and tells the shop manager to select the item in that slot.

- When an item is selected, the **Buy** button and the selected item appears. Clicking on the **Buy** button adds the item to the player's inventory, clears the selection, and removes the item from the slot.

# Leaving the shop

The player can purchase items from the shop (actually, they can buy anything as it's all free at the moment), but they are stuck in the shop, the doors and windows are barred, and the owner has a very stern face.

As the shop could be used from anywhere in the game, it would not make much sense to navigate through all the scenes of the game in a cycle to go back to the earlier scene. So, we need to add the ability to go back to the previous location the player was in, the place where his shop is located.

To implement this, we need to make a minor modification to the navigation manager to remember the last place where it was. Open the `NavigationManager` script from `Assets\Scripts\Navigation` and first add a new `using` statement to the beginning of the class, as follows:

```
using System.Collections.Generic;
using UnityEngine;
```

This will quickly enable us to discover what the current scene is. Next, add the following `static` property:

```
private static string PreviousLocation;
```

Then, in the `NavigateTo` method, we need to store the scene the player is travelling from before we change it; to do this, add the following line:

```
public static void NavigateTo(string destination)
{
    PreviousLocation = Application.loadedLevelName;
```

```
   if (destination == "Home")
   {
      GameState.PlayerReturningHome = false;
   }
   FadeInOutManager.FadeToLevel(destination);
}
```

Finally, we need to add a function to enable the scenes to tell the navigation manager to go back to the previous scene; this can be done using the following lines of code:

```
public static void GoBack()
{
   var backlocation = PreviousLocation;
   PreviousLocation = Application.loadedLevelName;
   FadeInOutManager.FadeToLevel(backlocation);
}
```

All this function does is that it gets the previous location to a separate variable, sets the current scene as the previous location (so if you go back again, you will return to the scene you just went back from), and then transitions to the previous scene.

Now that our navigation manager has the ability to go back, we can return to our shop scene to enable the user to leave the shop and go back to the real world.

Next, create another script named `BackButton` and place it in `Assets\Scripts\Shop` with the following contents, which just calls the new `Navigation` method:

```
using UnityEngine;

public class BackButton : MonoBehaviour {

   void OnMouseDown()
   {
      NavigationManager.GoBack();
   }
}
```

Attach the preceding script to the `BackButton` game object in the shop scene. Now, the player can click on the back button and leave the shop. Granted that this can only work once you enter the shop from another location, so let's look at how to get into the shop now.

# Entering the shop

We can buy items from the shop and we can leave the shop, but how do we get into the shop in the first place? As we did in *Chapter 6, The Big Wild World*, we just need to add trigger colliders where the user can enter the shop if they wish with the caveat that they can only enter when they are in front of the shop and have pressed a key (the up arrow button in this case).

To enable this, we need a very similar script to the `NavigationPrompt` script that we used in *Chapter 4, The Game World,* (always reuse) but with a few differences.

Create a new script named `ShopEntry` in `Assets\Scripts\Navigation`, then replace its contents to add a variable to control whether we can enter the shop or not; we do this using the following code:

```
using UnityEngine;

public class ShopEntry : MonoBehaviour {

    bool canEnterShop;
}
```

As with the `Navigation` script, we handle the changing of the state of this flag with a single function. So, if we need to change anything else, we can do so using the following code:

```
void DialogVisible(bool visibility)
{
    canEnterShop = visibility;
    MessagingManager.Instance.BroadcastUIEvent(visibility);
}
```

Next, we need trigger handlers to detect when the player is in front of a shop; refer to the following code that tells you how to add trigger handlers:

```
void OnTriggerEnter2D(Collider2D col)
{
    DialogVisible(true);
}

void OnTriggerExit2D(Collider2D col)
{
    DialogVisible(false);
}
```

Now that we can tell when the player is in front of the shop, we just need to capture whether they have pressed the up arrow button to enter the shop. We do that in the `Update` method as follows:

```
void Update()
{
  if (canEnterShop && Input.GetKeyDown(KeyCode.UpArrow))
  {
    if (NavigationManager.CanNavigate(this.tag))
    {
      NavigationManager.NavigateTo(this.tag);
    }
  }
}
```

Finally, we add a little GUI touch as follows to let the player know that they can enter the shop when they are in front of it:

```
void OnGUI()
{
  if (canEnterShop)
  {
    //layout start
    GUI.BeginGroup(
      new Rect(
        Screen.width / 2 - 150,
        50,
        300,
        50));

    //the menu background box
    GUI.Box(new Rect(0, 0, 300, 250), "");

    //Dialog detail—updated to get better detail
    GUI.Label(
      new Rect(15, 10, 300, 68),
    "Do you want to Enter the Shop?    (Press up)");

    //layout end
    GUI.EndGroup();
  }
}
```

Trying to enter the shop isn't going to get us very far if the game doesn't know it exists, so add this scene to the project's **Build Settings** and also update the `NavigationManager` script to include a new `Route` asset for the shop, as follows:

```
public static Dictionary<string, Route> RouteInformation = new
    Dictionary<string, Route>() {
    {"Battle", new Route {CanTravel = true}},
    {"World", new Route {RouteDescription = "The big bad world",
        CanTravel = true}},
    {"Cave", new Route {RouteDescription = "The deep dark cave",
        CanTravel = false}},
    {"Home", new Route {RouteDescription = "Home sweet home",
        CanTravel = true}},
    {"Kirkidw", new Route {RouteDescription = "The grand city of
        Kirkidw", CanTravel = true}},
    {"Shop", new Route {CanTravel = true}},
};
```

With the scripts in place, we now need to add them to the player's home in front of the shop. Open the `Home` scene and add a new empty game object named `Shop` as a child of the **WorldBounds** grouper game object (because it takes us out of the scene), attach the `ShopEntry` script, and add a **Box Collider 2D** component (set as a trigger), as shown in the following screenshot:

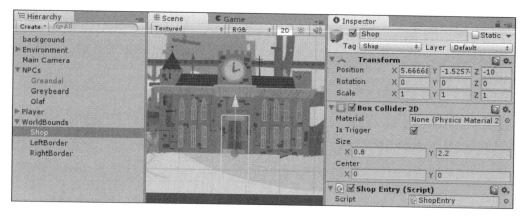

The collider just needs to be shaped or scaled enough so that our 2D character will collide with it when he passes in front of the shop.

Finally, to ensure that we navigate to the new **Shop** scene, we need to add a new tag named `Shop` and assign it to the new `Shop` game object, as shown in the following screenshot:

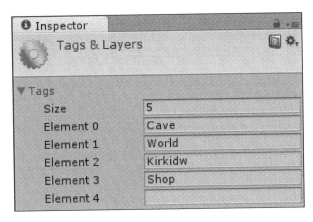

Now, when you run the `Home` scene and the player runs in front of the shop, you should get a nice new prompt in front of the shop; tapping the up arrow key will help you enter the shop and navigate inside it, as shown in the following screenshot:

# Managing your inventory

Now that you have got to grips with building a GUI with a 2D system as it stands, what about the existing GUI framework that Unity has? Well, as a comparison, let's put in a small player inventory viewer for the player and cover off the difficulties of using 2D with the GUI framework.

To start off, create a new script named `PlayerInventoryDisplay` in the `Scripts` root folder, `Assets\Scripts`, and replace its contents with the following code, adding some basic variables:

```
using UnityEngine;

public class PlayerInventoryDisplay : MonoBehaviour
{
  bool displayInventory = false;
  Rect inventoryWindowRect;
  private Vector2 inventoryWindowSize = new Vector2(150, 150);
  Vector2 inventoryItemIconSize = new Vector2(130, 32);

  float offsetX = 6;
  float offsetY = 6;
}
```

The names of each property should be fairly self-explanatory:

- A flag to confirm whether the inventory window is displayed or not
- Some sizes for the window and the inventory content sizes
- Offsets to space things out in the window

Next, we add an `Awake` function to set up the display of the inventory window as follows. Based on the size of the screen, it will be displayed on different devices (we don't want it to take up the whole screen):

```
void Awake()
{
  inventoryWindowRect = new Rect(
    Screen.width - inventoryWindowSize.x,
    Screen.height - 40 - inventoryWindowSize.y,
    inventoryWindowSize.x,
    inventoryWindowSize.y);
}
```

Then, in an OnGUI function, we will draw a button to open the inventory (this could instead be mapped to a key if you wish or both), and if the inventory is to be displayed, we will draw a custom window using the following code:

```
void OnGUI()
{
  if (GUI.Button(
    new Rect(
      Screen.width - 40,
      Screen.height - 40,
      40,
      40),
    "INV"))
  {
    displayInventory = !displayInventory;
  }
  if (displayInventory)
  {
    inventoryWindowRect = GUI.Window(
      0,
      inventoryWindowRect,
      DisplayInventoryWindow,
      "Inventory");

    inventoryWindowSize = new Vector2(
      inventoryWindowRect.width,
      inventoryWindowRect.height);
  }
}
```

For the main inventory window, we will use the custom ability of the Unity3D GUI to draw the window's contents (as opposed to the manual way, we applied it with the navigation prompt with BeginGroup and EndGroup). We implement this with a new function as follows, and this is where we but heads between the Unity3D GUI system and the new Unity3D 2D system:

```
void DisplayInventoryWindow(int windowID)
{
  var currentX = 0 + offsetX;
  var currentY = 18 + offsetY;
  foreach (var item in GameState.CurrentPlayer.Inventory)
  {
    Rect texcoords = item.Sprite.textureRect;
```

```
texcoords.x /= item.Sprite.texture.width;
texcoords.y /= item.Sprite.texture.height;
texcoords.width /= item.Sprite.texture.width;
texcoords.height /= item.Sprite.texture.height;

GUI.DrawTextureWithTexCoords(new Rect(
  currentX,
  currentY,
  item.Sprite.textureRect.width,
  item.Sprite.textureRect.height),
  item.Sprite.texture,
texcoords);


currentX += inventoryItemIconSize.x;
if (currentX + inventoryItemIconSize.x + offsetX >
  inventoryWindowSize.x)
{
  currentX = offsetX;
  currentY += inventoryItemIconSize.y;
  if (currentY + inventoryItemIconSize.y + offsetY >
    inventoryWindowSize.y)
  {
    return;
  }
}
    }
  }
}
```

In this window, we loop through all the items in the player inventory (if there are any) and display them as buttons. You could then wire up these buttons to actions, if the item has any, such as potions to be drank or bombs to be dropped.

Now, one thing to note is that the existing GUI system *does not natively support sprites*; we have to use the GUI `Texture2D` drawing function to pick up the specific sprite out of the spritesheet manually.

 The texture on the sprite is purely a reference to the full image the sprite came from. So, if your image is a single sprite, this is OK. However, in most cases, it will be from a spritesheet and will show the entire spritesheet.

So, we have to use the `GUI.DrawTextureWithTexCoords` function to grab the specific image region from the spritesheet. You should also note that we have to scale the region to the size of the full image because the coordinates given for the specific sprite are unscaled.

Thanks to one of the book reviewers, Trond Abusdal, for finding the preceding solution. I tried and couldn't get it to work. Fantastic find!

One warning is that if you try to read the pixels from the sprite's texture, you will get an **Access denied** message because of the way sprites are imported.

All is not lost, as in future, we will have the *all new* **Unity UI**, which will support sprites fully.

Alternatively, if you want, you can use separate sprites (losing some of the performance you get from spritesheets) for buttons, which makes the GUI implementation easier; alternatively, you can have separate textures for things you want to draw with the GUI system (just alter the import settings from **Sprite** to **Texture** and click on **Apply**).

With the script in place, just add it to the `Player` game object in the `Home` scene so the player can rummage through their pockets.

# Adding the Player inventory behavior

Now that we are done with the whole inventory saga, we need to ensure that when the player buys a weapon, they are able to use it and defend themselves when attacked.

There are a couple of ways of doing this as follows:

- Updating the player's statistics on acquiring the equipment
- Having assigned slots that affect the player's statistics
- All items in the inventory affect the statistics and are queried during the battle

The first step is the simplest as it requires no additional UI, which we will implement in the next code.

Open up the `Player` script under `Assets\Scripts\Classes` and add the following additional function:

```
public void AddinventoryItem(InventoryItem item)
{
  this.Strength += item.Strength;
  this.Defense += item.Defense;
  Inventory.Add(item);
}
```

The preceding code gives us a single point to control how the player's statistics are affected when we grant them a new inventory item in the game.

Ideally, you would want to add further control to this function, including making the player's **Inventory** property read only to avoid accidental direct access, which would bypass the calculation of the player's statistics.

Now that we have our helper function to control a player's **Inventory** property, we just need to update the `ShopSlot` script we created earlier to use the following new function:

```
public void PurchaseItem()
{
  GameState.CurrentPlayer.AddinventoryItem(Item);
  Item = null;
  var spriteRenderer = GetComponent<SpriteRenderer>();
  spriteRenderer.sprite = null;
  Manager.ClearSelectedItem();
}
```

Now, when the player receives a new weapon, their statistics will be improved. Our budding player is ready to return to the big bad world to take on those horrible goblins that block his way.

# Going further

If you are of the adventurous sort, try expanding your project to add the following features:

- Update the shop's setup to use `ScriptableObjects` to allow you to have more shop configurations or screens.

- Expand the player's **Inventory** options. Change it to use a 2D layout, such as the shop, instead of using Unity GUI.

- Update the **Inventory** items to have the type of inventory (weapons, armor, or potions) and then update the Inventory function of the player to assign different statistics for different items.

- Think about extending the inventory system. Presently, if I buy two weapons, I'll get two slots of additional statistics (the same as if I buy seven swords). Obviously, you may not want to be affected thus, but how could you prevent it?

- Have a go at adding money into the equation by making things cost money. In the purchasing section, display and act on it if the player does not have enough.

- Put a second view in the shop to allow the player to sell items back to the shop.

# Summary

In effect, the shopping or the inventory system is just a backdrop for this chapter. Its main purpose is to make you stop and think how you are going to actually make money from all your hard-earned efforts. With all the best will in the world, there has to be some return for all your labor, from recognition and sharing (which is what I mostly end up doing) to actually earning money. If you earn money, how are you getting paid, per installation, or a reoccurring revenue stream through in-app purchases?

Whichever way you go, stop and think carefully about it; don't leave it until you have finished, or in all likelihood you will be disappointed.

We covered monetization and what it means, building a GUI using the 2D system, the basic Unity3D GUI, and planning for an effective inventory system.

# 9
# Getting Ready to Fight

As we reach the end of our journey with the RPG game, we enter the last aspect of the framework itself. This brings to light one of the hardest parts of any game development: engagement. This centers on how you can keep the players playing the game in effect, how the game balances out to keep them challenged, and how to deliver enough varied content so they feel they are always experiencing something new.

So we'll start with a few finishing touches to the game's battle system itself and then look at deepening the background of the game.

Unlike previous chapters, the focus here will be on the implementation, showing you quite a few tips and tricks and helping you avoid some of the pitfalls of the sometimes strange Unity way of doing things. Also, as we have much to cover, this chapter will flow on to the next to give you time to pause, reflect, and then carry on.

The following is the list of topics that will be covered in this chapter:

- Preparing battle statistics and creating the game's UI
- Implementing the turn-based battle system
- Working with Mecanim in the code
- Building more advanced sprite 2D GUI systems

# Efficient RPG UI overlays

Taking stock of the various designs that have been floated around in RPG games, conveying important information such as health, stats, and other important details is crucial to any gameplay. If the information is too obscure, the player won't understand when they are close to death (and should run far away) or struggle to understand why their favorite magic trick just isn't going as well as it should. Similarly, if you make the UI too obtrusive, draw players' attention away too much, and obscure the real estate on the screen too much, then the result will be the same.

This balance is hard to maintain in any game, especially in RPG games, because we want to give as many capabilities as possible to our budding adventurer. It gets even harder once you start adding companions and hundreds of available skills and instant use items.

# The adventurer's overlay

Games such as *Baldur's Gate* (developed by Black Isle Studios) and many of the difficult and true RPG games from the 80s took the style of surrounding the player with everything at hand.

In the preceding screenshot, we see all the party members to the right, all the menu options to the left, and quick use items/skills laid at the bottom of the screen. Although functional, this style of design leaves only a small portion of the screen for the actual gameplay. As these were mostly PC titles and large screens were available, this wasn't too much of an issue.

Today, with smartphones and 10-inch tablets being the norm, this would create a large issue. Put simply, it doesn't scale well.

# A context-sensitive overlay

The developers of *Fallout* (developed by Interplay Entertainment) took a slightly different approach, taking a similar style to that of *Baldur's Gate*; it opted for an onscreen approach but were a bit more clever about the use of it.

In the preceding screenshot, we see a smaller overlay screen at the bottom of the screen, taking up a lot less real estate. In this game, it was possible to change the overlay based on what was selected, allowing the selection of a character of the player's party to be displayed on the screen; this helped to change the details shown to that character.

Buttons were added to provide pop-up sections for skills, character attributes, and the map.

It also provided two modes: one for traveling and one for battle, each distinctly different based on what the player would need at the time.

## Modern floating UI approach

A popular pattern that fits more modern titles is to use floating elements on the player's screen, taking advantages of the improvements that *Fallout* implemented and extending them much further.

Mobile games such as *Pylon* (developed by QuantumSquid Interactive) follow the standard of breaking up the important UI for the player and scaling/placing them on top of the main gameplay's screen. With this, the player can easily see their important stats, such as health/magic, and has easy access to actions and skills. Additionally, the map is informative and tapping on it brings out a fullscreen version.

Each of these elements only becomes active when the player needs them and are appropriately sized, so they don't get in the way too much.

# Balancing the need

As you can see, there are many choices as to how you can layout the important game UI; however, every game is different, so you will need to match up what the player needs to do against what they need to know in order to progress.

Above all, do not sacrifice the core of the gameplay at each point in the game just for a flashy screen element, unless it adds true value to the player.

# Putting it together

Now as I stated earlier, this section is going to be *big* and full of surprises. Some things are just what you need to do in order to flex Unity in the way we want to use it. Others are real gotchas that can leave you scratching your head and searching for the answer endlessly.

We'll start with the battle state machine, getting the player ready for the battle and then following up with some GUI interaction for the player to use in order to begin his or her assault in the battle. In the next chapter, we'll close the loop in the player's battle process and progress the state machine over to the opponents.

Let's begin!

# The battle state manager

Starting back in our **Battle** scene, we need to replace our temporary state machine with a proper one using all of Mecanim's handy features. Although we will still only be using a fraction of the functionality with the RPG sample, I advise you to investigate and read more about its capabilities.

Navigate to `Assets\Animation\Controllers` and create a new **Animator Controller** called `BattleStateMachine`, and then we can begin putting together the battle state machine. The following screenshot shows you the states, transitions, and properties that we will need:

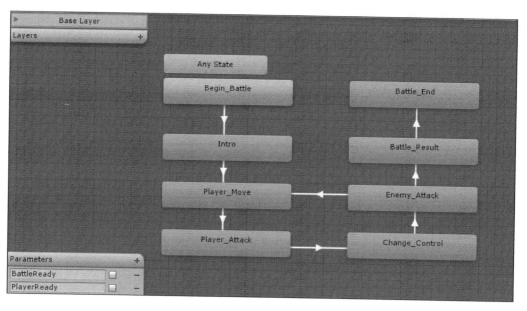

As shown in the preceding screenshot, we have created eight states to control the flow of a battle with two Boolean parameters to control its transition.

The transitions are defined as follows:

- From **Begin_Battle** to **Intro**
    - BattleReady = true (Transition Duration = 0)

- From **Intro** to **Player_Move**
    - Exit Time = 0.9 (Transition Duration = 2)

- From **Player_Move** to **Player_Attack**
    - PlayerReady = true (Transition Duration = 0)

- From **Player_Attack** to **Change_Control**
    - PlayerReady = false (Transition Duration = 2)

- From **Change_Control** to **Enemy_Attack**
    - Exit Time = 0.9 (Transition Duration = 2)

- From **Enemy_Attack** to **Player_Move**
  - BattleReady = true (Transition Duration = 2)

- From **Enemy_Attack** to **Battle_Result**
  - BattleReady = false (Transition Time = 2)

- From **Battle_Result** to **Battle_End**
  - Exit Time = 0.9 (Transition Time = 5)

Summing up, what we have built is a steady flow of battle, which can be summarized as follows:

- The battle begins and we show a little intro clip to tell the player about the battle
- Once the player has control, we wait for them to finish their move
- We then perform the player's move and switch the control over to the Enemy AI
- If there are any enemies left, they get to attack the player (if they are not too scared and have not run away)
- If the battle continues, we switch back to the player, otherwise we show the battle result
- We show the result for 5 seconds (or until the player hits a key), then finish the battle and return the player to the world together with whatever loot and experience they have gained

This is just a simple flow, which can be extended as much as you want, and as we continue, you will see all the points where you could expand it.

With our animator state machine created, we now just need to attach it to our battle manager so it will be available when the battle runs; follow the ensuing steps to do this:

1. Open up the **Battle** scene.
2. Select the **BattleManager** game object in the project hierarchy and add an `Animator` component to it.
3. Now drag the **BattleStateMachine** animator controller we just created into the `Controller` property of the `Animator` component.

The preceding steps attaches our new battle state machine to our battle engine. Now, we just need to be able to reference the **BattleStateMachine** Mecanim state machine from `BattleManager` script. To do this, open up the `BattleManager` script in `Assets\Scripts` and add the following variable to the top of the class:

```
private Animator battleStateManager;
```

Then, to capture the configured `Animator` component in our `BattleManager` script, we add the following to the `Start` function:

```
void Start () {
    battleStateManager = GetComponent<Animator>();
    if (battleStateManager == null)
    {
        Debug.LogError("No battlemanager Animator found");
    }
}
```

> Sadly, we have to assign it this way because all the functionality to interrogate the **Animator Controller** is built in to the `Animator` component. We cannot simply attach the controller directly to our `BattleManager` script and use it.

Now that it's all wired up, let's start using it.

# Getting to the state manager in the code

Now that we have our state manager running in Mecanim, we just need to be able to access it from the code. However, at first glance, there is a barrier to achieving this. The reason being that the Mecanim system uses hashes (integer ID keys for objects) not strings to identify states within its engine (still not clear why, but for performance reasons probably). To access the states in Mecanim, Unity provides a hashing algorithm to help you, which is fine for one-off checks but a bit of an overhead when you need per-frame access.

A simple solution to this is to generate and cache all the state hashes when we start and then use the cache to talk to the Mecanim engine.

First, let's remove the placeholder code from *Chapter 7, Encountering Enemies and Running Away,* for the old `enum` state machine, so remove the following code from the top of the `BattleManager` script:

```
enum BattlePhase
{
    PlayerAttack,
```

```
    EnemyAttack
}
private BattlePhase phase;
```

Also, remove the following line from the `Start` method:

```
phase = BattlePhase.PlayerAttack;
```

There is still a reference in the `OnGUI` method, but we will replace that shortly; feel free to remove it as well now if you wish.

Now, to begin working with our new state machine, we need a replica of the available states we have defined in our Mecanim state machine. For this, we just need an enumeration using the same names (you can create this either as a new C# script or simply place it in the `BattleManager` class), as follows:

```
public enum BattleState
{
    Begin_Battle,
    Intro,
    Player_Move,
    Player_Attack,
    Change_Control,
    Enemy_Attack,
    Battle_Result,
    Battle_End
}
```

It may seem strange to have a duplicate of your states in the state machine and in the code; however, at the time of writing, it is necessary. Mecanim does not expose the names of the states outside of the engine other than through using hashes. You can either use this approach and make it dynamic, or extract the state hashes and store them in a dictionary for use.

Mecanim makes the managing of state machines very simple under the hood, and it is extremely powerful, much better than trawling through code every time you want to update the state machine.

Next, we need a location to cache the hashes the state machine needs and a property to keep the current state so we don't constantly query the engine for a hash. So, add a new `using` statement to the beginning of the `BattleManager` class, as follows:

```
using System.Collections;
using System.Collections.Generic;
using UnityEngine;
```

Then, add the following variables to the top of the `BattleManager` class:

```
private Dictionary<int, BattleState> battleStateHash
  = new Dictionary<int, BattleState>();
private BattleState currentBattleState;
```

Finally, we just need to interrogate the animator state machine we have created. So create a new `GetAnimationStates` method in the `BattleManager` class as follows:

```
void GetAnimationStates()
{
  foreach (BattleState state in (BattleState[])System.Enum.
    GetValues(typeof(BattleState)))
  {
    battleStateHash.Add(Animator.StringToHash
      ("Base Layer." + state.ToString()), state);
  }
}
```

This simply generates a hash for the corresponding animation state in Mecanim and stores the resultant hashes in a dictionary that we can use without having to calculate them at runtime when we need to talk to the state machine.

Sadly, there is no way at runtime to gather the information from Mecanim as all the classes for interrogating the animator are only available in the editor.

You could gather the hashes from the animator and store them in a file to avoid this, but it won't save you much.

To complete this, we just need to call the new method in the `Start` function of the `BattleManager` script by adding the following:

```
GetAnimationStates();
```

Now that we have our states, we can use them in our running game to control both the logic that is applied and the GUI elements that are drawn to the screen.

Now add the `Update` function to the `BattleManager` class, as follows:

```
void Update()
{
  currentBattleState = battleStateHash[battleStateManager.
    GetCurrentAnimatorStateInfo(0).nameHash];

  switch (currentBattleState)
```

```
{
  case BattleState.Intro:
    break;
  case BattleState.Player_Move:
    break;
  case BattleState.Player_Attack:
    break;
  case BattleState.Change_Control:
    break;
  case BattleState.Enemy_Attack:
    break;
  case BattleState.Battle_Result:
    break;
  case BattleState.Battle_End:
    break;
  default:
    break;
  }
}
```

In Unity 5, you will have to use the fullPathHash property instead of just nameHash when checking an animator state.

Thankfully this is the only change required in this entire title that is needed for Unity 5* :D (*at the time of writing).

This code gets the current state from the animator state machine once per frame and then sets up a choice (`switch` statement) for what can happen based on the current state. (Remember, it is the state machine that decides which state follows which in the Mecanim engine, not nasty nested `if` statements everywhere in code.)

Next, replace/add the OnGUI function with the same pattern to control which GUI elements would be displayed, as follows:

```
void OnGUI()
{
  switch (currentBattleState)
  {
    case BattleState.Begin_Battle:
      break;
    case BattleState.Intro:
      break;
    case BattleState.Player_Move:
      break;
    case BattleState.Player_Attack:
      break;
    case BattleState.Change_Control:
      break;
```

```
    case BattleState.Enemy_Attack:
      break;
    case BattleState.Battle_Result:
      break;
    default:
      break;
  }
}
```

If you need a quick way to generate a `switch` statement code from an enum state (as shown in the preceding code), there is a simple shortcut to do so using Visual Studio's built-in snippets:

Just type `switch` and when the snippet prompt appears, tab it twice. Then, type in the property name that has a type of an enum state (the `currentBattleState` property in this case which is of the type, `BattleState`). Finally, hit the down arrow key and your case statements will be automatically generated for you!

Neat, eh!

With these in place, we are ready to start adding in some battle logic.

# Starting the battle

As it stands, the state machine is waiting at the `Begin_Battle` state for us to kick things off. Obviously, we want to do this when we are ready and all the pieces on the board are in place.

When the current **Battle** scene we added in *Chapter 7, Encountering Enemies and Running Away*, starts, we load up the player and randomly spawn in a number of enemies into the fray using a coroutine function called `SpawnEnemies`. So, only when all the nasty goblins are ready and waiting to be chopped down do we want to kick things off.

To tell the state machine to start the battle, we simple add the following line just after the end of the `for` loop in the `SpawnEnemies IEnumerator` coroutine function:

```
battleStateManager.SetBool("BattleReady", true);
```

Do not ask me why we can affect the properties just by using their string names and cannot do the same with the states; it just baffles me. I hope they change this in a future release.

Now when everything is in place, the battle will finally begin.

# Adding a little flair

In an ode to the fantastic game *Star Command* (http://www.starcommandgame. com/), when a battle starts there is a little introductory animation that introduces the two parties in battle, I added the Intro state sequence, which currently just displays a message about the battle.

 I was going to add a full animation to zoom and highlight the player and the goblins and then show the vs message, but I'll leave that up to you to play with. Can't have all the fun now, can I?

Currently, the state machine pauses at the Intro state for a few seconds, so while it's paused, let's add a simple GUI dialog to tell the player about the impending battle. Simply add the following to the case line of the Intro state in the OnGUI function:

```
case BattleState.Intro:
    GUI.Box(new Rect((Screen.width / 2) - 150 , 50, 300, 50),
        "Battle between Player and Goblins");
    break;
```

Now the player is informed that a battle is about to happen whether they like it or not (and now he cannot run away again, yet!).

 Now when you run the game in the Unity editor and bring up the **Animator** tab, you will see that the animation states change as the battle commences; it changes from **Begin | Intro | Player_Move**, indicating that it's now the player's turn to act.

If you wish, you can also re-add the **Run Away** button for the player into the Player_Move state in the OnGUI function as well:

```
case BattleState.Player_Move:
  if (GUI.Button(new Rect(10, 10, 100, 50), "Run Away"))
  {
    GameState.PlayerReturningHome = true;
    NavigationManager.NavigateTo("World");
  }
  break;
```

As the battle is now in progress and the control is being passed to the player, we need some interaction from the user. So let's give them something to click on with a smarter GUI.

# Bring on the GUI

Before we can start acting on the state machine, we first need to add something for the player to interact with, namely, the weapons the player possesses to knock those pesky goblins into the middle of the next week.

To do this, we will add a nice 2D graphical command bar with button placements using the 2D system instead of the aging Unity GUI system. The following is a sample of what we will be building:

The system is also flexible and dynamic enough to work in any portion of the screen, with any number of buttons, even with multiple columns and rows if you wish.

CommandBar (the container) manages the placement, and the state of the bar can contain any number of command buttons; each button will display the item it is managing and its input control.

As the command bar and command buttons are codependent, our code won't compile until they are both implemented, so let's start with the CommandBar class and then add the button definition to it.

The command bar and button code was refactored and updated to 2D from an existing open source project; it can be found at `github.com/fholm/unityassets/tree/master/ActionBars`.

The full 3D implementation also has several other features you might like to implement in the command bar, such as cooldowns, multiselects, and descriptors. So check it out if you wish.

You might also want to check out the rest of Fredrik's other free assets in the repository.

# The command bar

Starting with the command bar manager, create a C# script called `CommandBar` in `Assets\Scripts` and replace its contents with the following class definition and properties:

```csharp
using UnityEngine;
using System.Collections;

public class CommandBar : MonoBehaviour {

    private CommandButton [] commandButtons;

    public float buttonSize = 1.28f;
    public float buttonRows = 1;
    public float buttonColumns = 6;
    public float buttonRowSpacing = 0;
    public float buttonColumnSpacing = 0;

    public Sprite DefaultButtonImage;
    public Sprite SelectedButtonImage;

    private float ScreenHeight;
    private float ScreenWidth;
}
```

Remember, where `CommandButton` is referenced, it will show as an error until we add the `CommandButton` class to the next section.

The properties should speak for themselves: an array for the buttons that the bar is managing, settings related to button's positioning, two images to use for the base button backdrops, and finally a couple of properties to manage the screen's real estate that the command bar will be drawn in.

Next, we need a few controlled properties. These will be accessible in the code but not visible in the editor because they are not marked as [SerializeField]:

```
public int Layer
{
  get { return gameObject.layer; }
}

float Width
{
  get
  {
    return (buttonSize * buttonColumns) +
      Mathf.Clamp((button ColumnSpacing * (buttonColumns - 1)),
      0, int.MaxValue);
  }
}

float Height
{
  get
  {
    return (buttonSize * buttonRows) +
      Mathf.Clamp((button ColumnSpacing * (buttonRows - 1)),
      0, int.MaxValue);
  }
}
```

 For more information about class attributes and editor tags, such as [SerializeField], check out *Chapter 12, Deployment and Beyond*, and *Appendix, Additional Resources*.

The preceding code just enables us to discover the layer the command bar is assigned to and ensure any child elements we add can be assigned to the same layer. The remaining expose the calculated width and height for the entire command bar.

If you create a public variable, it will be visible in the code and the editor, for example:

```
public float myPublicVariable;
```

If you create a private variable, it will only be visible within the current class in the code, for example:

```
private float myPrivateVariable;
```

If you create a variable property with a public property getter (get), it will be visible to any reference in the class but *not* in the editor, for example:

```
private float myPrivateVariable;
public float  myPublicProperty
{
   get { return  myPrivateVariable; }
}
```

The pattern you use is up to you, based on how you need to access/ control the property.

You can also customize the visibility of the properties in the editor using the ([SerializeField] and [HideinInspector]} attributes; more information on this will be provided in *Chapter 12, Deployment and Beyond*, and *Appendix, Additional Resources*.

To ensure that we can also anchor the command bar to a region on the screen, we will enable it to be placed relative to a fixed position such as top-left and bottom-right. To do this, we will first need a new enum state for all the positions we are going to support. So, create a new script in Assets\Scripts\Classes called ScreenPositionAnchorPoint and replace its contents with the following:

```
public enum ScreenPositionAnchorPoint
{
    TopLeft,
    TopCenter,
    TopRight,
    MiddleLeft,
    MiddleCenter,
    MiddleRight,
    BottomLeft,
    BottomCenter,
    BottomRight
}
```

Now returning to the `CommandBar` script, we can add the following variables to the top of the script to track the desired anchor point on the screen using this new `enum`:

```
public bool anchor = true;
public Vector2 anchorOffset = Vector2.zero;
public ScreenPositionAnchorPoint  anchorPoint =
  ScreenPositionAnchorPoint.BottomCenter;
```

Then, to work out where exactly on the screen the command bar should be based on this anchor point, we just need a simple helper function. So, add the following to the bottom of the `CommandBar` script:

```
Vector2 CalculateAnchorScreenPosition()
{
  Vector2 position = Vector2.zero;

  switch (anchorPoint)
  {
    case ScreenPositionAnchorPoint.BottomLeft:
      position.y = -(ScreenHeight / 2) + Height;
      position.x = -(ScreenWidth / 2) + buttonSize;
      break;

    case ScreenPositionAnchorPoint.BottomCenter:
      position.y = -(ScreenHeight / 2) + Height;
      position.x = -(Width / 2);
      break;

    case ScreenPositionAnchorPoint.BottomRight:
      position.y = -(ScreenHeight / 2) + Height;
      position.x = (ScreenWidth / 2) - Width;
      break;

    case ScreenPositionAnchorPoint.MiddleLeft:
      position.y = (Height / 2);
      position.x = -(ScreenWidth / 2) + buttonSize;
      break;

    case ScreenPositionAnchorPoint.MiddleCenter:
      position.y = (Height / 2);
      position.x = -(Width / 2);
      break;
```

```
case ScreenPositionAnchorPoint.MiddleRight:
   position.y = (Height / 2);
   position.x = (ScreenWidth / 2) - Width;
   break;
case ScreenPositionAnchorPoint.TopLeft:
   position.y = (ScreenHeight / 2) - Height;
   position.x = -(ScreenWidth / 2) + buttonSize;
   break;

case ScreenPositionAnchorPoint.TopCenter:
   position.y = (ScreenHeight / 2) - Height;
   position.x = -(Width / 2);
   break;

case ScreenPositionAnchorPoint.TopRight:
   position.y = (ScreenHeight / 2) - Height;
   position.x = (ScreenWidth / 2) - Width;
   break;
}
return anchorOffset + position;
}
```

With all the settings in place for the command bar, we next need to initialize it. So, add an `Awake` function as follows:

```
void Awake()
{
   ScreenHeight = Camera.main.orthographicSize * 2;
   ScreenWidth = ScreenHeight * Screen.width / Screen.height;
}
```

This simply displays the current screen's size, which will be used to scale the command bar to the screen.

Finally, to complete the initialization, we need to set up the available buttons based on the settings for the command bar. This is done in three parts:

- Looping through the columns and rows for the command bar
- Creating new command bar buttons for each position
- Aligning the display position for each button

Like with the inventory system, there is a cooperative relationship between the CommandBar class and its command bar buttons. So, the code won't be compiled until we are done. Bear this in mind as we progress.

First we need to be able to create a button, so add the following function:

```
CommandButton CreateButton()
{
    // Create our new game object
    GameObject go = new GameObject("CommandButton");

    // Add components
    go.AddComponent<SpriteRenderer>();
    go.AddComponent<BoxCollider2D>();

    go.transform.parent = transform;

    // Init
    CommandButton button = go.AddComponent<CommandButton>();
    button.Init(this);

    return button;
}
```

This function performs the following:

- Creates a new empty game object (and names it CommandButton)
- Adds two game components (SpriteRenderer2D and BoxCollider2D) that are required for the CommandButton game object to function; more on this later
- Makes the button a child of the command bar by setting its parent transform
- Creates and assigns the CommandButton script we created earlier to the new button
- Calls the Init function of the button (this doesn't exist yet; we will come back to this later)
- Once everything is ready, it returns the new CommandButton game object to whoever called it

Now we have the ability to create buttons; we will also need the ability to re-position them within the command bar. For this, we will add another function:

```
void InitButtonPositions()
{
  int i = 0;
  float xPos = 0;
  float yPos = 0;

  for (int r = 0; r < buttonRows; ++r)
  {
    xPos = 0;

    for (int c = 0; c < buttonColumns; ++c)
    {
      commandButtons[i].transform.localScale = new
        Vector3(buttonSize, buttonSize, 0);
      commandButtons[i].transform.localPosition = new
        Vector3(xPos, yPos, 0);

      i++;
      xPos += buttonSize + buttonColumnSpacing;
    }

    yPos -= buttonSize + buttonRowSpacing;
  }
}
```

This function will simply loop through all the buttons assigned to the command bar and then scale and position them accordingly. We then have a set of arranged buttons within the command bar according to the row and column settings we configured.

With all the helper functions defined, we can now actually complete the initialization of the CommandBar class. To do this, add the following function:

```
void InitCommandButtons()
{
  commandButtons = new CommandButton[(int)buttonRows *
    (int)buttonColumns];

  for (int i = 0; i < commandButtons.Length; i++)
  {
    var newButton = CreateButton();
```

```
      if (i < GameState.CurrentPlayer.Inventory.Count)
      {
        newButton.AddInventoryItem(GameState.CurrentPlayer.
          Inventory[i]);
      }

      commandButtons[i] = newButton;

  }

  InitButtonPositions();
}
```

Here, we simply set up the button array based on the configured rows and columns, and then added a new empty command bar button to each element using the preceding `CreateButton` function. Once all the buttons have been created, we then use the `InitButtonPositions` function to position them correctly within the command bar.

Then, if the player has any weapons in their inventory, it will add that item to the button using a simple helper function (which we'll add in the next section).

All that is left is to ensure that the command bar is positioned correctly on the screen according to the anchor point. To do this, we first need another helper function to set the position:

```
void SetPosition(float x, float y)
{
  transform.position = new Vector3(x, y, 0);
}
```

We put this in a separate function so that if we need to apply offsets for the `CommandBar` class for different platforms, we can do it from this central helper instead of doing it throughout the code.

With the new helper in place, we need to replace/add the `Update` function that will ensure the bar is drawn to the correct portion of the screen's space:

```
void Update () {
  Vector2 position = Vector2.zero;

  if (anchor)
  {
    position = CalculateAnchorScreenPosition();
  }
  else
```

```
{
  position = transform.position;
}
SetPosition(position.x, position.y);
}
```

> We still use the SetPosition function here as this method places the command bar relative to the position in the screen space we want it to be drawn in. This still may need further offsetting if a particular platform is needed, such as Ouya or Xbox.

With this, each frame simply gets the intended position of the command bar, either from the anchor point or the position set in the editor, and uses our helper function to push it to the correct part of the screen.

Finishing off, we need to call our InitCommandButtons function in the preceding code when the script starts:

```
void Start () {
  InitCommandButtons();
}
```

# The command button

Next we'll add the CommandButton class; firstly create a new C# script in Assets\ Scripts called CommandButton and replace its contents with the following:

```
using UnityEngine;
using System.Collections;

[RequireComponent(typeof(SpriteRenderer))]
[RequireComponent(typeof(BoxCollider2D))]
public class CommandButton : MonoBehaviour
{
  private CommandBar commandBar;
  public InventoryItem Item;
  bool selected;
}
```

> Note the additional attributes placed on this class for the SpriteRender and BoxCollider2D components. This is just Unity's way of stating that these items are mandatory for this object when used in the scene. If you forget, Unity will warn you.

We have defined a tight reference for the `CommandBar` class that the button is a child of so that the button knows what is controlling it and they can communicate accordingly. This enables the button to tell the `CommandBar` class when it is selected, and the `CommandBar` class will be able to clear its selection, if need be.

We also have a property for `InventoryItem` as we are going to use this bar to activate items for use in the battle (the player's sword), and lastly, a flag to track whether the button is selected or not.

As described, we are using tight coupling between the button and the command bar because of their relationship, as opposed to the loose coupling we did before using messaging. We will still use messaging for some actions, but we will do that later.

It's important to understand when you should tightly couple objects and when you shouldn't using the appropriate pattern as required.

Basically, if a parent needs to manage its children, then you should tightly couple them so they can communicate effectively. If the two objects have no direct relationship, then either of them uses static functions, central state classes, or messaging to route information between them.

Next, we'll add the `Init` function that we called earlier to the `CreateButton` function:

```
public void Init(CommandBar commandBar)
{
    this.commandBar = commandBar;
    gameObject.layer  = commandBar.Layer;

    var collider = gameObject.GetComponent<BoxCollider2D>();
    collider.size = new Vector2(1f, 1f);

    var renderer = gameObject.GetComponent<SpriteRenderer>();
    renderer.sprite = commandBar.DefaultButtonImage;
    renderer.sortingLayerName = "GUI";
    renderer.sortingOrder = 5;
}
```

When initializing the button's contents, we are setting up all the components this object has assigned to it; they are as follows:

- First we define a tight reference for the `CommandBar` class itself because each button is managed by the `CommandBar` class.

- Next we set the layer of the new button to be the same as the command bar.

- Then we get the `BoxCollider2D` game object and set its size appropriately. (The default is actually the same as we are setting it, but it is worth being prudent and ensuring it is the size we want; don't assume!)

- Finally, we get `SpriteRenderer`, give it the default button image, and set its sorting parameters as required; if this is not the case, you won't see it because it will be drawn behind everything else.

In an odd peculiarity (that can leave you scratching your head for hours), if you try setting up the preceding code in line with where you are using it (in the `CommandBar` script) instead of within the class script (as in the preceding code), it will not actually work. It will create the new game object, but anything else just gets forgotten when used. Try it for yourself if you wish.

So now we can manage what the `InventoryItem` button is managing; we'll add another function to do this in a controlled way. This is because there is a fair amount of setup required in order for us to display the item on top of the button:

```
public void AddInventoryItem(InventoryItem item)
{
    this.Item = item;
    var childGO = new GameObject("InventoryItemDisplayImage");
    var renderer = childGO.AddComponent<SpriteRenderer>();
    renderer.sprite = item.Sprite;
    renderer.sortingLayerName = "GUI";
    renderer.sortingOrder = 10;
    renderer.transform.parent = this.transform;
    renderer.transform.localScale *= 4;
}
```

So when the `CommandBar` class requests to put `InventoryItem` in a button, it creates a new empty game object and adds a sprite renderer to it with the relevant settings for it to display. We also keep a reference for the item being displayed so that we can reuse its properties later (like how much damage our sword would bring about).

## Adding the command bar to the scene

Open up the **Battle** scene if you haven't done so already so that we can add the new command bar to the **Battle** scene. The command bar we have built is part of the battle controller, so we will add the new script to the `BattleManager` game object as a second script.

So, select the `BattleManager` game object and either drag the `CommandBar` script to it, or click on **Add Component** and navigate to **Scripts | Command Bar**; the inspector should now look as follows:

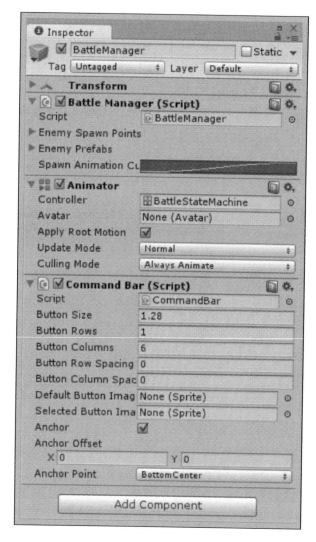

Next, we'll need the images for our buttons. In the assets that accompany this title, you will find a `button1.png` spritesheet that contains four button highlights, as shown in the following screenshot:

Add this to the project in the UI folder under Assets\Sprites\ from the assets included with this title, set **Sprite Mode** to **Multiple**, and open up **Sprite Editor**. Next, use the **Grid** slicing mode and set both the pixel size settings for $X$ and $Y$ to 128; this gives us a nice 2 x 2 split of the sprite with our four button images as shown in the following screenshot:

Now if we return to the CommandBar script we added to our BattleManager script, we can configure it as shown in the following screenshot:

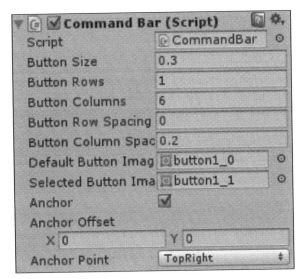

You can play with these settings if you wish to meet your own style and flavor. If you run the project now, six new buttons will appear floating at the top-right corner of our screen.

Granted, unless you visit the shop first, no weapons will appear in the command bar. What I recommend (unless you want to keep visiting the shop you keep testing) is to add a new property to the CommandBar script so that you can add a debug inventory item, as follows:

```
public InventoryItem debugItem;
```

Then, add this item to the players inventory when the script starts, as follows:

```
void Awake()
{
#if UNITY_EDITOR
  GameState.CurrentPlayer.AddinventoryItem(debugItem);
#endif

}
```

This way you will always see a weapon while you're testing, and it will only be added to the editor, thanks to the #if UNITY_EDITOR precompiler directive.

For more details on the precompiler directives supported in Unity, see http://docs.unity3d.com/Manual/PlatformDependentCompilation.html.

# Selecting the weapon

Now that we have our command bar with a selection of buttons and items to display, it would be good if we could actually use it as well.

The pattern I opted for with this bar is to make it so you can only select a single button at a time (clicking on another button will clear any existing selected items). This is just one pattern of course, and you could update/modify the code in this section as you wish. For now, let's see what's involved in managing this selection and also inform the battle manager that something has been selected.

In brief, what we will do is the following:

- Use the OnMouseDown function on a command button to detect a user's click

- This will cause a message to be fired to tell the BattleManager state that a button has been clicked

- The `BattleManager` state will then take whichever inventory item has been selected and use it as an active weapon
- If the user clicks on another button, this will override the previous selection, even if it is empty

So let's see what's involved in doing that.

# Selecting a command button

To complete the story of the button, we need to add a couple of handlers to let it be clicked; change its selection state, the button's sprite, and a function to safely clear the button's selection state.

First, we'll add the `UpdateSelection` function to the `CommandButton` script:

```
void UpdateSelection()
{
  var renderer = gameObject.GetComponent<SpriteRenderer>();
  renderer.sprite = selected ? commandBar.SelectedButtonImage :
    commandBar.DefaultButtonImage;
}
```

Here, we simply get the `SpriteRenderer` component or the button itself (not its child item) and assign the correct button sprite, either the selected or unselected image configured for the command bar.

Next, we add the `ClearSelection` function:

```
public void ClearSelection()
{
  selected = false;
  UpdateSelection();
}
```

This simply sets the selected state to `false` and then calls the `UpdateSelection` function to set the button sprite appropriately.

Finally, we add the `OnMouseDown` function to react to the `BoxCollider2D` component we have on the button and receive *clicked* events:

```
void OnMouseDown()
{
  if (commandBar.CanSelectButton)
  {
    selected = !selected;
    UpdateSelection();
```

```
        commandBar.Selectbutton(selected ? this : null);
    }
}
```

So now when the user clicks, it will flip the selected state for the button and then call the `UpdateSelection` function to set the correct button sprite. You will note that this function depends on a property in the `CommandBar` script that doesn't exist yet. This is there so that if for some reason the command bar is disabled or input is not allowed, then we can ignore any clicks; we'll add this shortly.

Once the user has selected the button, we tell the command bar about it. We then let it manage what happens to the selection after that. We could handle it within the button itself, but this would mean lots of complicated code in this very simple class; it's best to leave it up to the manager. This function doesn't exist yet in the command bar, so let's add it now.

# Managing the selections from the command bar

As the command bar manages all the buttons that can be selected and we only want one item to be selected at a time (in the weapon bar at least), we need a way to unselect all the buttons (if the player changes their mind and wants to select another button). The buttons do not know about each other; only the command bar knows about all its children. This might also be used to clear any selections once we move on to a different phase of the battle.

First we need some additional variables and properties to manage what is selected in the command bar, so open up the `CommandBar` script and add the following variables to the top of the script, just under the existing variables:

```
private bool canSelectButton = true;
private CommandButton selectedButton;

public bool CanSelectButton
{
  get
  {
    return canSelectButton;
  }
}
```

Now we can track which button is currently selected.

As we will need a way to clear the current selection (for the enemies turn or the player's next turn) to avoid having to duplicate the code everywhere, we will reuse the `ResetSection` function to set a new selection if we have one. So let's add this public function as follows:

```
public void ResetSelection(CommandButton button)
{
  if (selectedButton != null)
  {
    selectedButton.ClearSelection();
  }
  selectedButton = button;
}
```

This will simply clear the existing selection if there is one and then track the new selection. If the user has simply cleared their last selection, then this would just be `null`.

Now we just need to be able to actually select a button, but first we need a few things.

# Updating the BattleManager state with selections

Now that the command bar can select and deselect buttons, we need to be able to tell the `BattleManager` state that the player has selected a weapon. For this, we'll use messaging as there is no direct relationship between the command bar and the `BattleManager` state.

First we'll need to beef up the `MessagingManager` script with a new event we want to publish as we have done previously with the Dialog and UI events.

So, open up the `MessagingManager` script and add the following:

```
private List<Action<InventoryItem>> inventorySubscribers = new
List<Action<InventoryItem>>();

// Subscribe method for Inventory manager
public void SubscribeInventoryEvent
(Action<InventoryItem> subscriber)
{
  if (inventorySubscribers != null)
  {
    inventorySubscribers.Add(subscriber);
  }
}
```

```
// Broadcast method for Inventory manager
public void BroadcastInventoryEvent(InventoryItem itemInUse)
{
  foreach (var subscriber in inventorySubscribers)
  {
    subscriber(itemInUse);
  }
}

// Unsubscribe method for Inventory manager
public void UnSubscribeInventoryEvent(Action<InventoryItem>
  subscriber)
{
  if (inventorySubscribers != null)
  {
    inventorySubscribers.Remove(subscriber);
  }
}

// Clear subscribers method for Inventory manager
public void ClearAllInventoryEventSubscribers()
{
  if (inventorySubscribers != null)
  {
    inventorySubscribers.Clear();
  }
}
```

With the message in place, we just need to broadcast this new message when the player selects a button. We will add a new SelectButton method to the CommandBar script to complete the journey, as follows:

```
public void Selectbutton(CommandButton button)
{
  if (selectedButton != null)
  {
    selectedButton.ClearSelection();
  }
  selectedButton = button;
  if (selectedButton != null)
  {
    MessagingManager.Instance.BroadcastInventoryEvent
      (selectedButton.Item);
  }
}
```

```
    else
    {
        MessagingManager.Instance.BroadcastInventoryEvent(null);
    }
}
```

To finish off the `CommandBar` script while we are updating its messaging, let's also subscribe to the UI event's message and link it to the `canSelectbutton` variable/property we added earlier.

So, create a new delegate method called `SetCanSelectButton`:

```
void SetCanSelectButton(bool state)
{
    canSelectButton = !state;
}
```

Then, update the `Start` function in the `CommandBar` script as follows:

```
void Start () {
    InitCommandButtons();
    MessagingManager.Instance.SubscribeUIEvent(SetCanSelectButton);
}
```

Don't forget to unsubscribe the event from it as well when the command bar is destroyed by adding the `OnDestroy` method:

```
void OnDestroy()
{
    if (MessagingManager.Instance != null)
    {
        MessagingManager.Instance.UnSubscribeUIEvent
            (SetCanSelectButton);
    }
}
```

Now whenever the UI is locked, we ensure that no further button presses are allowed, such as for events when the player has attacked the enemy.

# Updating the BattleManager state with a weapon

Finally, we return to the `BattleManager` script and decide what to do with this new weapon the user has selected. First we need a variable to store the selected weapon in, so add the following to the top of the `BattleManager` script with the rest of the variables:

```
private InventoryItem selectedWeapon;
```

Next we need a handler function to store the new selected weapon:

```
private void InventoryItemSelect(InventoryItem item)
{
  selectedWeapon = item;
}
```

Then, we have to wire up this function to the event we are broadcasting from the `BattleManager` state in the `Start` method:

```
MessagingManager.Instance.SubscribeInventoryEvent
  (InventoryItemSelect);
```

Now we know what the player is fighting with, let's update the UI with some instructions.

So far, when the battle starts in the state machine, an intro is shown and then two seconds later, it is the player's turn; however, at the moment, the player is completely unaware of this, so let's update the `OnGUI` method in the `BattleManager` script as follows:

```
void OnGUI()
{
  switch (currentBattleState)
  {
    case BattleState.Begin_Battle:
      break;
    case BattleState.Intro:
      GUI.Box(new Rect((Screen.width / 2) - 150, 50, 300, 50),
        "Battle between Player and Goblins");
      break;
    case BattleState.Player_Move:
      if (GUI.Button(new Rect(10, 10, 100, 50), "Run Away"))
      {
        GameState.PlayerReturningHome = true;
        NavigationManager.NavigateTo("World");
      }
```

```
  if (selectedWeapon == null)
  {
    GUI.Box(new Rect((Screen.width / 2) - 50, 10, 100, 50),
      "Select Weapon");
  }
  break;
case BattleState.Player_Attack:
  break;
case BattleState.Change_Control:
  break;
case BattleState.Enemy_Attack:
  break;
case BattleState.Battle_Result:
  break;
default:
  break;
}
}
```

In the `Intro` part, we display a simple message to inform the player about the battle, and when it is the player's turn, we display the **Select Weapon** message until they have selected one.

# Going further

As we reach the halfway mark in the battle implementation, we can take stock of what we have and also look forward to more things we could include at this point.

Try expanding the battle to include the following:

- Add more weapons, items, potions, and other things that the player can use in the battle and decide just how many actions they can have. Can they only use one thing in a turn or are potions free to use?

- Add more command bars with different items. Return to the inventory view and use it for the command bar as well.

- Add player/enemy health stats and display them on the screen for your particular game style, using the tricks learned from the command bar.

# Summary

Getting the battle right based on the style of your game is very important as it is where the player will spend the majority of their time fighting. Keep the player engaged and try to make each battle different in some way, as receptiveness is a tricky problem to solve and you don't want to bore the player.

Think about expanding the shops and the items they stock. From here, you should have enough to finish the game design itself. Possibly, look to have different types of inventory items, potions, shields, and so on.

We covered the following in this chapter:

- What makes a battle
- Planning to expand your game and how it should look
- Working with state machines in the code
- Working with better 2D GUI elements, such as the command bar

In the next chapter, we will continue the battle and set out to teach those pesky goblins a lesson or two.

# 10
# The Battle Begins

The previous chapter was so big that it had to be split in twain.

We left the previous chapter at a point where the player was just about ready for battle, with a sword (or axe) in hand, staring down at the Goblin horde, ready to hack them away. Let's finish this round; select a not-so-willing target and do some damage to it.

The following topics will be covered in this chapter:

- What it means to battle
- Planning for longevity
- Enhancing the enemy AI
- Particle systems in 2D and other gotchas
- More animation know-how

## Proving ground

What sets aside a really good RPG from a run-of-the–mill point-and-click adventure are the battles (well, unless you count the insult sword fighting scene in the *Secret of Monkey Island* series at `http://monkeyisland.wikia.com/wiki/Insult_Sword_Fighting`).

Battles can take many forms, from real-time, hack-and-slash, nonstop action to the more strategic turn-based battle systems. Each appeals to a different audience and dramatically alters how your game is perceived. In many cases, the battles (apart from the story) will make up the heart and soul of your game; if you get this wrong, it's a quick one way - try to uninstall purgatory.

No matter which path you choose, the enemies that the player will face have to be challenging at all times. This doesn't mean they should level up at the same time as the player (in some titles, there is a flat progression between the player and his or her enemies; avoid this at all cost as it will quickly become boring), but then they should challenge the player in different ways.

There are several things you need to plan for; they are as follows:

- Animations
- Player actions
- Enemy defenses and reactions
- Special moves
- Interactions

Each of these provides an engaging experience to the player and makes the battle feel worthwhile. If you don't focus on each area, players might feel bored when playing the game.

# Leveling up

While it's not always critical for games to have the story or progression on to the next area as the focus, in most cases, it's important to ensure that the player feels they are achieving something as they progress. This may be in how much gold they collect from the fallen enemies to buy swanky new gear and that Level 20 battle sword with flame powers they have had their eye on for weeks. It could also be about increasing the statistics or skills of the player, enabling them to take on more powerful enemies with a wave of their wrist.

Invariably, it is a mix of all of the previous things that makes a game stand out. In fact, in some titles, this is the whole focus of the game; you spend more time planning what skills to have or upgrade as you progress on to explore/fight.

One piece of advice I would give is to ensure that you have some sort of whole-world experience system, not just focus on the battles. This will make you stand out from the crowd. You can have skills and strengths the player can use to affect the whole game; it should be about the game experience and not just the fight. Many big RPG games spend a lot of their development effort getting this right, but that's not to say this cannot be applied to smaller or even episodic games.

# Balancing

By far the most difficult thing to implement in any game is balancing. If done right, you will spend over 50 percent of your development efforts testing, tweaking, retesting, and retweaking the game.

Don't use just one focus group to test your game, but use people from all walks of life. Have kids and public audiences, even your wife, husband, or partner to play your game, and gauge their feedback. The more number of people test your game, the better the balance of the game will be.

Finding that sweet spot between difficulty, playability, engagement, and fun is always hard, so do not underestimate it. Remember, just because you play the game in a certain way doesn't mean everyone else will play in the same way.

# Putting it together

Following on from the previous chapter, we will continue on our journey of the battle and kick off with some target practice.

## Preparing the BattleManager script

As we prepare to attack our foe, we recognize that the player can only target one Goblin at a time with his trusty sword or axe (there could be some splash damage or knock - on attack later, but let's focus on our player's attack first). So, we'll add some variables to `BattleManager` to manage this.

We will also add some other elements to spruce up the battle, such as a selection circle or a target identifier, and add a variable to set a prefab for this.

So, open the `BattleManager` script and add the following variables to the top of the class:

```
private string selectedTargetName;
private EnemyController selectedTarget;
public GameObject selectionCircle;
private bool canSelectEnemy;

bool attacking = false;

public bool CanSelectEnemy
{
  get
  {
```

```
        return canSelectEnemy;
    }
}

public int EnemyCount
{
    get
    {
        return enemyCount;
    }
}
```

> We haven't created the `EnemyController` class yet, so it will show as an error. We will add that next.

So, we have added properties to hold the selected target as we did with the selected weapon, a flag, and a property to track whether we can actually select an enemy (as the player needs to select a weapon first); additionally, we've added a variable to maintain a record of just how many enemies are left in the battle, which the enemy AI will use to decide how chicken they are or not.

> Instantiating prefabs in the code requires the prefab to be in the `Resources` folder, because they are associated with the asset-bundling features. With Unity Pro, you can also download the asset bundles from the Web and include them in your project at runtime. With the free version, however, you can only use what is in your project already.
>
> For single objects, it's easier to attach a prefab to the editor and use it from there (either on an existing class or a static editor class).

# Beefing up the enemy

At the moment, Goblin is just a sprite drawn on the screen with an AI system that just sits idle in the background. So, let's expand on this and give our Goblins some muscle power. Player, be warned!

As stated previously, to keep the player engaged, you need to have a varied amount of enemies in the battle, and they need to be challenging enough to make the player think and apply tactics.

# The enemy profile/controller

First, we'll create a new profile for the enemies, starting off with a new enumeration for the enemy class. Create a new C# script named `EnemyClass` in `Assets\Scripts\Classes` and replace its contents with the following code:

```
public enum EnemyClass
{
  Goblin,
  Ork,
  NastyPeiceOfWork
}
```

I've used just a couple of examples, as we will only be using the `Goblin` for now. Next, create a new `Enemy` C# script in the same folder, as follows:

```
public class Enemy : Entity
{

  public EnemyClass Class;
}
```

The preceding code just extends the base `Entity` class for our enemies and adds the `EnemyClass` enumeration we just created.

Now that we have a profile for the enemy, we need a controller to make the enemy perform actions in a controlled way. So, create another C# script named `EnemyController` in `Assets\Scripts`, starting with the following variables:

```
using System.Collections;
using UnityEngine;

public class EnemyController : MonoBehaviour {

  private BattleManager battleManager;
  public Enemy EnemyProfile;
  Animator enemyAI;

  public BattleManager BattleManager
  {
    get
    {
      return battleManager;
    }
    set
    {
```

```
            battleManager = value;
        }
    }
} .
```

The preceding code gives us the missing `EnemyController` class that we used in the `BattleManager` script with the following properties:

- A tight reference to the `BattleManager` script, which is needed because the enemies are directly affected by the battle as it is ensued
- The enemy profile
- A reference to the AI animator controller we created in *Chapter 7, Encountering Enemies and Running Away*

As the AI needs information about the battle, we need to ensure that it has kept each frame up to date. So, for this, we add an `UpdateAI` method and call it from the `Update` method to keep the AI up to date, as follows:

```
void Update()
{
    UpdateAI();
}

public void UpdateAI()
{
    if (enemyAI != null && EnemyProfile != null)
    {
        enemyAI.SetInteger("EnemyHealth", EnemyProfile.Health);
        enemyAI.SetInteger("PlayerHealth",
          GameState.CurrentPlayer.Health);
        enemyAI.SetInteger("EnemiesInBattle",
          battleManager.EnemyCount);
    }
}
```

The preceding code just sets the properties of the AI to the current values. As the values change, the AI will react based on the transitions that are defined. For example, if the Goblin's health drops below 2 and the player's health is greater than 2, it will transition to `Run Away`. Granted we are not doing anything with the states yet, but we will come on to that later.

Next, we need to grab the reference to the AI that is currently configured against the game object that will be used by the previous `UpdateAI` function in the `Awake` method:

```
void Awake()
{
    enemyAI = GetComponent<Animator>();
    if (enemyAI == null)
    {
        Debug.LogError("No AI System Found");
    }
}
```

There are several logging options in Unity, from the basic `Log` to the more detailed `LogWarning` and `LogError`. These logging options provide us with more detail while debugging our project, so use them wisely.

To save sanity when you are adding more content to the game, it is worthwhile to add `Debug` comments, surrounding them with important components or scripts required by an object. Using them this way does not affect the performance and can save you hours of searching for the reason for a crash because you forgot to add something.

However, as stated before, do not use `Debug.Log` extensively or in the normal operation of your game. This is because it kills the performance!

Another approach is to write your own utility function to perform logging, which can be controlled by a single flag. So, instead of `Debug.Log`, you will call `DebugUtility.Log` or `DebugUtility.LogWarning`, which will then call `Debug.Log` if it was enabled. This allows you to place the logging code throughout your project and have a single place where you can turn it all on or off.

Nice tip from our reviewer, Fredrik Kellerman!

# Updating the Goblin prefab

The **Goblin** prefab we created earlier now needs this new `EnemyController` class attached to it. Select the **Goblin** prefab from `Assets\Prefabs\Characters`, click on the **Add Component** button in the **Inspector** window, and navigate to **Scripts | EnemyController**, as shown in the following screenshot:

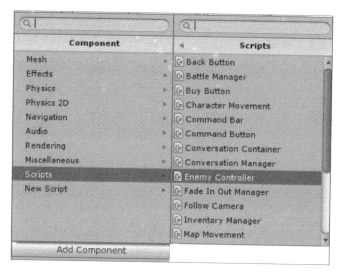

Once added, the updated **Goblin** will look like the following screenshot in the **Inspector** window:

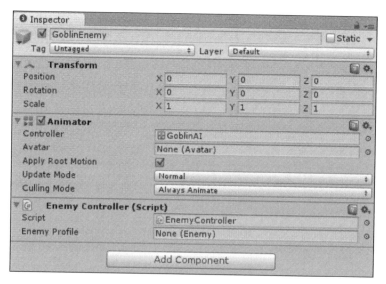

As you can see, we cannot currently edit the **Enemy Profile** tab from the editor (as this requires a custom inspector, which will be covered in *Chapter 11, Onward Wary Traveler*). Hence, we are doing it through the code. You can use a scriptable object asset and assign it to the tab, and I've already shown you how to do this. Feel free to change it later if you wish.

# Setting up the enemy profile in the code

Returning back to the `BattleManager` script, the area where we push our Goblins into action is in the `SpawnEnemies` coroutine. Now, instead of just throwing sprites at the screen, we can add some real danger to the mix for our humble player and his itty-bitty sword using the following code:

```
IEnumerator SpawnEnemies()
{
  //Spawn enemies in over time
  for (int i = 0; i < enemyCount; i++)
  {
    var newEnemy = (GameObject)Instantiate(EnemyPrefabs[0]);
    newEnemy.transform.position = new Vector3(10, -1, 0);
    yield return StartCoroutine(
    MoveCharacterToPoint(EnemySpawnPoints[i], newEnemy));
    newEnemy.transform.parent = EnemySpawnPoints[i].transform;

    var controller = newEnemy.GetComponent<EnemyController>();

    controller.BattleManager = this;

    var EnemyProfile = ScriptableObject.CreateInstance<Enemy>();
    EnemyProfile.Class = EnemyClass.Goblin;
    EnemyProfile.Level = 1;
    EnemyProfile.Damage = 1;
    EnemyProfile.Health = 2;
    EnemyProfile.Name = EnemyProfile.Class + " " + i.ToString();

    controller.EnemyProfile = EnemyProfile;
  }
  BattleStateManager.SetBool("BattleReady", true);
}
```

Now, as we loop through the number of enemies being added to the battle, we grab the `EnemyController` class attached to the **Goblin** prefab, create a new `EnemyProfile` class, give it some values, and finally initialize the controller with the new `EnemyProfile` class.

Ideally, you should change this generation to something that is a bit more structured instead of just initializing it this way, but you should get the picture.

Now that we have a stronger opponent, let's select it and start with the attack.

# Selecting a target

Like with `CommandBar`, the player needs some visual representation to confirm whether their actions actually have an effect in the game. To this end, let's add some selection logic for our enemies and a nice visual effect in 2D. First, we'll create the prefab for this with a little animation and then get ready to attach our `BattleManager` script using the variable we added earlier.

## The selection circle prefab

First off, I created the following selection circle with my graphics skills (aka programmer art :D ):

This is nothing fancy, but it will look better once we get it in the game. So, add `SelectionCircle.png` to your project from the assets that accompany this title to `Assets\Sprites\Props`.

Next, we'll create a prefab of this sprite in our scene for later use. This simply sets up how we want to use it visually, and since we are going to use it several times over in the scene, using prefabs means that there will only be one instance with many copies.

Now, drag the `SelectionCircle` image on to the scene (if it doesn't work, you are looking at the game view, which means that you need to switch to the **Scene** tab) and set the properties as shown in the following screenshot:

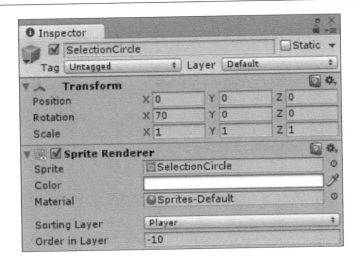

Finally, drag the object from the **Scene** hierarchy into `Assets\Prefabs\Props` to create the prefab, ensuring its name is `SelectionCircle`. Then, delete the object from the scene as we no longer need it.

Now, in the **Battle** scene, in the editor, select the **BattleManager** game object in the **Project** hierarchy; once you do this, drag the `SelectionCircle` prefab on to the **Selection Circle** property for the `BattleManager` script to attach it to the **BattleManager** game object.

# Adding selection logic to the EnemyController class

With everything set up in the **BattleManager** game object, we can now return to the `EnemyController` script and repeat the process we used with `CommandButton` so the player can click on the Goblins to highlight them.

First, we need a couple of properties in the `EnemyController` script to keep a reference to our `SelectionCircle` prefab and determine whether the current enemy is selected or not. So, add the following to the top of the `EnemyController` class:

```
private bool selected;
GameObject selectionCircle;
```

Now, to liven the selection process a bit, let's add some spin to the selection circle when it is on the screen. To do this, we'll add a simple coroutine to constantly update the selection circles' rotation transform (simple and effective). We could have used the 2D animation system to do the same thing, but it's a bit too much for a simple rotation (unless you want to do more fancy things with the selection circle, such as add particles, have the circle jump up and down while spinning, and so on).

So, in the EnemyController script, add the following coroutine function:

```
IEnumerator SpinObject(GameObject target)
{
  while (true)
  {
    target.transform.Rotate(0, 0, 180 * Time.deltaTime);
    yield return null;
  }
}
```

Nothing fancy; you just need to rotate the object on its *z* axis over time.

If you want the circle to spin faster or slower, just alter the amount of *z* axis rotation you apply. Here, I have it set to spin 180 degrees every second, one full spin every 2 seconds.

Next, when the player clicks, we use the combination of the BoxCollider2D and OnMouseDown functions to select the Goblin and display the selection circle.

Add a new BoxCollider2D component to the **Goblin** prefab and then add the following function to the EnemyController script:

```
void OnMouseDown()
{
  if (battleManager.CanSelectEnemy)
  {
    var selection = !selected;
    battleManager.ClearSelectedEnemy();
    selected = selection;
    if (selected)
    {
      selectionCircle = (GameObject)GameObject.Instantiate(
        battleManager.selectionCircle);
      selectionCircle.transform.parent = transform;

      selectionCircle.transform.localPosition = Vector3.zero;
      StartCoroutine("SpinObject", selectionCircle);
```

```
            battleManager.SelectEnemy(this, EnemyProfile.Name);
        }
    }
}
```

Here, we store what the current state of the selected Goblin is (if we click on the same one twice, unselect it); make sure there are no other Goblins selected (you may want to change this behavior if you have weapons that can target more than one enemy). If it is a new selection, perform the following steps:

1. Create a clone of the SelectionCircle prefab.

2. Set its transform and position local to the selected Goblin.

3. Start SelectionCircle, spinning with its coroutine.

4. Tell the **BattleManager** game object that we have selected a target to destroy.

 The new functions don't exist on the BattleManager script yet, so we will return to those shortly.

Like with CommandButtons, we need a final function to clear the selection state of this enemy if required, so add the ClearSelection method to the EnemyController script, as follows:

```
public void ClearSelection()
{
    if (selected)
    {
        selected = false;
        if (selectionCircle != null)
        DestroyObject(selectionCircle);
        StopCoroutine("SpinObject");
    }
}
```

We are done with the EnemyController script now.

To finish off the selection logic, let's return to the BattleManager script and add the two missing functions as follows:

```
public void SelectEnemy(EnemyController enemy, string name)
{
    selectedTarget = enemy;
    selectedTargetName = name;
}
```

```
public void ClearSelectedEnemy()
{
  if (selectedTarget != null)
  {
    var enemyController =
      selectedTarget.GetComponent<EnemyController>();
    enemyController.ClearSelection();
    selectedTarget = null;
    selectedTargetName = string.Empty;
  }
}
```

Both the functions are very simple. They either set the two variables we created earlier for the selectedTarget and the selectedTargetName variables, or clear these values, get the EnemyController component for the selected target, and use the ClearSelection function we just added.

However, we still can't select the enemy to attack yet, as our BattleManager script does not let us do it. Since we want to control the flow of what the player does, we do not enable this until they have first selected a weapon; if there is no selected weapon, there is no enemy selection.

To enable you to select an enemy and then progress on to the battle, we need to update our OnGUI method again for the additional actions. So, alter the case BattleState.Player_Move section of the OnGUI method as follows:

```
case BattleState.Player_Move:
if (GUI.Button(new Rect(10, 10, 100, 50), "Run Away"))
{
  GameState.PlayerReturningHome = true;
  NavigationManager.NavigateTo("World");
}
if (selectedWeapon == null)
{
  GUI.Box(new Rect((Screen.width / 2) - 50,10,100,50),"Select
    Weapon");
}
else if (selectedTarget == null)
{
  GUI.Box(new Rect((Screen.width / 2) - 50, 10, 100, 50), "Select
    Target");
  canSelectEnemy = true;
}
```

```
else
{
  if (GUI.Button(new Rect((Screen.width / 2) - 50, 10, 100, 50),
    "Attack " + selectedTargetName))
  {
    canSelectEnemy = false;
    battleStateManager.SetBool("PlayerReady", true);
    MessagingManager.Instance.BroadcastUIEvent(true);
  }
}
break;
```

Now the battle can ensue. The player selects a weapon and a target, and they have a nice (well, a nice GUI) button to tap to say they are happy with their choice. So, let the battle commence.

We also inform anyone listening to the GUI events that the GUI is now locked, and the player cannot do anything until it is their turn again.

Now, when you run the project, the flow of the battle will be as follows:

1. The battle begins.
2. The introduction is played, informing the player about the impending doom.
3. The player is asked to select a weapon.
4. The selected weapon is highlighted.
5. The player is asked to select a target.
6. The selected enemy gets the red ring of death circling their feet, and they probably get a sense of foreboding.
7. The `Battle` state manager gets informed that the player has completed their move and that they are ready by setting the `PlayerReady` property in the state machine to `true`.

So, when you run the project, your scene should look like this:

# Attack! Attack!

Now that the player has committed themselves into the fray, we can play through their selected action. For now, this is just a single action, but if you have more characters/moves, then this could be extended further.

As the attack is a loop that is played until the player (or his party) runs out of attacks, we use a simple coroutine to perform the attack itself. So, let's add the following function to the BattleManager script:

```
IEnumerator AttackTarget()
{
  int Attacks = 0;
  attacking = true;
  bool attackComplete = false;
  while (!attackComplete)
  {
    GameState.CurrentPlayer.Attack(selectedTarget.EnemyProfile);
    selectedTarget.UpdateAI();
    Attacks++;
    if (selectedTarget.EnemyProfile.Health < 1 || Attacks >
      GameState.CurrentPlayer.NoOfAttacks)
```

```
        {
          attackComplete = true;
        }
        yield return new WaitForSeconds(1);
    }
}
```

The following is what the previous code is doing:

1.  It sets the initial states for the battle. It tells us how many attacks have been performed, the fact that we are attacking (disable non-attacking code such as the GUI), and that the attack has not yet finished.

2.  Then, until we are finished, we keep attacking:

    ○ We call the `Attack` function for the player against the selected enemy (this was defined in the `Entity` class; all the attacks are standard, so if you want to modify them, ensure they are done correctly in the class so that all the attacks are the same)

    ○ We update the AI state for the selected enemy (let them have access to bad news, if any)

3.  If the enemy is dead or the player has run out of attacks, mark the battle as complete.

4.  Wait for the end of the frame to attack again or end the loop.

It's all very neat logic and central in one place. If you are unsure about what is happening in a battle, then you only have one place to check (unless it's about damage).

All that is left is to call this function now when the player clicks on the Attack button in the `Update` method of the **BattleManager** game object. So, update the `case BattleState.Player_Attack` section as follows:

```
case BattleState.Player_Attack:
    if (!attacking)
    {
        StartCoroutine(AttackTarget());
    }
    break;
```

Now that the attack has commenced and no doubt some Goblins were at least hurt in the ensuing battle, let us provide the player with some visual feedback.

# The pesky Goblin reacts with 3D particles

The player has made his or her move, and the Goblin has been affected in some way; it would be nice to see what happened.

In this case, the player's sword (or axe, if you added the axe) has a damage level of 5 and the player's strength is only 1; however, this will still give him a total attack damage of 6. The lazy Goblin didn't get any armor today while he was out pillaging in the woods with his pals (unless he's alone and they ditched him), and his default health is of 1. The formula for this is as follows:

*Health 1 – Attack Strength 6 = dead*

So, the poor Goblin has to go and meet his maker in the worst way possible. This brings us to one of the last troublesome issues with the new 2D system, that is, particles. To make the death animation nice, we are going to add a particle effect when the Goblin is killed along with some other animation.

# Mixing up 2D and 3D

Now, as all of the 2D rendering in Unity is actually performed in 3D with some nice jazzy helpers to make it look seamless, it is possible to add 3D objects to your 2D scenes. This is possible, provided you still follow the normal pattern to balance the performance in your scene; a large 2D scene that performs well is still going to have its performance slaughtered if you throw lots of complex 3D models in the background. It is no different than 3D in that respect.

However, what you do have to be content with is the drawing order (a good old z buffer fighting for its return) of 3D elements in the scene as if they were 2D. The area that is most impacted by this are **particle effects**.

# Particle effects and 2D

Like other 3D elements, particle effects will work fine in a 2D scene, provided you set them up correctly. To show this, we are going to define a new particle effect to use in our Goblin's death scene. We will also add a new sprite to mark the Goblin's demise and leave its mark on the world.

 Surprisingly, however, unlike the GUI system, particles can understand sprites. So, we don't need to mess with the texture import settings when using sprites for particle effects.

# Adding the deathly sprites

In the `Sample` assets folder, you will find the following two sprites:

A blood splat effect image called
"bloodSplat.png"

A tombstone image called
"Tombstone.png"

Now perform the following steps:

1.  Add the blood splat to `Assets\Sprites\FX`.
2.  Add the tombstone to `Assets\Sprites\Props` and set its **Pivot** field to **Bottom** so that it is the same as all the Character sprites.

# Creating the material for the particle effect

For particle effects to work, they need a material defined, not just the raw texture/ sprite itself. So, navigate to `Assets\Materials` (create it if you haven't done so already) and right-click on it to create a new material and name it `BloodSplatter`.

Next, click on the **Select** button on the material properties in the **Inspector** window for the new `BloodSplatter` material and select the `bloodSplat.png` image we just imported.

Lastly, change the shader the material uses to the **Transparent/Diffuse** shader (this is because our sprite has transparent sections. If we didn't use a shader that supports transparency, any section that is transparent would be drawn in black) by clicking on the dropdown next to the **Shader** property of the `BloodSplatter` material, and then navigate to **Transparent | Diffuse**.

Your material should now look like the following screenshot:

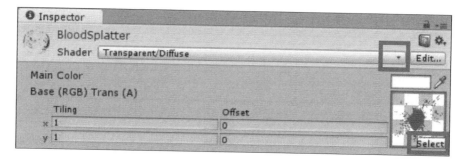

# Restructuring the Goblin prefab

Now, because of the way the 2D animation system works, animating child objects from a parent is fine; animating the child of child objects does not work, and also animating both the parent and the child does not work as well. Basically, the transforms and parentage do not play nice together.

This isn't a big issue; it just means you need to plan ahead more when you create objects that will have multiple sprites or supporting objects that will all interact on the same animation.

To start off, perform the following steps:

1.  Create a new and empty game object in the scene called `GoblinEnemy`.
2.  Drag the existing **Goblin** prefab from `Assets\Prefabs\Characters` on to the scene as a child of the new and empty game object (so we can reuse it); be sure to reset the transform on the new child.
3.  Delete the old prefab; we don't need it any more.
4.  Remove the `Animator`, `EnemyController`, and `Box Collider 2D` scripts from the old **Goblin** prefab and add them on to the new and empty game object called `GoblinEnemy`, setting them up as before. There are some components you can drag between game objects; then, there are others that you need to remove and re-add manually. It's trial and error to see which components support this behavior. In this instance, the `EnemyController` script can be dragged over. Now, you should be left with just the sprite renderer on the Goblin game object.
5.  Check that `Box Collider 2D` on the **GoblinEnemy** game object is positioned over the Goblin, adjusting the **Center X & Y** values.

6. Drag the **Tombstone** sprite from `Assets\Sprites\Props` on to the `GoblinEnemy` game object. Set its position transform to **0** for all the values, set **Scale transform** where **X** is **0.2** and **Y** is **0.2**, and set **Sorting Layer** to `Player`.

7. Set the color of the Tombstone SpriteRenderer where **A** (alpha) is **0** (click on the color box and reduce the **A** scale to **0**); we don't want to see it by default.

8. Create another empty game object and call it `BloodParticles`, then drag it to the `GoblinEnemy` game object as a child. Make sure to also set its position transform to **0** for all the values.

> If you are using Unity 4.5, you can create child game objects quicker by selecting the `GoblinEnemy` game object, the **Create Empty Child** option under **GameObject**, or the hotkey *Alt + Shift + N*.

This gives a nice new framework for the life cycle of the Goblin's enemy; it also allows you to use the same layout but switch out the particles you use in death scenes or the marker that they leave behind in death.

## Adding the particles

Now on to the crux of this section. Select the **BloodParticles** game object and add a new particle system by clicking on **Add Component** and selecting **Particle System** under **Effects**.

Straightaway, we can see a problem.

2D view

3D view

When the particles render, by default, they are always rendered behind the 2D view, and no setting in the editor, by default, can change that for 3D renderers. It is only available for a 2D sprite renderer.

To resolve this, we need to apply a script to either the particle system itself or when we play the particle system in the code. For simplicity's sake, I've implemented it as a script on the particle system; this way, it is always in effect, and I do not need to worry about configuring it.

So, create a new script called `ParticleSortingLayer` in `Assets\Scripts` and replace its contents with the following:

```
using UnityEngine;

[ExecuteInEditMode]
public class ParticleSortingLayer : MonoBehaviour
{

  void Awake()
  {
    var particleRenderer = GetComponent<Renderer>();
    particleRenderer.sortingLayerName = "GUI";
  }
}
```

Here, the script simply sets the sorting layer on the underlying renderer for the particle system; in this case, I've hardcoded it to the GUI sprite layer.

The `[ExecuteinEditMode]` attribute just enables you to see the effect in the editor as well. More on editor functionality is covered in *Chapter 11, Onward Wary Traveler.*

Script libraries, such as the awesome **UnityToolbag** by Nick Gravelyn, also provide the previous functionality and are worked into a more reusable script; it's well worth checking it out at `https://github.com/nickgravelyn/UnityToolbag`.

Another one of these libraries will also expose the hidden `SortingLayer` properties for 3D renderers in the editor. For more information, you can read about it at `https://github.com/nickgravelyn/UnityToolbag/tree/master/SortingLayer`.

Now just attach this script to the particle system and it will be transformed into what is shown in the following screenshot, with the particles now in front of the background:

Now that we have our particle system working and rendering, we can configure it for the game. The following are all the settings we need to change:

- **Name**: BloodParticles
- **Rotation**: X: -90
- **Duration**: 1.00
- **Looping**: false (unchecked)
- **Start lifetime**: 0.5
- **Speed**: 2 / 3 (random between two constants)
- **Start Rotation**: 10 / 50 (random between two constants)
- **Gravity Multiplier**: 0.5
- **Inherit Velocity**: 200
- **Play On Awake**: false (unchecked)
- **Shape**: Radius: 0.2
- **Color Over Lifetime**: Gradient - Alpha (v) 255 -> 0
- **Size over Lifetime**: progressive curve
- **Renderer**: Material: BloodSplatter material

To change a value to an alternate setting, such as **Random Between Two Constants**, use the drop-down button to the right of the property:

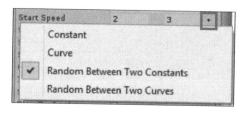

The curve editor appears at the bottom of the particle editor inspector.

Check the sample project in the Chapter9-10 folder for what the completed particle system looks like in the **Inspector** window.

# The death animation

Now that we have all the parts constructed for our live Goblin and some extra bits for his death, let's create a new GoblinDeath animation and add it to our Goblin's AI.

With our new GoblinEnemy structure in the **Project** hierarchy, select it and bring up the **Animation** tab (**Window | Animation** in the menu). Then, click on the **Clip** dropdown and select **[Create New Clip]**. When prompted, save the new animation in Assets\Animation\Clips and call it GoblinDeath.

If the **Clip** dropdown is grayed out, then remember to click on the **Record** button to enable editing.

The following is what we are aiming for in the animation, a simple alpha transition to fade the Goblin out and then fade the tombstone in:

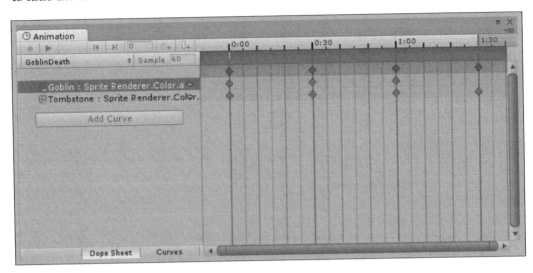

To recreate this, perform the following steps:

1. Click on **0:00** on the timeframe to select the start point.

2. Make sure the record button is enabled.

3. Select the **Goblin** game object in the hierarchy.

4. Open the **Color** editor for the **SpriteRenderer** (by clicking on the color box) and alter the **A** (alpha) value; it doesn't matter to what. This just adds the property to the animation curve.

5. At position **0:00**, set the value of **Goblin : Sprite Renderer.Color.a** to **1**.

6. At position **0:30**, set the value of **Goblin : Sprite Renderer.Color.a** to **0.5**.

7. At position **1:00**, set the value of **Goblin : Sprite Renderer.Color.a** to **0**.

8. Select the position **0:00** in the timeframe.

9. Select the **Tombstone** game object in the hierarchy.

10. Open the **Color** editor for the SpriteRender and alter the **A** (alpha) value.

11. At position **0:00**, set the value of **Tombstone: Sprite Renderer.Color.a** to **0**.

12. At position **0:30**, set the value of **Tombstone: Sprite Renderer.Color.a** to **0** (you might have to set it to **1** first and then reset it back to **0** to stick).

13. At position **1:00**, set the value of **Tombstone: Sprite Renderer.Color.a** to **0.5**.

14. At position **1:30**, set the value of **Tombstone: Sprite Renderer.Color.a** to **1**.

This gives us the positions we want; however, if you look at the curve for the **Tombstone** fade - in animation, it will not look quite right, as shown here:

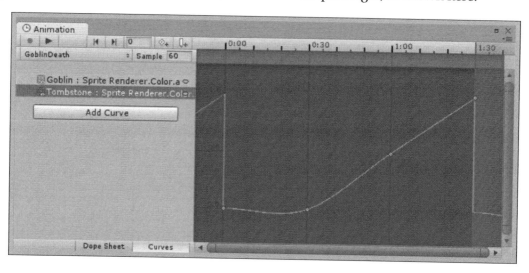

This is just because the curve system is doing its best to figure out what you want based on your recordings. To give us a flatter line at the beginning of our animation and a more linear line while the tombstone fades in, we just need to override the default behavior for the first two animation keys. To do this, we set the tangents for each animation key appropriately, as follows:

1.  Switch to the **Curves** view by clicking on the **Curves** button; then, right-click on the animation key (a small diamond in the view) for **Tombstone: Sprite Renderer.Color.a** at the position **0:00** and select **Right Tangent | Constant**.

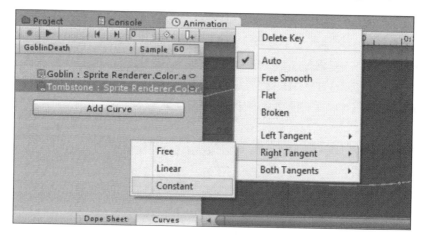

2. Right-click on the key of **Tombstone: Sprite Renderer.Color.a** at the position **0:30** and select **Left Tangent | Linear**.

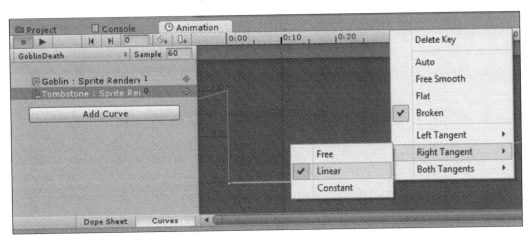

This gives us a nice overlapping transition between the Goblin and the Tombstone. The Goblin fades out, and halfway through this, the Tombstone fades in and our curve now looks better, as it appears in the following screenshot:

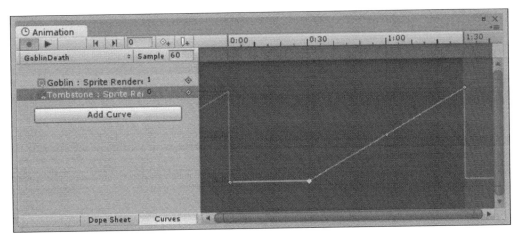

# Adding particles to the animation

So that the particles are played at the beginning of the animation, we need to add an **Animation** event to the timeline. When the event is fired, it will call a custom function against the object it is attached to.

Sadly, we still cannot call particle systems directly from the Animator Dope sheet, so we have to work around this with these Animation events.

Before we can add the event, we first need to add the function and its corresponding code of the particle system to the `EnemyController` script that the animator is working from.

First, add a new variable to the top of the class to store a reference to the particle system:

```
private ParticleSystem bloodsplatterParticles;
```

Next, we will grab the reference to the particle system from the component added to the game object the script is attached to in the `Awake` function:

```
void Awake()
{
  bloodsplatterParticles =
    GetComponentInChildren<ParticleSystem>();
  if (bloodsplatterParticles == null)
  {
    Debug.LogError("No Particle System Found");
  }
  enemyAI = GetComponent<Animator>();
  if (enemyAI == null)
  {
    Debug.LogError("No AI System Found");
  }
}
```

Finally, we will add the following function that will cause the particle system to play (and also clear the selected enemy from `BattleManager`):

```
void ShowBloodSplatter()
{
  bloodsplatterParticles.Play();
  ClearSelection();
  if (battleManager != null)
  {
    battleManager.ClearSelectedEnemy();
  }
  else
  {
    Debug.LogError("No BattleManager");
  }
}
```

With these in place, we return to the **Animation** view, right-click on **0:00** in the dark gray bar of the timeline, and select **Add Animation Event**, as shown in the following screenshot:

This will bring up the **Edit Animation Event** window, shown in the following screenshot, where you can select the function we just created:

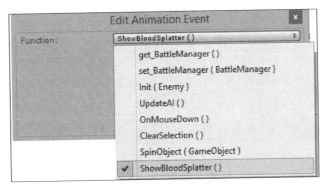

Now, when the animation begins, it will also trigger the particle effect to start spawning and explode the blood particles in a very tastily manner.

# Connecting the dots

If you now select the **GoblinEnemy** game object in the **Hierarchy** window and open the **Animator** tab (**Window | Animator** in the menu), you will see the new animation clip as a new state in the **GoblinAI** animator sheet.

However, it is not connected to anything just yet, as we want to play the animation when the Goblin dies. We just need to hook this up to the **Any** state for when the Goblin's health drops to 0 or below.

So, right-click on the **Any** state, create a new transition, and connect it to the new **GoblinDeath** state. Then, set the condition for this transition so that **EnemyHealth** is less than **1**.

To tidy things up, we also need to fix the transition from the **Idle** state to the **Any** state because we only want the Any state to be used when the Goblin is leaving the scene (either in a box or as fast as his little legs will take him). This is because the Idle state is the default state and it will begin there, so we only need control when the Goblin goes into a defense mode or attacks the player. To do this, we need to perform the following:

1. Remove the transition between the Idle state and the Any state.
2. Add a new transition from **Attack** to **Idle** with the condition **playerSeen = false**.
3. Add a new transition from **Defend** to **Idle** with the condition **playerSeen = false**.

This closes the loop a bit more cleanly between the action and exit states (it also stops a bug where the state machine could hop directly from **Idle** to **Death**).

The final Goblin AI Animator view should now look like this:

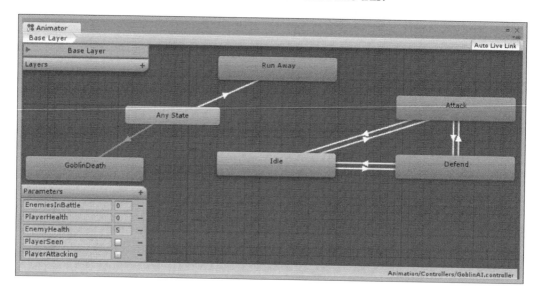

# Making the new GoblinEnemy game object a prefab and adding it to the battle

Now that we have the new base for the Goblin, drag the **GoblinEnemy** game object to `Assets\Prefabs\Characters` (delete the old one if you haven't already). When it's created, delete the original `GameObject` from the **Project** hierarchy as we will only use the prefab from now on.

Check over all the game objects in the prefab to ensure all the position transforms are set to **0, 0, 0**. This will avoid too much head-scratching when they don't draw in the correct place.

Return to the **BattleManager** game object and add the new prefab to the **EnemyPrefabs** property of the `BattleManager` script. We need to replace the one we just deleted.

# Houston, we have a problem!

Despite our best laid-out plans, we actually have problems now; if you run the project at this point, you will notice two very annoying bugs:

- The Goblins spawn into the battle horrendously and die instantly
- Their death isn't finite as they keep dying repeatedly

Now, this isn't truly a problem for our budding adventurer and is arguably fun to watch, but this isn't what we were really going for; there should at least be some challenge.

## Mecanim AI considerations

The answer to the first problem is simple enough: it takes time for `EnemyController` to update the **EnemyAI** state machine for the first time (several frames actually, just a Unity thing). As the AI isn't updated, the initial state of **EnemyHealth** is **0**. So, when the state machine starts, the initial condition for the transition to **GoblinDeath** is met because **EnemyHealth** is less than **2**. To resolve this, simply set the default state machine's value for **EnemyHealth** to something more than the default condition, as shown in the following screenshot (for example, I set the default value to 5):

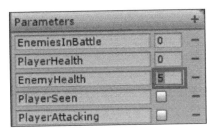

 When using the Mecanim system for AI, be sure to always check your default values for properties.

## Animation, states, and looping

The second issue is a bit more conventional and just requires a bit more knowledge about the new animation system, as by default, all the animations will loop forever.

To stop an animation from looping, you would normally just transition it to another animation state in the Mecanim animator view when it is complete (the condition **Exit Time = 0.9**). However, in this case, our animation is the final resting state, and as stated, with nowhere to go, the animation state will just loop forever.

To change this, we simply need to alter the animation clip's import settings to denote it is a static animation and not a looping one (by turning off looping).

So, navigate to `Assets\Animation\Clips` and select the **GoblinDeath** animation clip. Then, in the **Inspector** window, uncheck the **Loop Time** option as shown in the following screenshot:

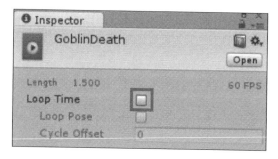

There are several other import properties for animation clips, but these are mainly for 3D models.

# The final run-through

Running the project now in the battle scene won't get you very far unfortunately; you will need to switch back to the home scene and play through from there. You can perform the following actions in your game:

1. Beginning at home.
2. Going to the shop and buying a weapon.
3. Leaving the shop and going to the big bad world.
4. Wandering until you encounter a battle.
5. Selecting a weapon to attack with.
6. Selecting a Goblin enemy.
7. Clicking on **Attack**.

Once this is done, only then will you be able to see how the full effect of the battle animation will unfold.

 Alternatively, add a code set in `Debug` style to the `BattleManager` script to give the player a sword when the script starts; just don't leave it there when you run your game properly.

# Going further

Now, you are probably thinking at this point, "What about the rest of the battle?" Put simply, I leave that up to you.

You are now armed with everything you need to know to be able to complete the rest of the battle scene. You should not just stop there, however, and you should see just how far along you can get.

Try expanding the battle to include various states using the following steps:

1. Add an onscreen GUI to inform that the control is now changing hands in the **Change Control** battle state.

2. Loop through the Goblins and let them attack the player; rough him or her up a bit.

3. Check whether the battle is complete, and accordingly, either transition back to the **Player Move** state or set the `BattleReady` state variable to `false` to transition to the Battle Result state.

4. Display a 2D GUI to summarize the battle results and grant the user some experience, perhaps with some gold, each time an enemy is slain.

5. Transition back to the map when the battle is over.

# Summary

This is a chapter with lots of new code, features, and tips and tricks. Hopefully, you have learned a lot.

From here on, you should look at planning for some sort of skill tree and putting a simple UI in place that the user can access to either spend the experience he or she has gained or level up certain skills.

The sample has more features implemented if you want to see the end result, but I'll recommend reusing what you have learned and build it yourself. The best way to learn is through re-enforcement and testing yourself.

We covered the factors that make a battle, a more advanced GUI with 2D, mixing 2D and 3D and what to look out for, working with particle effects and animation, and more animation know-how.

In the next chapter, we will look at packaging your game and making it a bit more than just a couple of game screens.

# 11
# Onward Wary Traveler

You have a game; it looks good, plays well, and everyone loves it. The only problem is that it is still not a finished project.

In this chapter, we will look at how we can extend Unity to help make the content easier and better, and finally, package up the game and surround it with menus and other features that will make it whole.

As they say, the finishing of a project can take up to 80 percent of the time needed to polish it. Be warned! This is usually right. To wrap up, we will cover the tricky art of persisting the player's data as they play both on the device and on the cloud.

The following topics will be covered in this chapter:

- The editor and how to make the most out of it
- Packaging your game with menus and additional screens
- Saving, loading, and persistence for your game

## Extending the editor

Everyone who uses Unity knows about the editor. It's the core place where you will spend a great deal of time putting your game together. You will spend the rest of your time in the choice of your code editor, patching things together, adding values, and working around with what most see as limitations of the editor itself. This, however, is not the case.

The people at Unity realized early that they couldn't do everything, since everyone wanted something different or little tweaks here and there; if they had tried to do everything, nothing would have ever left their doors.

So, from the ground up, Unity was designed to be extensible, and they exposed much of what is needed to build your own editor in effect within Unity itself.

If you browse the asset store (`https://www.assetstore.unity3d.com/en`), you will see a lot of assets that take advantage of this, and they have produced some really snazzy bolt-ons for the editor. These can reduce the need to code and just build things using the editor GUI.

These aren't magical things and don't even require low-level C++ coding to achieve (although some do). You can update your editor to fix your game very easily, and you can do this in any of the languages that Unity supports.

The scripting framework behind the editor is broken up into several distinct layers that can be combined to give you almost any effect you need to build your content.

# The property drawers

The editor only has a basic way of looking at the properties in the **Inspector** pane based on the classes and objects used in your game. If you are using an existing Unity class, such as a string, color, or curve, Unity already has readymade property drawers (or visual handles) to manage these with their own editor windows in some cases (such as the curve editor). The majority of these are also built on the extensible framework that Unity exposes and is available to you as well.

Other classes such as vectors and numbers have a basic implementation, which is usually fine, but sometimes you would just prefer it in a different way.

This is where the property drawers come in. They can either replace the existing property viewer for a single field or for a type of object entirely. If you want a slider to alter a value between two values, add a `PropertyDrawer` attribute to the property to show a slider instead of just `int` or `float` as follows:

```
[Range (0, 100)]
public float health = 100;
```

The preceding code example shows a range slider instead of a single float value as you can see here:

For a more advanced example, check out the post on the Unity blog, which shows several different patterns to use your property drawers and even create them. The post is available at `http://blogs.unity3d.com/2012/09/07/property-drawers-in-unity-4/`.

While building the property drawers, you will use the `EditorGUI` controls to draw the elements on the screen. The `EditorGUI` class provides a rich collection of controls that can be used. For the list of available controls, visit `https://docs.unity3d.com/Documentation/ScriptReference/EditorGUI.html`.

The property drawers can only use the default layouts in the `EditorGUI` class. For performance reasons, they cannot use the automatic controller found in the `EditorGUILayout` class, which is used in `EditorWindows`.

For more information on property drawers, see the Unity reference guide at `https://docs.unity3d.com/Documentation/ScriptReference/PropertyDrawer.html`.

If you want to see some more creative uses of the property drawers, check out the simple little GitHub repository at `https://github.com/tenpn/ChestOfPropertyDrawers`.

# Property drawers examples

Using the NPC script in `Assets\Scripts\Classes`, let's see the effect of adding some simple property drawers to our NPCs in the **Inspector** pane.

## Built-in property drawers

Starting simply, we can decorate some of the properties of the NPC class in our game with the `Range` attribute by adding the following code:

```
public string Name;
[Range(10, 100)]
public int Age;
public string Faction;
public string Occupation;
[Range(1, 10)]
public int Level;
```

The preceding code has the following effect on the editor inspector:

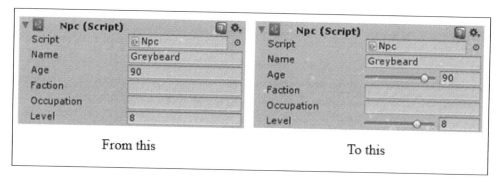

From this                                To this

This just makes it easier to manage your settings and makes it a little prettier to look at. Now, let's look at something that is a little more complicated.

## Custom property drawers

Creating your own property drawer is certainly a bit more advanced. However, once you have learned the basics, it is quite easy to build your own.

For this example, we will create a simple pop up that takes an array of values for the possible selection, as shown here:

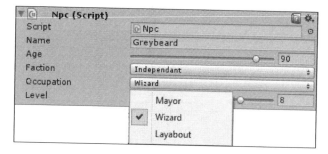

First, we need a property type or attribute that we want to control. This could be a set of parameters (such as the `Range` property, which has a beginning and an end), a validation string, or even an enumeration.

 The property type or attribute you want to control has to live in your project folder and **not** in the special `Editor` folder. The Unity documents are not clear enough on this.

So, create a new folder named `Properties` in `Assets\Scripts\Classes`. Then, create a new C# script named `PopupAttribute` in the `Properties` folder and replace its contents with the following code:

```
using UnityEngine;
public class PopUpAttribute: PropertyAttribute
{
  public string[] value;
  public PopUpAttribute(params string[] input)
  {
    value = input;
  }
}
```

Note that your `property` class must be derived from the `PropertyAttribute` class, and it must have a constructor with the same number of parameters required for your attribute (for example, the `Range` attribute has two `int` values).

> In a strange (I suspect reflection) circumstance, you can either call your class by its name or suffix it with the word `Attribute` (as shown in the preceding code); both will be recognized by the name alone.
>
> For example, `PopUpAttribute` can be recognized as `PopUp` or `PopUpAttribute`.

With the property in place, we can now add our custom property drawer code. Unlike the property we just created, this does have to live in the special `Editor` folder.

So, create a new folder named `PropertyDrawers` in the `Assets\Scripts\`**Editor** folder and create a new script named `PopUpCustomPropertyDrawer`, replacing its contents with the following code:

```
using UnityEditor;
using UnityEngine;

[CustomPropertyDrawer(typeof(PopUpAttribute))]
public class PopUpCustomPropertyDrawer : PropertyDrawer {

  PopUpAttribute popUpAttribute {
    get { return ((PopUpAttribute)attribute); } }
}
```

The preceding code gives us the basic framework for our custom property drawer (the `public` property I've added isn't mandatory, but provides quick and easy access to the underlying property type we are enabling). Next, we need to add the `OnGUI` function that will draw our custom property UI using the following code:

```
public override void OnGUI(Rect position, SerializedProperty prop,
    GUIContent label)
{
    if (prop.propertyType != SerializedPropertyType.String)
    {
        throw new UnityException("property " + prop + " must be string
            to use with PopUpAttribute ");
    }

    var popupRect = EditorGUI.PrefixLabel(position,
        GUIUtility.GetControlID(FocusType.Passive), label);

    var currentItem = prop.stringValue;
    var currentIndex = popUpAttribute.value.Length - 1;
    for (; currentIndex >= 0; currentIndex--)
    {
        if (popUpAttribute.value[currentIndex] == currentItem)
            break;
    }

    int selectedIndex = EditorGUI.Popup(popupRect, currentIndex,
        popUpAttribute.value);
    prop.stringValue = selectedIndex < 0 ? "" :
        popUpAttribute.value[selectedIndex];
}
```

Walking through the preceding script is quite simple; it is described as follows:

- The class is decorated with a `CustomPropertyDrawer` attribute and the type of class it is targeted at.
- As stated, the class is derived from the `PropertyDrawer` class.
- A helper property (`popUpAttribute`) gets the correct type of class from the attribute property of the `PropertyDrawer` base class (optional).
- We override the `OnGUI` function for the property drawers.
- We then check whether the target property (the variable you will attach this to) is of the correct type (in this case, a string). It returns `UnityException` if it is not correct.

- A `Rect` variable is defined for where we want to draw the output from our property drawer (a requirement to use the `EditorGUI.Popup` control).

- We get the current value for the property we are attached to and compare it with the possible values for the item. We do this only because we have a list of options and need to know which the current one is. For other types, this may not be needed.

- We draw a pop-up control using the `EditorGUI.Popup` control.

- Lastly, we set the property we are attached to with the value the user has selected.

> We could have used an `enum` object instead of an array to give us a more programmatic approach, in which case the preceding steps would be very similar. However, this approach allows us to set the scope of the selection for each property.

With the property and our custom property drawer in place, we can decorate the variables in our `NPC` class to achieve the result I pictured earlier, as follows:

```
public string Name;
[Range(10, 100)]
public int Age;
[PopUp("Imperial", "Independant", "Evil")]
public string Faction;
[PopUp("Mayor", "Wizard", "Layabout")]
public string Occupation;
[Range(1, 10)]
public int Level;
```

It may seem like a lot of fuss. However, once it's complete, you can tune the Unity editor to work for you more efficiently.

# Custom editors

Say you want to control the entire scope of a single class or `ScriptableObject`; this is where `CustomEditor` scripts come in.

They can be used against any script that can be attached to a game object to alter how it works in the Unity editor inspector.

As an example of these (the best way to show custom editors is through code), we will add some functionality to a camera to provide us with better control over it in a scene.

First, we'll need a very simple camera script that will point the camera to a specified target, starting at 0, 0 ,0. So, create a new script named `CameraLookAt` in `Assets\Scripts` and replace its contents with the following code:

```
using UnityEngine;

public class CameraLookAt : MonoBehaviour
{
  public Vector3 cameraTarget = Vector3.zero;

  void Update()
  {
    transform.LookAt(cameraTarget);
  }
}
```

We can then define a `CustomEditor` script that will be run by the editor whenever it detects a game object with the script attached to it.

 As with a lot of editor features, remember (as a good rule of thumb) that if a class requires the `UnityEditor` namespace, it will need to live in the special `Editor` folder in your project.

So, create a new C# script called `CameraTargetEditor` in `Assets\Scripts\Editor` in your project and replace its contents with the following code:

```
using UnityEngine;
using UnityEditor;

[CustomEditor(typeof(CameraLookAt))]
public class CameraTargetEditor : Editor
{
    public override void OnInspectorGUI()
    {
        CameraLookAt targetScript = (CameraLookAt)target;

        targetScript.cameraTarget =
          EditorGUILayout.Vector3Field ("Look At Point",
            targetScript.cameraTarget);
        if (GUI.changed)
            EditorUtility.SetDirty(target);
    }
}
```

This script doesn't do much yet; we now have a `Vector3` handle in our script that displays the position of the camera's target (the specific point it is looking at). What is very nice here is that you can edit the values and the camera will automatically transform itself to look at the new point. To demonstrate this, create a new scene named `EditorDemos` in `Assets\Scenes` and attach the `CameraLookAt` script to **Main Camera**. If you then select the **Main Camera** game object in the hierarchy, you will see the following settings in the **Inspector** pane:

This is a lot easier than messing with the rotation values of the ordinary camera. Let's continue to add more functionalities that will blow your mind.

 If the custom editor script depends on certain properties or components being available on the game object you attach it to, then be sure to use the `RequireConponent` attribute on the base class (not the `CustomEditor` script).

To make it even more useful, we can also represent this selection in the scene view as a control handle. To do this, we simply add another function to our `CameraTargetEditor CustomEditor` script; add the following `OnSceneGUI` function to the script:

```
void OnSceneGUI()
{
    CameraLookAt targetScript = (CameraLookAt)target;

    targetScript.cameraTarget = Handles.PositionHandle(
            targetScript.cameraTarget, Quaternion.identity);

    if (GUI.changed)
        EditorUtility.SetDirty(target);
}
```

Just as the `OnGUI` method draws in to your game, this function will draw in to the editor scene. Using the `Handles.PositionHandle` control, it will draw a regular handlebars control in the scene at the point you have specified, in this case, the camera's look-at target, as seen here:

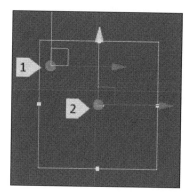

Camera Target (1) and Camera Transform (2)

Want more?? You can then alter how the handlebars will look on the screen with the following code:

```
void OnSceneGUI()
{
    CameraLookAt targetScript = (CameraLookAt)target;

    targetScript.cameraTarget = Handles.PositionHandle(
targetScript.cameraTarget, Quaternion.identity);
    Handles.SphereCap(0, targetScript.cameraTarget,
Quaternion.identity, 2);
    if (GUI.changed)
        EditorUtility.SetDirty(target);
}
```

As shown in the following screenshot, this simply alters the handlebars we are drawing, decorating them with a sphere. There are several other options as well should you choose to explore them.

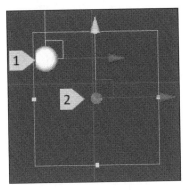

(1) Camera Target Sphere, (2) Camera Transform

For more information about custom editors, see the Unity reference guide at `http://docs.unity3d.com/Documentation/ScriptReference/Editor.html`.

For more information about handles and what you can do with them, see the Unity reference guide at `http://docs.unity3d.com/Documentation/ScriptReference/Handles.html`.

# The editor window

Quite simply, Unity editor windows are just separate containers for collections of editor GUI controls. These windows are a more advanced version of the property drawers described previously, and as such use a different set of custom controls.

The **Inspector**, **Game**, and **Scene** windows, and in fact, pretty much every other dockable window in the Unity editor, are editor windows. In fact, they are all built in the same way using the same scripting framework.

As stated previously, remember that any script that uses the editor functionality or the `UnityEditor` namespace must be placed in a special project folder titled `Editor`.

To implement your own editor window, you simply need to create a class that is derived from `EditorWindow` instead of `MonoBehaviour`. The script must also live in the special `Editor` folder within the project structure, so create a new script called `MyEditorWindow` in `Assets\Scripts\Editor`, as follows:

```
using UnityEditor;
using UnityEngine;

public class MyEditorWindow : EditorWindow
{
string windowName = "My Editor Window";
bool groupEnabled;
bool DisplayToggle = true;
float Offset = 1.23f;

}
```

I've added some properties to give some depth to the example.

With your new window in place, you then need to implement a function to display the window when it is called inside the new `MyEditorWindow` class:

```
[MenuItem ("Window/My Window")]
public static void ShowWindow ()
{
    EditorWindow.GetWindow(typeof(MyEditorWindow));
}
```

It doesn't matter what the preceding function is called; it's just an editor reference attribute attached to the function that shows where the option will appear in the Unity editor menu.

If you want more control over the size and position of your editor window, instead of using the preceding `GetWindow` function, you can use the following `GetWindowWithRect` function:

```
[MenuItem ("Window/My Window")]
public static void ShowWindow ()
{
    EditorWindow.GetWindowWithRect(typeof(MyEditorWindow),
      new Rect(0, 0, 400, 150));
}
```

This will set the position and size of the window to a fixed point on the screen, but as with all other editor windows, it can then be resized and docked like any other window. This method is more useful to display a collection of properties in the scene view to edit nodes or other position-based visual configuration.

Lastly, you need some GUI code. This is pretty much the same as the normal GUI code, but with a few editor extensions because it is being drawn in the editor. This goes in to an OnGUI method, for example:

```
void OnGUI()
{
    // Your custom Editor Window GUI code
    GUILayout.Label("Base Settings", EditorStyles.boldLabel);
    windowName = EditorGUILayout.TextField("Window Name",
      windowName);

    groupEnabled =
      EditorGUILayout.BeginToggleGroup("Optional Settings",
        groupEnabled);

    DisplayToggle =
      EditorGUILayout.Toggle("Display Toggle", DisplayToggle);

    Offset = EditorGUILayout.Slider("Offset Slider",
      Offset, -3, 3);
    EditorGUILayout.EndToggleGroup();
}
```

The preceding example will show the following menu window:

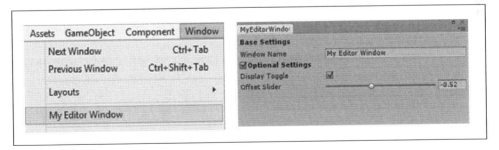

When you put GUI elements together in an editor window, you can use either the basic `EditorGUI` controls or the more advanced `EditorGUILayout` controls, which implement some additional automatic layout features on top of the basic controls.

For more details on the controls available with `EditorGUILayout`, check out the Unity reference at `https://docs.unity3d.com/Documentation/ScriptReference/EditorGUILayout.html`.

For more information on editor windows, see the Unity reference guide at `https://docs.unity3d.com/Documentation/ScriptReference/EditorWindow.html`.

# Gizmos

With custom editors, you could also have handles to represent a control in the scene view, extending the **Inspector** features in to the scene.

We also have another way to have class-based features that are only available in the editor through the use of Gizmos.

Gizmos offer a much richer graphical way to add visual elements to the scene to aid the use of a class, unlike custom editors, which are only added to your base class that the editor will then make use of.

`OnDrawGizmo` functions are only available on classes that are derived from `MonoBehaviour`, not the `Editor` classes.

For example, we can amend the `CameraLookAt` script we created earlier and make it draw a Gizmo line from the camera to the target's look-at point by adding the following code to the script:

```
void OnDrawGizmos()
{
    Gizmos.color = Color.yellow;
    Gizmos.DrawLine(transform.position, cameraTarget);
}
```

The code produces the result as follows:

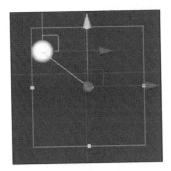

Now, when you return to the editor and move the look-at point or the camera, there will be a yellow line drawn between them.

 If you collapse the script in the **Inspector** pane, this will turn off the Gizmo. This is handy if you want to just hide it.

If you don't want the Gizmo drawn all the time, you can also track when the user has the Gizmo selected using the OnDrawGizmosSelected method, as follows:

```
void OnDrawGizmosSelected()
{
    Gizmos.color = Color.red;
    Gizmos.DrawLine(transform.position, cameraTarget);
}
```

Now when the game object the script is attached to is selected in the editor, the line will be drawn in red instead of yellow. Alternatively, just use the OnDrawGizmosSelected function on its own to only draw a line when selected.

 For more information on Gizmos, see the Unity reference guide at http://docs.unity3d.com/Documentation/ScriptReference/Gizmos.html.

For fantastic additional resources and tutorials, check out the article on CatLike Coding's blog at http://catlikecoding.com/unity/tutorials/editor/star/.

Or, you can check out the excellent Gimzo-driven design tutorial at http://code.tutsplus.com/tutorials/how-to-add-your-own-tools-to-unitys-editor--active-10047.

# Building your editor menus

Another way of extending in to the editor is to customize it by adding your own menus. We covered little bits of this in previous chapters by adding extra options to create your assets and such, but there is much more to it.

>  MenuItem functions must be declared as Static functions, else they will not be recognized, and scripts must be placed in the special Editor folder.

## Adding a MenuItem attribute

The main way of adding a new menu item is to define a script in Assets\Scripts\ Editor and append the MenuItem attribute to a static method within it. So, create a new script called MyMenu in this folder and replace its contents with the following code:

```
using UnityEditor;
using UnityEngine;
public class MyMenu
{
    // Add a menu item named MenuItem1 to a Menu option called
    // MenuName in the menu bar.
    [MenuItem ("MenuName/MenuItem1")]
    static void EnableMyAwesomeFeature ()
    {
        Debug.Log ("I am a leaf on the wind. Watch how I soar.");
    }
}
```

This code simply creates a new top-level menu option called MenuName with a single item called MenuItem1, as shown here:

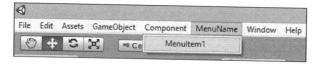

From here, you can execute whatever you need to.

 When you return to Unity after adding a menu script, it may sometimes not show up immediately. You can either click on the menu bar or restart the editor to make it appear (it just needs a nudge).

# Enabling/disabling a MenuItem attribute

We can extend this further by adding a validation logic method to support a `MenuItem` attribute. This controls whether the menu option is enabled or not.

For this, you need to create a pair of the following items:

- A menu item
- A menu item validator

 The menu item and the menu item validator must have the same menu path. So, if the menu item (as declared previously) is `[MenuItem ("MenuName/MenuItem1")]`, the validator must have the same menu definition as follows:

```
[MenuItem ("MenuName/MenuItem1", true)]
```

Validators do not add menu items. They only extend or validate the existing menu items.

So, using the menu item we just added earlier, we can add a validator menu function. It must have a return type of `bool` and an additional flag set against the function attribute, as follows:

```
[MenuItem ("MenuName/MenuItem1", true)]
static bool CheckifaGameObjectisselected() {
    // Return false if no transform is selected.
    return Selection.activeTransform != null;
}
```

This simple validator just checks whether you have a game object selected in the editor; if not, then `MenuItem1` is disabled.

This new validation function is evaluated by the editor whenever it displays the menu item of the same name. By setting the `bool` flag at the end of the `MenuItem` attribute, it tells the editor that this function provides the validation logic for a `MenuItem` attribute of the same name. Then, the editor will enable or disable that `MenuItem` attribute based on the return of the validator function.

# Adding shortcut keys to a MenuItem attribute

If you add % and a letter to the end of your `MenuItem` attribute, Unity will also enable a shortcut key for that letter.

So, %g would enable a shortcut of *Ctrl + G* on Windows and *cmd + G* on a Mac.

For example, add a new function to our `MyMenu` script as follows:

```
[MenuItem ("MenuName/MenuItem2 %g")]
static void EnableMyOtherAwesomeFeature()
{
    Debug.Log ("Find my key and win the prize - g");
}
```

This will show us an additional option with the shortcut defined, as you can see here:

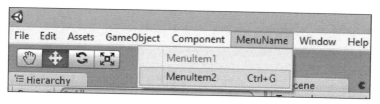

# Adding contextual MenuItems

The last bit of trickery you can perform is to add menu items to the existing features of Unity, even **Inspector**.

You do this with a custom name for the `MenuItem` attribute and a different signature for the function. So, we add the following method to our `MyMenu` script:

```
[MenuItem("CONTEXT/Transform/Move to Center")]
static void MoveToCenter(MenuCommand command)
{
    Transform transform = (Transform)command.context;
    transform.position = Vector3.zero;
    Debug.Log("Moved object to " +
      transform.position + " from a Context Menu.");
}
```

The preceding script attaches itself to any transform component (in this case, the **Inspector** pane). Then, when it is run, the parameter on the function receives the instance of the object it was run on and lets you interrogate or alter it, resulting in the following screenshot:

The structure of the special `MenuItem` name is as follows:

- **CONTEXT**: This is a fixed item to identify the menu as a contextual item
- **Object**: This is the type of object this context menu will be available on
- **Name**: This is the name of the menu item

You can just add extra dimensions/children to context menus by adding additional "/" characters.

However, if there is an error or the depth of your menus is too deep, Unity won't show the error; it just won't display the menu item (leaving you scratching your head). If this happens, try setting a shorter or different menu name.

Context menus can be added to just about any object/component in the Unity editor, including your own objects.

 For more information on the MenuItem class and its use in Unity Editor, see the Unity scripting reference guide at https://docs.unity3d.com/Documentation/ScriptReference/MenuItem.html.

# Running scripts in the Editor folder

The last little tidbit you should be aware of surrounds scripts and their execution.

If you put a script in the Editor folder, it will be executed when you are in the editor. However, what about all your other scripts?

Sure you can run the game and see the script running, but that doesn't help you when you are in the editor. What if you want to see the effect of your script while manipulating game objects in your scene? If you are using GUI controls, this becomes even more critical when you are trying to place controls on the screen.

Thankfully, there is a way to force the editor to run your script, and all it takes is yet another attribute called ExecuteInEditMode added to your class. To show this, let's open the CommandBar script under Assets\Scripts in our project and add the [ExecuteInEditMode] attribute to that class as follows:

```
using UnityEngine;
using System.Collections;

[ExecuteInEditMode]
public class CommandBar : MonoBehaviour
{
```

Now when you open up the Battle scene, CommandBar will always be drawn as shown here:

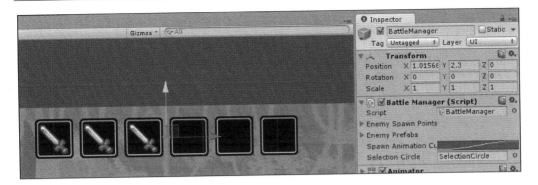

If you are applying this to the GUI that repositions itself to the scene like with `CommandBar`, the visual aspect you see in the editor may not be the same as when the game is running. So, things may position differently. You either manage it in the code or live with it in the editor; it's up to you.

If you have portions of your script that rely on other components that may not be active in the editor, be sure to check for null references in your code to avoid nasty errors in the console that may lead you down a dark path.

For example, in the `CommandBar` script, we need to have `null` checking on the `MessagingManager` calls and the `SetPosition` function, which have been updated in the sample app.

Also, any calls to `Static` classes in the `OnDestroy` method may generate errors/warnings when they are run in the editor; so just be aware!

## Alternative approaches

There is always more than one way to cut the cheese as they say, and so too it is with Unity. Some more advanced options to run the scripts in the editor include the following methods.

# The [InitialiseOnLoad] attribute

Another advanced feature with the editor is to make use of the `[InitialiseOnLoad]` attribute. What this attribute does is run whatever class or script it is attached to when the editor opens or when a build event occurs (such as after you edit a script or run the project). Most developers use this for tracking purposes or to have background processes run whenever something is changed. This is especially useful if you have some level data stored in a custom file and need to regenerate a scene or level based on that configuration.

Unlike `[ExecuteInEditMode]`, the `[InitialiseOnLoad]` attribute is an editor-only feature, and the scripts using it must be placed in the special `Editor` folder in your project.

It is recommended that you combine the use of the `[InitialiseOnLoad]` attribute together with a static constructor to ensure the script will run before any other scripts in the scene or project.

If you are loading resources in an `[InitialiseOnLoad]` class, beware that the filesystem may not be initialized when the script starts. It's recommended you delay it until the first editor update (using the following method). For more details, check out the detailed post at `http://bit.ly/InitiliseOnLoadResources`.

# The EditorApplication callbacks

The editor, like a lot of things in Unity, also comes adorned with several callbacks to mark when things happen. Exposed through the `EditorApplication` class, you can gain access to the following events:

| Event/delegate | Description |
| --- | --- |
| `Update` | This event is called every time the editor window is updated or refreshed. Note that this is more often that the game or scene update calls. |
| `projectWindowItemOnGUI` | This event is called for each project item in view of the **Project** window when it is drawn to the screen. |
| `hierarchyWindowItemOnGUI` | This event is called for each item in the **Hierarchy** window when it is drawn to the screen. |
| `projectWindowChanged` | This event is called whenever an item is changed in the **Project** window. |
| `hierarchyWindowChanged` | This event is called whenever an item is changed in the **Hierarchy** window. |

| Event/delegate | Description |
|---|---|
| `playmodeStateChanged` | This event is called when you start or stop the game in the editor. |
| `searchChanged` | This event is called whenever the search criteria is changed in any **Editor** window. |
| `modifierKeysChanged` | This event is used to track when a modifier key (*Alt*, *cmd*, *Ctrl*, and so on) is pressed. So, you need to change a view when a modifier key is pressed, and you need to watch for this event/delegate. |

These events can be added to any class/script in your `Editor` project folder, so you can hook up a functionality to run when these events occur using the following syntax. For example, let's employ the following methods in an editor script to fire whenever we change the project's hierarchy:

```
void OnEnable()
{
    // Event / delegate registration, usually put in the OnEnable
    //or other function
    EditorApplication.hierarchyWindowChanged +=
        HierarchyWindowChanged;
}

//callback function for when event occurs
void HierarchyWindowChanged()
{
    //Scan hierarchy for new items
    //If found add something to the editor window
}

void OnDestroy()
{
    // Don't forget to unregister the delegate when it goes out of
    //scope or is not needed
    EditorApplication.hierarchyWindowChanged -=
        HierarchyWindowChanged;
}
```

This gives your editor scripts the ability to react to whatever the editor does by attaching to the `hierarchyWindowChanged` event when the script is enabled (making sure to unattach it when the script is disabled).

# Mixing it up

In more advanced cases, you can build a framework that combines with the previous approaches effectively to create a complete editor manager. This needs to be implemented in a class with a static constructor so that it is initialized as soon as the editor starts.

To demonstrate this, let's create a simple script that will save the scene for us when we hit the play button. First, create a new script called `SaveSceneOnPlay` in `Assets\Scripts\Editor` and replace its contents with the following code:

```
using UnityEditor;
using UnityEngine;
[InitializeOnLoad]
public class SaveSceneOnPlay
{
    // Static class constructor,
    // this is initialized as soon as Unity Starts
    static SaveSceneOnPlay()
    {

    }
}
```

This gives us the framework for an `[InitializeOnLoad]` script that will run when Unity starts. Then, we add our static function to do the work of saving the scene:

```
static void SaveSceneIfPlaying()
{

    if (EditorApplication.isPlayingOrWillChangePlaymode &&
      !EditorApplication.isPlaying)
    {

        Debug.Log("Automatically saving scene (" +
          EditorApplication.currentScene +
            ") before entering play mode ");

        EditorApplication.SaveAssets();
        EditorApplication.SaveScene();
    }
}
```

This method checks whether the editor is about to change the play state and is not being played currently; if this is the case, then it saves the current changed assets and the current scene.

Next, we hook up this function with the `playmodeStateChanged` event delegate in the static constructor as follows:

```
static SaveSceneOnPlay()
{
    EditorApplication.playmodeStateChanged += SaveSceneIfPlaying;
}
```

Now, with this script in our project, whenever we hit play, the script will automatically save the project for us.

# Building in-game menu structures

Usually left as an afterthought or slapped on at the end, menu systems are just as important as your game in most aspects. How the user interacts/starts or walks through all the sections of your game leading to the actual gameplay can radically change how the user feels about your game. There's no point in having a world-beating game if the first thing the user sees on starting your game is a roughly drawn or shabby-looking menu system. The best menu systems I've seen are actually seamlessly built into the game mechanics themselves.

## The screens

First off, you need to work out the structure of your menu systems in advance; it doesn't need to be heavy, just understand the flow of your game from start to finish and then iterate on that design until it looks impressive and easy to use. The kinds of screens and areas that you need to focus on are covered in the next section.

## Splash screens

Splash screens tell the user about you and your brand; it's the first thing they always see. If you animate a splash screen, try to keep it under 3 seconds; a good baseline is to aim for between 1-2 seconds—anything shorter and users won't pay attention, longer and you could just annoy them waiting to start the game.

A big debate I've seen between studios is whether you should allow the user to skip splash screens, and there doesn't seem to be any firm sway either way.

A general piece of advice though is to not allow skipping as it can devalue your brand.

Splash screens can either be separate screens or just fullscreen GUI textures that are drawn using the GUI.DrawTexture function in your menu scripts as follows:

```
public Texture m_texture;
void OnGUI()
{
    GUI.DrawTexture(new Rect(0, 0, Screen.width, Screen.height),
        m_texture,
        ScaleMode.ScaleToFit,
        true);
}
```

Either method will work; the direction you take will largely depend on the style of your game.

## Loading screens

Plan to have a loading screen in advance. You may not actually use it initially, but when your game runs on lower spec devices, you will find that the loading times will increase, sometimes dramatically. Be prepared!

A good example of a loading scene tutorial can be found at http://chicounity3d. wordpress.com/2014/01/25/loading-screen-tutorial/.

## The main menu

The main menu is the obvious focal point when the player starts your game. Ideally, this should flow in to your game rather than look like a bolt on. Try to use game elements and moving/animated features.

This screen will be the first true impression of your game on the player.

Ensure that the player has a **Continue** option that returns them to their last point in the game so that they start playing in as few clicks/taps as possible. If you support the saving option, have a **Continue** button to jump on to the last save. If you use levels, jump on to the next level that they can play.

Don't force the player to wade through mountains of screens just to continue playing. I'm not saying don't have a new button or an option to select levels; just add an additional **Continue** option so they can jump straight in to the game.

# Save slots/level selections

The norm these days is just to have a grid array with masses of numbers plastered across the screen. These aren't bad per se; however, if you want to stand out, think differently. Surprise the player and stylize these screens as much as possible, and animate them and make them exciting/interactive.

# Settings pages

Every game usually has an array of settings to control various elements of the game itself. However, don't fall foul of some platform requirements with regards to these.

If you use audio, always have options to control the volume and a quick mute option; you may find you have to set this programmatically on some platforms.

If you use location services, then you must have an option to turn this on or off. It's a mandatory requirement on some platforms. Have a backup plan if the location is not available.

Try and support closed captioning; it is fairly easy to do this, and it means you open up your game to an even wider audience. Then, just have a setting to enable/disable it. Highlight it in your description on the store; you'll get extra credit for this from your users and reviewers.

# About the screen

There are so many games that leave this out. This is not essential by any means, but you can have a page that describes your game studio, the developers, any extra credit for artists, resources, and so on. This screen generally doesn't have to be fancy, but it helps.

# Privacy policy

In an ever-growing world of security, privacy, and data protection, even if your game doesn't use any online features or store any data about the user, it is still essential to include a privacy policy.

On some platforms, it is becoming mandatory to have your policy stated somewhere in the app/game.

**Do not ship your game without some form of privacy policy.**

Policies do not have to be extensive, and there are numerous examples of different types of policies out there; a quick search or a good lawyer will put you in good stead.

The following site lists several generators; just pick the one that is right for you to get started:

```
http://www.applicationprivacy.org/do-tools/privacy-policy-generator/
```

## Pause screens

Like a lot of common screens used throughout your game, from scene to scene, one of the most common panels the player will see is the pause menu.

Whether it is a simple "on hold" screen or a full navigation system, you should take care of how you design it. Some games truly build the pause screen into the game and make it part of the game experience, while others just stop everything and throw up a panel.

Think different and don't just do what is necessary if possible.

Unity provides a delegate that is called when the Unity player receives a Pause event (if the platform supports it), which you can implement in the script as follows:

```
using UnityEngine;
using System.Collections;

public class ExampleClass : MonoBehaviour {
    public bool paused;
    void OnGUI() {
        if (paused)
            GUI.Label(new Rect(100, 100, 50, 30), "Game paused");

    }
    void OnApplicationPause(bool pauseStatus) {
        paused = pauseStatus;
    }
}
```

If you are using a state machine (such as in this title), you should then also progress it to a paused state as well.

 A simple way to stop all of the game updating is to set `Time.timeScale = 0`; but if you have logic that requires updates on the screen, then this may not work.

# Additionals (purchasing, achievements, leaderboards, and so on)

Generally shown as big lists on screens, these areas are your main way to entice the player to keep playing, whether it's to compete with friends for the highest scores or work toward a number of achievements (for the completionists out there). You should try to make these screens fun and informative. For levels, think about linking it with friends of the player to see how they compete with each other, or offer deals/promotions with what your game has to offer. As per a repeated statement in this chapter, think about what makes your game different and go beyond the norm.

# Social

In an ever-increasing social world, games need to react to this and think beyond the boundaries of just the game. Whether you are enabling simple bragging on levels/scores or if you are using social networks to find friends online and suggest games, you have to consider the social link-in with your game to stay competitive.

Not that social integration is the be all and end all, but an ever increasing number of players now actively look for it, so you should consider it at some level.

# The flow

When you have decided on all the screens within your game, the next step is to visualize (before cutting code) how they will all fit together. It doesn't take long and can save you hours of head-scratching later.

You can either grab a piece of paper or download some of the many free tools out there such as Freemind (a Mindmap tool at `http://freemind.sourceforge.net/wiki/index.php/Main_Page`) and Expression design (now free from MS at `http://www.microsoft.com/en-gb/download/details.aspx?id=36180`).

In the end, you want to have written down how each screen will connect to each other, what state the game will be in for that transition, and any key information that will need storing to prevent failure (since your game could be closed at any point by the user). At all states (based on how your game is intended to work), the player's current state should be preserved; whether you save it once or progressively will be impacted by how your screens fit together.

The following diagram shows a very simple example in the Mindmap tool of a game screen flow:

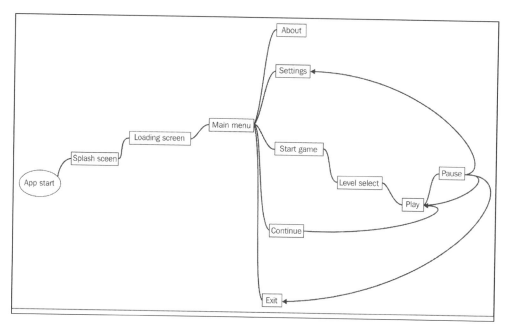

# Working with settings

Saving data is always important, especially in games where you need to keep track of the player's progress or at the very least a track record of scores, plays, and other important data.

Within Unity, there is only one method of storing data natively, and that is `PlayerPrefs`. It is very simple to use and very flexible, although it does have a hard limit of 1 MB of storage for the web player. It is possible to serialize data into `PlayerPrefs` (and some developers do this), but generally if you need to serialize, most developers build their own system.

# Using PlayerPrefs

`PlayerPrefs` is simply a key dictionary to store individual variables as a key in the Unity runtime data store. On its own, it has to read each and every scene at runtime, which is why most games use a static class to keep the state stored in `PlayerPrefs` and only use it between scenes for scene-specific configuration.

Using `PlayerPrefs` is very easy and simple. The process is the same as any other dictionary to save a setting for your call:

```
PlayerPrefs.SetInt("PlayerScore", currentScore);
PlayerPrefs.SetFloat("PlayerDamage", currentDamage);
PlayerPrefs.SetString("PlayerName", currentPlayerName);
```

Loading it back again when you need it again involves the following code:

```
currentScore = PlayerPrefs.GetInt("PlayerScore");
currentDamage = PlayerPrefs.GetFloat("PlayerDamage");
currentPlayerName = PlayerPrefs.GetString("PlayerName");
```

You can also supply defaults to values with a second parameter if the setting does not yet exist, as follows:

```
currentScore = PlayerPrefs.GetInt("PlayerScore", 0);
currentDamage = PlayerPrefs.GetFloat("PlayerDamage", 0);
currentPlayerName = PlayerPrefs.GetString
   ("PlayerName", "New Player");
```

By default, Unity will save the settings to disk when the application is closed. However, it's recommended that you save them intermittently when possible by calling the following:

```
PlayerPrefs.Save()
```

Saving settings in Unity isn't necessarily a given and should not be treated as safe. The settings file has a hard limit of 1 MB of storage on the web player. If this is exceeded, it will throw an exception. This limit is per application.

So, you can either drastically limit what settings you store (recommended) or wrap your SET `PlayerPrefs` calls in a `try/catch` statement to be safe if you plan to deploy to the web player.

Other platforms do not have this limitation.

There are also delete functions to remove either a single key or to clear the cache completely.

For more information about `PlayerPrefs`, see the Unity reference guide at https://docs.unity3d.com/Documentation/ScriptReference/PlayerPrefs.html.

# Serializing your data

To store any kind of complicated data or structure, you need to serialize it into a concatenated format. The result can then be stored in `PlayerPref` as mentioned previously or saved on a disk or the Web.

There are several types of serializers you can use, including the following:

- **Binary serialization**: This is binary-formatted output and is non-human readable
- **XML serialization**: This is the basic text output formatted into XML and is human readable
- **JSON serialization**: This is a compressed standalone output in XML format; it is human readable and allows you to have a manual implementation
- **Custom serialization**: This is DIY and is used to build your own serialized output

Each serializer has performance or security gains. There isn't a one size fits all; just choose the serializer that fits your purposes.

For our example, we will enhance our game to save our player's state. First, we will create a helper function to do the serialization for us, so create a new script called `SerializationHelper` in `Assets\Scripts\Classes` and replace its contents with the following code:

```
using System.IO;
using System.Xml.Serialization;

public class SerilizerHelper {
}
```

Now, in this script, we will add two functions: one to serialize our player (pack it up) and one to deserialize it (unpack it). The serialize function is as follows:

```
public static byte[] Serialise<T>(T input)
{
    byte[] output = null;
    //Create an XML formatter
    var serializer = new XmlSerializer(typeof(T));
    try
    {
```

```
            //Create an in memory stream to hold our serialized output
            using (var stream = new MemoryStream())
            {
                //Serialize the data
                serializer.Serialize(stream, input);
                //Get the serialized output
                output = stream.GetBuffer();
            }
        }
        catch { }


        //Return the serialized output
        return output;
    }
```

I've implemented the serialization function using C# generics (type <T>). This allows you to build a function that will work for any type of class you supply it with. This saves us from creating a serialization function for each and every type of data we want to serialize.

To learn more about generics (a fairly advanced topic), check out the MSDN documentation at http://msdn.microsoft.com/en-gb/library/512aeb7t.aspx.

Not all platforms support all serializers, and also, some classes (such as MemoryStream) are not available on all platforms. You will sometimes have to tailor the approach you use to work with other platforms. If you do, however, make sure you do it within the helper classes so that all the platform-variant code is in one place and does not clutter up your game. More on supporting multiple platforms is covered in *Chapter 12, Deployment and Beyond*.

The code is commented to explain what each step actually does. If you wish, you can store the output of this function in PlayerPrefs. It's more likely, however, that you will either save it to the Web or to a disk using a different buffer than MemoryStream (see the following section). Other serializers work pretty much the same way using a different formatter (for example, binary serialization uses BinarySerialiser).

To deserialize the data, we simply do the reverse:

```
public static T DeSerialise<T>(Stream input)
{
    T output = default(T);
    //Create an XML formatter
    var serializer = new XmlSerializer(typeof(T));
```

```
try
{
    //Deserialize the data from the stream
    output = (T)serializer.Deserialize(input);
}
catch { }
//Return the deserialized output
return output;
}
```

So as you can see, both patterns are very similar; this just reverses the flow (doesn't cross the streams).

Serialization is important as it can be used anywhere you need to package data to be saved or even transmitted over the wire for a cloud backup or even network play.

For more information about serialization, see the MSDN .NET reference guide at `http://msdn.microsoft.com/en-us/library/ms172360(v=vs.110).aspx`.

# Saving data to disk

A better way to manage your games to save data is to serialize it to disk, a method you will use to determine how fast and secure this is.

Instead of using `PlayerPrefs`, it is better to manage the saving and loading of your player data to a disk (or the Web; see the following sections). Thankfully, Mono (the C# engine behind Unity3D) and JS provide common functions to access the disk across all the platforms that Unity supports.

 There are exceptions, however, due to platform limitations or specializations in some platforms (such as Windows 8, where all disks access are accessed asynchronously). In these cases, Unity provides special classes to access platform components, for example, the `UnityEngine.Windows` namespace.

You can also write your disk access routines that are more platform-specific if you wish to make them more performant, but this requires you to write an interface and your platform-specific code for each routine (see *Chapter 12, Deployment and Beyond*, for information on DLL import).

# Modeling your saved data

If we look to add the saving and loading options to our game, we need to take a few things into account first. Consider that we just had a basic class for our player's state; the following is just an example:

```
[Serializable]
public struct Player {

    public string Name;
    public int Age;
}
```

We attach the [Serializable] attribute to the class to tell the serializer that it is serializable data. This isn't mandatory as most sterilizers will work with most public classes and serialize the public properties of that class, but not private properties though.

We could then simply save the class directly to the disk. However, because our player definition inherits from our common Entity class and the Entity class inherits from ScriptableObject (so we could use it as a common base for all the characters of our game), this means we cannot perform a simple serialization.

If you wish, you could change this implementation, moving all the properties from the Entity class to the Player class and then marking it as [Serializable]; it's your choice. I've kept it this way to show you the considerations needed to also serialize ScriptableObject. This is especially useful when (like we have in this game) ScriptableObjects are attached to our player, in this case, the player's inventory (the inventory items are part of the project, and we attach them to the player).

So, as the data we want to serialize is more complex, the best thing to do is build a separate Save State class, which will model the data we want to save.

By defining a Save model, we can also tailor it to contain more than just one type of data; it could contain other specific save information, such as the time in the world, enemy progress (if the enemy AI is also marching through the world), and the current state of the global economy. There is something you should keep in mind: it is a fairly common practice to create a separate Save model to save data.

Alternatively, it is also a good practice to have several save files, some of which you save very frequently (game/world state) and others you only write when the player asks to (the main save). The implementation comes down to your type of game and your saving/loading needs.

To create a `Save` model based on our player class in the game, create a new script called `PlayerSaveState` in `Assets\Scripts\Classes` and replace its contents with the following code:

```
using System;
using System.Collections.Generic;
using UnityEngine;

[Serializable]
public struct PlayerSaveState {

    public string Name;
    public int Age;
    public string Faction;
    public string Occupation;
    public int Level;
    public int Health;
    public int Strength;
    public int Magic;
    public int Defense;
    public int Speed;
    public int Damage;
    public int Armor;
    public int NoOfAttacks;
    public string Weapon;
    public Vector2 Position;
    public List<string> Inventory;
}
```

This gives us the basic `Save` model for our player. Note that some of the properties are different, specifically the player's inventory. We'll come back to this later.

Now that we have our model, we need a way to convert an active class in the game, such as the player in it to its savable state and back again. Now we can write static methods in the preceding class; however, there is a better way to do this using `Extension` methods (like we did with `WorldExtensions` to convert WorldSpace to ScreenSpace coordinates).

So, add the following code to the very end of the preceding class (you could also just create a new script for this as before, but for now, let's just add it to the same class; this is just so we can see all of the conversion code in one place):

```
public static class PlayerSaveStateExtensions { }
```

Next, we need another extension method to convert a `Player` class into the new `PlayerSaveState` class. So, add the following code to the `PlayerSaveStateExtensions` class:

```
public static PlayerSaveState GetPlayerSaveState(this Player
   input)
{
    PlayerSaveState newSaveState = new PlayerSaveState();
    newSaveState.Age = input.Age;
    newSaveState.Armor = input.Armor;
    newSaveState.Damage = input.Damage;
    newSaveState.Defense = input.Defense;
    newSaveState.Faction = input.Faction;
    newSaveState.Health = input.Health;
    newSaveState.Level = input.Level;
    newSaveState.Magic = input.Magic;
    newSaveState.Name = input.Name;
    newSaveState.NoOfAttacks = input.NoOfAttacks;
    newSaveState.Occupation = input.Occupation;
    newSaveState.Position = input.Position;
    newSaveState.Speed = input.Speed;
    newSaveState.Strength = input.Strength;
    newSaveState.Weapon = input.Weapon;

    newSaveState.Inventory = new List<string>();
    foreach (var item in input.Inventory)
    {
        newSaveState.Inventory.Add(item.name);
    }

    return newSaveState;
}
```

This is fairly simple; we are just copying the properties across. Of course, you only need to copy savable properties. If there are values the player cannot affect, then there is no need to save them. Of note is that for the player's inventory, where we only capture the asset name of each item. This is because we don't need to serialize `InventoryItems` themselves (the game already knows about them), only the ones the player has.

If you have items that can wear out, then you will also need to create a savable state for `InventoryItem` so you can save just the important bits or changeable values.

Instead of creating a `Save` model, you can simply tag each property you want to serialize with a `[SerializeField]` attribute (including private variables) and those that you don't want to serialize with a `[NonSerialized]` attribute.

However, in practice, this can cause trouble or confusion when debugging your saved data. In my personal experience, it's better to define a separate `Save` model so that you always know what you are dealing with.

Then, you simply need another extension method to do the reverse, as follows:

```
public static Player LoadPlayerSaveState(this PlayerSaveState
    input, Player player)
{
    player.Age = input.Age;
    player.Armor = input.Armor;
    player.Damage = input.Damage;
    player.Defense = input.Defense;
    player.Faction = input.Faction;
    player.Health = input.Health;
    player.Level = input.Level;
    player.Magic = input.Magic;
    player.Name = input.Name;
    player.NoOfAttacks = input.NoOfAttacks;
    player.Occupation = input.Occupation;
    player.Position = input.Position;
    player.Speed = input.Speed;
    player.Strength = input.Strength;
    player.Weapon = input.Weapon;
    player.Inventory = new List<InventoryItem>();
    foreach (var item in input.Inventory)
    {
      player.Inventory.Add(
        (InventoryItem)Resources.Load("Inventory Items/" + item));
    }
    return player;
}
```

This is pretty much the same in reverse, except for the inventory. We cannot simply create a new inventory item because each `InventoryItem` is a `ScriptableObject` that we created in our game in the editor.

So to give the player the correct InventoryItems from our game's library, we call Resources.Load to pull the item from our game project, passing the path to InventoryItem and its name (which we saved earlier). Then, we add them to the player's inventory.

Hopefully, you can see why I stuck with the previous model to give you a more in-depth look at how to manage ScriptableObjects with serialization.

# Making your game save and load functions

Using the serialization helper we created earlier and our Save model, we can now implement our Save and Load functions. So, open up the GameState script from Assets\Scripts\Classes and add the following property to mark our save location on the disk:

```
static string saveFilePath =
Application.persistentDataPath + "/playerstate.dat";
```

This just saves us from writing this over and over again. Alternatively, if you are using a slot-saving system, then this will need to be a list that would also need to be saved (probably in a PlayerPrefs property). Next, we will add the Save function as follows:

```
public static void SaveState()
{
    try
    {
        PlayerPrefs.SetString("CurrentLocation",
          Application.loadedLevelName);
        using (var file = File.Create(saveFilePath))
        {
            var playerSerializedState =
              SerializerHelper.Serialise<PlayerSaveState>
                (CurrentPlayer.GetPlayerSaveState());
            file.Write(playerSerializedState,
                0, playerSerializedState.Length);
        }
    }
    catch
    {
        Debug.LogError("Saving data failed");
    }
}
```

So, when we need to save our game, we perform the following actions:

1. Save the player's current location to `PlayerPrefs` as it is very simple data.
2. Create a save file using Unity's `File` function (passing in the path to its location).
3. Create a serialized copy of our player in a new `PlayerSaveState` property.
4. Finally, we write our serialized data to our save file.

 With any operation that writes data outside of your game, always wrap it in a `try`/`catch` block. This will ensure your game doesn't crash when one out of a million bad things could happen.

This is all very simple. Then, to retrieve the saved data from the disk, first we'll add a little helper function to tell us whether a save file already exists, which we can also use elsewhere in the game, as follows:

```
public static bool SaveAvailable
{
    get { return File.Exists(saveFilePath); }
}
```

This just uses another function of the `File` class to test the existence of a file. Now, we can add the `Load` method as follows:

```
public static void LoadState(Action LoadComplete)
{
    try
    {
        if (SaveAvailable)
        {
            //Get the file
            using (var stream = File.Open(saveFilePath,
                FileMode.Open))
            {
                var LoadedPlayer =
                    SerializerHelper.DeSerialise<PlayerSaveState>
                        (stream);
                CurrentPlayer =
                    LoadedPlayer.LoadPlayerSaveState(currentPlayer);
            }
        }
    }
```

```
   catch
   {
       Debug.LogError("Loading data failed, file is corrupt");
   }
   LoadComplete();
}
```

Again, this is just the reverse of saving the file with one difference: you have to test whether the save file exists first, else it will result in an error in the worst way possible.

You should note that we do not return the saved data directly back to the calling function; instead, we use a delegate to tell the caller when it is finished. The reason for this is simple: accessing the disk is slow. So, we need to ensure we have finished loading all of our data before we continue with our game, which is obviously very important. You can, if you want, also do this with the Save function if you wish as well.

# Testing your Save and Load functions

As a simple test for our saving and loading functions, we can add a basic menu to our game. So, create a new scene named MainMenu in Assets\Scenes and a new script called MainMenu in Assets\Scripts and replace its contents with the following code:

```
using UnityEngine;

[ExecuteInEditMode]
public class MainMenu : MonoBehaviour {

    bool saveAvailable;
    void Start()
    {
        saveAvailable = GameState.SaveAvailable;
    }
}
```

Here, we simply start by using a variable to see whether we have a saved file when the menu is loaded.

Then, we just add an OnGUI method as follows:

```
void OnGUI () {

GUILayout.BeginArea(new Rect((Screen.width / 2) -
    100,(Screen.height / 2) - 100, 200,200 ));
```

```
if(GUILayout.Button("New Game"))
{
  NavigationManager.NavigateTo("Home");
}
GUILayout.Space(50);
if (saveAvailable)
{
  if (GUILayout.Button("Load Game"))
  {
    GameState.LoadState(() =>
    {
      var lastLocation = PlayerPrefs.GetString(
        "CurrentLocation", "Home");
        NavigationManager.NavigateTo(lastLocation);
    });
  }
}
GUILayout.EndArea();
}
```

This is a very simple menu with two buttons. The first uses the NavigationManager script to load the Home scene, and the other only displays whether there is a load available and then performs the following operations:

1. Loads the current state of the game.

2. Once the Load delegate is complete, it also retrieves the player's last location from PlayerPrefs.

3. Then, it navigates to the last scene the player was in.

Attach the script to the camera, save the scene, and add it to the **Build** settings, and we are almost set.

The last thing to do is ensure that we save the game. You could do this by implementing it via a pause menu in the game, but for simplicity, I just added it to the NavigationManager script to save the game whenever the player moves from scene to scene.

So, open up the NavigationManager script and add GameState.SaveState() before the call to FadeInOutManager in both the NavigateTo and GoBack methods.

# Backing up to the Web

An alternative to the basic saving of data to a disk, a lot of games now (especially if they are targeting multiple platforms) support a web backend to store a player's data. It doesn't need to be heavy; just use a player name/ID key and store the serialized data.

The benefit of this approach is that the player can continue playing on any device, regardless of which device they were last playing on.

*Halo Spartan Assault* implemented this feature and its sales skyrocketed because players on Windows Phones could switch to playing on their desktop or Xbox when they got home or vice versa. A big selling point!

Implementing this approach depends on the backend service you use for your data; whether you roll your own or use Azure MWS, Amazon Web Services, or Parse, which all have plugins that work for Unity3D.

The simplest approach is to use the serialization methods described previously and post your data to a backend web service using the Unity WWW class. As a full example would be too complex to demonstrate, what follows are just some code snippets of the available Unity functions.

Granted you will have to write your web service on a server to accept this data, which is out of scope of this book, but if you search on www.codeproject.com or stackoverflow.com, you will find many good examples of such implementations.

You could post the serialized data direct to a service using a function similar to the following code (as an example only):

```
void UploadSaveData1()
{
   string url = "http://mybackendserver.com/Upload.php";
   var playerSerializedState =
     SerializerHelper.Serialise<PlayerSaveState>
   (CurrentPlayer.GetPlayerSaveState());
   WWW www = new WWW(url, playerSerializedState);

   StartCoroutine(WaitForRequest(www));
}
```

```
IEnumerator WaitForRequest(WWW www)
{
  yield return www;

  //check for errors
  if (www.error == null)
  {
    Debug.Log("Successful: " + www.text);
  }
  else
  {
    Debug.Log("Error: " + www.error);
  }
}
```

This simply takes the byte array of the serialized saved data and posts it to your server.

Alternatively, you can post data to the server as a form (more common):

```
void WebPost2()
{
  string url = "http://mybackendserver.com/Upload.php";
  var playerSerializedState =
    SerializerHelper.Serialise<PlayerSaveState>
  (CurrentPlayer.GetPlayerSaveState());
  var data = Convert.ToBase64String(playerSerializedState);

  WWWForm saveForm = new WWWForm();
  saveForm.AddField("saveData", data);
  WWW www = new WWW(url, saveForm);

  StartCoroutine(WaitForRequest(www));
}
```

This makes a traditional HTTP post with parameters in the body of the request.

Getting the data from the server is much simpler. To do so, write a simple coroutine to download the data that you can call when it's needed:

```
IEnumerator GetSavedDataFromWWW()
{
  string url = "http://mybackendserver.com/DownloadSaveData.php";
  WWW www = new WWW(url);
  yield return www;

  if (www.error == null)
  {
    var restoredData = DeserializePlayerState(www.bytes);
  }
  else
  {
    Debug.LogError("Error: " + www.error);
  }
}
```

Note that the examples are over-simplified to show you how the WWW class works.

For more information about the WWW class, see the Unity scripting reference guide at https://docs.unity3d.com/Documentation/ScriptReference/WWW.html.

If you would rather not roll your services, you can use backends such as Azure for which some budding teams have put together plugins for Unity3D. Check them out at http://www.bitrave.com/azure-mobile-services-for-unity-3d/.

There is even a promising Unity implementation that connects to Google Services as well at https://github.com/kimsama/Unity-GoogleData.

I've not seen any implementation for AWS as yet, but keep an eye out for this or use the previous examples as a primer to start your own; if you do see any, please share!

# Going further

If you are of the adventurous sort, try expanding your project to add the following features:

- Either add the property drawers or even a complete custom editor for the dialogues in the conversation system covered in *Chapter 5, NPCs and Interactions*.

- Extend the Enemy classes in *Chapter 9, Getting Ready to Fight*, to better configure them in the editor.

- Build your menus either in a single scene or multiple ones. Manage the transition between each menu state/view.

- Take one of your own game ideas and plan the flow of the game from end to end using a Mindmap tool. Go beyond just the menu and sketch out the entire game.

# Summary

As we look to make best use of the editor, we look to extend and expand on the default views that Unity gives us.

Through the course of this chapter, we looked at all of the capabilities that Unity gives us to make best use of these features. With these tools in hand, we can make building our games a lot easier and customize Unity to fit our game (rather than the other way a round). The editor is there to help us build our game, so why not improve it.

Several developers graciously share their editor scripts and work in open source libraries, so be sure to look around; you don't need to start from scratch.

We also looked into what is involved in finishing and packaging the game itself with menus and important touch points if you want to stand out.

We covered editor customization, property drawers, custom editors, editor windows, and Gizmos. We also covered architecting the game package with screens and menus and working with saving and loading data.

In the next chapter, we look at packaging the game on to several platforms and extending our game out on to the platform itself and providing platform-specific features either in the game or beyond.

# 12
# Deployment and Beyond

Building a game is one thing, and showing it to your friends and family is another. However, eventually, you are going to want to ship and sell your game in one of the most challenging markets, games!

Your title has to shine—it has to enable features that other titles don't have to stand out and be noticed.

In this chapter, we will take a deep dive into what it takes to try and take advantage of native platform features and make them available to your game that is running in Unity3D. This could be for notifications support, active or live tiles, location capabilities, or even in-app purchasing (Unity doesn't support in-app purchases currently, and it only supports full purchase).

The following topics will be covered in this chapter:

- Getting to Unity from a native platform
- Giving Unity access to a native platform
- Plugins and what they offer, including building your own
- Building your asset projects (and making a fortune on the asset store)
- Hints and tips for marketing and shipping

# Handling platform differences

Unity does a lot for developers to abstract us from the many platforms you can deploy to. Most of the common functions, such as memory management, audio, controller inputs, purchasing, and so on, are all implemented with a single generic interface with Unity3D. This means you do not need to write a separate code to play an audio file, or draw to the screen for each and every device or platform that you want to support and deploy to. It really is a big time saver (ask anyone who has written their own engine just how much fun they had doing everything multiple times for each platform).

Unity does a lot, but it doesn't do everything. For the following fringe areas, you will have to do the leg work to get these features implemented:

- Social integration (Facebook and so on)
- In-app purchasing
- Alternate physics or networking implementations

The list goes on. In a lot of cases, there are already pre-made assets on the Unity store that have done the hard work to build these implementations. A fair few, you will note, do not support all platforms. In these cases, it will get you most of the way, but you will either have to wait for them to support platform X or write it yourself.

In all cases, assets need to integrate tightly with the underlying platform. They have made use of the interoperability features available in Unity, which this chapter will go through in detail, what each asset has to offer, and what it brings to the table. Some are simple to perform, others not so much. Also, in some cases, you will have to work with the Unity platform build system to push your changes onto the platform (though not absolutely necessary, this will save you from having to repeat every build or if you want to create your assets). The following diagram shows the layout of how Unity works with the platforms it supports:

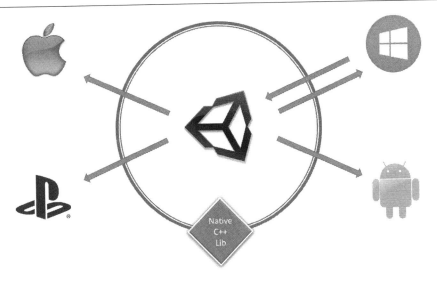

In general, the patterns you need to support are as follows:

- Using different code paths with directives
- Accessing the native platform from Unity
- Calling the platforms from Unity
- Implementing reusable libraries that are natively compiled to work on all platforms

# Preprocessor directives

When you want the code to run in a particular way on one platform and in a different way on another, you can use the precompiler directives to tell Unity to pick one section of code over another (when it builds the project), or to simply ignore the sections of the code. This is also true for the editor, which Unity considers a platform, just like any other. So, we can have the code to run and deploy in the editor, but restrict its execution when it's deployed to another platform. You could say the special editor classes do this, but you may also want to do this with any other code.

The preprocessor directives (or the platform defines) that Unity recognizes are listed in the following table:

| Statement | Description |
|---|---|
| UNITY_EDITOR | This code will run only in the editor, not on a platform |
| UNITY_EDITOR_WIN | This code specifically targets the editor on Windows (if you have the code that runs differently than on a Mac) |
| UNITY_EDITOR_OSX | This code specifically targets the editor on Mac (if you have the code that runs differently than on a PC) |
| UNITY_STANDALONE | This code targets the desktop platforms (Windows/Mac/Linux) |
| UNITY_STANDALONE_OSX | This code targets Mac OS X only (this includes Universal, PPC, and Intel architectures) |
| UNITY_DASHBOARD_WIDGET | This code targets the Mac OS X dashboard widget deployments |
| UNITY_STANDALONE_WIN | This code targets the Windows desktop only (excluding Windows 8) |
| UNITY_STANDALONE_LINUX | This code targets the Linux desktop clients only |
| UNITY_WEBPLAYER | This code targets the Web players |
| UNITY_WII | This code targets the Wii platform only |
| UNITY_IPHONE | This code targets the iPhone platform only |
| UNITY_ANDROID | This code targets the Android platform only |
| UNITY_PS3 | This code targets the PlayStation 3 platform only |
| UNITY_XBOX360 | This code targets the Xbox 360 platform only |
| UNITY_FLASH | This code targets the Adobe Flash platform only |
| UNITY_BLACKBERRY | This code targets the BlackBerry10 platform only |
| UNITY_WP8 | This code targets the Windows Phone 8 platform only |
| UNITY_WP_8_1 | This code targets the Windows Phone 8.1 app or Universal projects on Windows Phone 8 |
| UNITY_METRO / NETFX_CORE | This code targets the Windows Store 8.0, Windows Store 8.1, and Universal 8.1 apps |
| UNITY_METRO_8_0 | This code targets the Windows 8.0 platform only |
| UNITY_METRO_8_1 | This code targets the Windows 8.1 apps or Universal projects on Windows 8.1 |
| UNITY_WINRT | This code targets all the RT-based platforms, including Windows Phone and Windows 8, regardless of the version |

| Statement | Description |
|---|---|
| UNITY_WINRT_8_0 | This code targets all the RT-based platforms, including Windows Phone 8.0 and Windows 8.0 |
| UNITY_WINRT_8_1 | This code targets all the RT-based platforms, including Windows Phone 8.1, Windows 8.1, and the Universal apps |

> It's worth noting that you are not limited to just the Unity preprocessor directives. You can use Visual Studio's directives or even create your own by adding the following class to the top of your #define MyDirective class (no semicolon). Then, you can block out sections of your code by enabling or disabling this line. If a directive does not exist, it will always be skipped.

To use these directives, we will simply declare them with an #if statement to surround the code we want to target. For example, if you recall in *Chapter 11, Onward Wary Traveler*, we learned that File classes don't work for Windows 8 because the OS does not have the File class or more specifically, the System.IO class (if you build the project for Windows 8 currently, you will get lots of such errors). So, to be able to load the files for Windows 8, you need to use different code.

# Updating the save system for another platform

To walk through the use of preprocessor directives, let's handle one such platform that needs some attention, that is, Windows 8. In Unity's implementation on Windows 8 (due to its asynchronous way of working), they have added some specialized classes because the default implementations of these classes are not available on Windows 8 (in this case, the File class). On Windows 8, you need to use the UnityEngine. Windows.File class instead of the normal UnityEngine.File class.

So, open up the GameState script and update the following code by adding the highlighted snippet:

```
public static void SaveState()
{
  try
  {
    PlayerPrefs.SetString("CurrentLocation",
      Application.loadedLevelName);
    var playerSerializedState =
      SerializerHelper.Serialise<PlayerSaveState>
```

```
(CurrentPlayer.GetPlayerSaveState());
#if UNITY_METRO
UnityEngine.Windows.File.WriteAllBytes(saveFilePath,
  playerSerializedState);
#else
using (var file = File.Create(saveFilePath))
{
  file.Write(playerSerializedState, 0,
    playerSerializedState.Length);
}
#endif
  }
  catch
  {
    Debug.LogError("Saving data failed");
  }
}
```

In the preceding code, we have added a preprocessor directive for the UNITY_METRO target (and moved up the playerSerializedState variable as it can be used by all platforms).

Now when you build for Windows 8, it will use the first block of code. For all other platforms, it will use the second block.

We have to perform something similar for the LoadState class as follows:

```
public static void LoadState(Action LoadComplete)
{
  PlayerSaveState LoadedPlayer;
  try
  {
    if (SaveAvailable)
    {
      #if UNITY_METRO
      var playerSerializedState =
        UnityEngine.Windows.File.ReadAllBytes(saveFilePath);
      LoadedPlayer = SerializerHelper.DeSerialise<PlayerSaveState>
      (playerSerializedState);
      #else
      //Get the file
      using (var stream = File.Open(saveFilePath,
        FileMode.Open))
      {
```

```
            LoadedPlayer =
               SerializerHelper.DeSerialise<PlayerSaveState>
               (stream);
         }
      #endif
         CurrentPlayer =
            LoadedPlayer.LoadPlayerSaveState(CurrentPlayer);
         }
      }
   catch
   {
   Debug.LogError("Loading data failed, file is corrupt");
   }
   LoadComplete();
}
```

Additionally, since the `File` class on Windows 8 only returns a byte array (`byte[]`), we need an additional `deserialize` function to work with the byte arrays instead of a stream. So, open the `SerializationHelper` script and add the following method:

```
public static T DeSerialise<T>(byte[] input)
{
   T output = default(T);
   //Create an XML formatter
   var serializer = new XmlSerializer(typeof(T));
   try
   {
      //Create an in-memory stream with the serialsed data in it
      using (var stream = new MemoryStream(input))
      {
         //Deserialize the data from the stream
         output = (T)serializer.Deserialize(stream);
      }
   }
   catch { }

   //Return the deserialized output
   return output;
}
```

 If you want to keep things simple, you can also convert the `load` function to always pass a byte array for all platforms, and get rid of the first deserialization method.

Finally, one last fix. If you build for Windows 8 now, you will still have one error that remains in the `SerializationHelper` script. This is because the implementation of the `MemoryStream` class on Windows 8 doesn't have a `GetStream` method. Now, you can use another preprocessor directive and use a different implementation for Windows 8. However, in this case, if you simply switch to using the `ToArray()` method, it'll give you the result you want.

 This may not always be the case! If you need to encode data for text or images, you may find that using `ToArray` doesn't fit because it can output the data differently, and you may potentially lose some data in certain formats. Just test and check whether it still behaves as you require!

# Build note

Currently, there have been a few inconsistencies among the builds of Unity. In some builds, the project works fine; in others, it crashes when you try to use the singleton classes.

In testing, it seems as though the execution order of singletons is altered, and they are actually destroyed after they are created. This mostly seems to affect the .NET-based builds.

If this happens, you will need to compensate with a minor update to the singleton script in `Assets\Scripts\Classes` and update the `OnDestroy` method with the following code:

```
public void OnDestroy()
{
  #if !UNITY_METRO
  applicationIsQuitting = true;
  #endif
}
```

By specifying `!UNITY_METRO`, we are stating that this code should be run on all platforms except Windows 8 (in the last tested build 4.5.2, Windows phone was unaffected). If you find this occurring on other platforms, add them to the ignore list. Consider the following instance:

```
#if !UNITY_METRO && !UNITY_ANDROID
```

This process doesn't actually destroy the singleton script as it is recreated each time it is used (if it has already been destroyed). However, this flag is there to ensure that it is not recreated when the application is actually shutting down.

# Getting access to Unity

The first and simplest bridge between the platforms is to allow access to your Unity game from a native platform. As you can see in the following diagram, the first challenge is to enable a platform to talk to your Unity package:

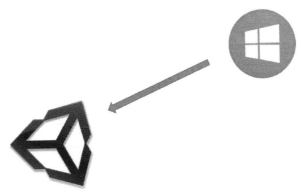

On the .NET platforms such as Windows and Windows phone, the following two patterns are used to access the game embedded within the Unity player directly from the host platform:

- The UnityEngine namespace from the Unity player
- The static classes in your Unity project

## Accessing the UnityEngine namespace

Once you have built a project for the .NET platforms, you have a ready-to-run solution.

The player that deploys with the project also gives you indirect access to all the components and game objects within your scenes through the UnityEngine namespace.

For the game objects, you can simply query with the GameObject.Find method, as shown in the following code example:

```
var _cube = UnityEngine.GameObject.Find("Cube");
```

The preceding code will give you a game object that you can manipulate however you wish to, as if you were in Unity itself.

Alternatively, if you want to access scripts or non-standard content, you will need to cast the objects you search for to use them properly. Refer to the following example:

```
var mainScript = (MainScript)
    UnityEngine.GameObject.FindObjectOfType(typeof(MainScript));
```

This will give you a reference to an instance of a class of the `MainScript` type in your current scene.

> All the functions are not scene aware. So, if you have to access the items in specific scenes, you will need to track that manually through a static property or through events (refer to the next section).
>
> Additionally, if your script is used on several objects in the scene, be sure to perform the search from an instance of an object.

# The static classes

The second method to access your Unity project from .NET platforms (such as Windows) is to expose specific variables outside the confines of your game or app.

To do this, declare a static variable within a class in your project, as shown in the following example:

```
public class MyExternalCass : MonoBehaviour
{
  public static bool TurnOnAds;
}
```

Then, from your project, once you have built it, you can access this variable using the following code:

```
MyExternalClass.TurnOnAds = false;
```

You will then have the logic in your game to make use of these variables.

> It is highly recommended that you use classes that are single scripts to expose variables in this fashion. Do not use this method on the reusable classes.

# Access to the platform

If you reverse the previous implementation, there are cases where you need to access a specific behavior on the native platform itself.

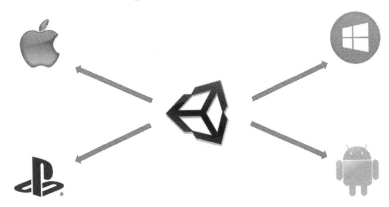

If you need a bit more interactivity from your Unity project, and you wish to enable Unity to communicate directly to the platform, then the following are the two common methods to achieve this:

- Static events (.NET platforms only)
- Plugins

## Static events in your Unity project

We covered events back in *Chapter 5, NPCs and Interactions*, to enable a loose coupling between an action and a dependency. We can reuse events to bridge the gap between Unity and the .NET platforms such as Windows and Windows Phone.

We will begin by defining a `static` event in Unity, which is intended to indicate an action the project needs the native platform to enact:

```
public static EventHandler PurchaseRequested;
public static void Purchase(string productID)
{
  if (PurchaseRequested != null)
  {
    PurchaseRequested(productID, null);
  }
}
```

The previous code sets up a delegate that can be used to enact an in-app purchase on the native platform. When requested in code, it tells whatever object is listening that the user wishes to purchase an item in the game.

Then, in the platform project, you will hook up to the delegate to perform the action when the event is raised, for example, on Windows Phone to complete a purchase, you would need to use the following code:

```
private void Unity_Loaded()
{
   //Hook up the IAP request to platform
   InAppPurchase.PurchaseRequested += PurchaseRequested;
}
private void PurchaseRequested(object sender, EventArgs e)
{
   var ProductId = (string)sender;
   //Purchase requests must be done on UI thread so use dispatcher
   Dispatcher.BeginInvoke(() => PurchaseItem(ProductId));
}

private async void PurchaseItem(string productID)
{
   //Do stuff to purchase the item from the store
}
```

The code hooks up to the previous PurchaseRequested event in the InAppPurchase class, and when a purchase is requested, it is routed to the UI thread and the item is purchased.

 Each platform handles in-app purchase differently, or you could choose to use a third-party in-app solution such as Lotaris. The final implementation is up to you.

The example is kept simple just to demonstrate one method for your Unity project to communicate with the platform solution.

# Embedding platform DLLs

The only other method to enable the platform features in your Unity project is to create your platform class library and embed that library in your project.

To enable this, Unity has even more special folders in the `Assets` folders. The root folder of this structure is the `Plugins` folder, shown as follows:

- `Plugins` (editor plugins)
- `Plugins\x86` (Pro only)
- `Plugins\x86_64` (Pro only)
- `Plugins\Android`
- `Plugins\iOS`
- `Plugins\BlackBerry`
- `Plugins\WP8`
- `Plugins\Metro`

> On the mobile platforms, `Plugins` are supported in the free version.
>
> You will need Unity Pro to build plugins for desktop systems (targeted at x86/x64/any CPU).
>
> Plugins are not supported on the current web player for security reasons; there's no information yet whether this will also be true for WebGL in U5.

To enable your plugin to work for each platform, you will need to install it in each of the previous folders per platform.

However, on the .NET platforms, you also need an attritional editor plugin (explained in detail in the next section) that provides the basic interface for your plugin due to the way .NET plugins are compiled.

## The editor plugin (.NET only)

The editor plugin is just a shell or interface for how your plugin will operate. Unity will use this while in the editor for testing/editing purposes.

The mock interface needs to resemble what your real plugin interface will look like in order for other scripts and code to be able to access the real plugin on each platform.

For the DLL that is going to be placed in `Assets\Plugins`, it must be a .NET 3.5 Framework class library. Just be sure to select this framework while creating the editor Plugin DLL.

As a simple example, create a new `Class Library` project in your code editor (Visual Studio or MonoDevelop), and then create a new C# class (usually, there is a default `Class1.cs` class created with the class library). You can then define a plugin interface in the new class for the editor that looks like the following code:

```
namespace MyAwesomePlugin
{
  public class MyPluginClass
  {
    public static string GetPlatform
    {
      get
      {
        return "This is the Editor";
      }
    }
  }
}
```

This simple class just exposes a static string to return the name of the platform.

## The platform plugin

For the platform plugin, we will create another Class Library, which targets the level of framework required by the target platform. For example, a Windows 8 (store app) class library for the Windows 8.0 platform.

Then, create a new class (or reuse the default class) and enter the following code:

```
namespace MyAwesomePlugin
{
  public class MyPluginClass
  {
    public static string GetPlatform
    {
      get
      {
```

```
            return "Welcome to Windows 8";
        }
    }
  }
}
```

As you can see, it has the same namespace, same class name, and same property as our editor class, but now the implementation has changed.

 This is just a very simple example; the real platform implementation could have any platform-specific code within it, as it will be executed against the platform when deployed.

## Accessing the plugin

So, we have our editor (mock) and platform (Windows 8) plugins defined; you just need to copy them to your Unity project. Now, perform the following steps:

1. Copy the DLL from the Windows 8 class library to `Assets\Plugins\Metro`.

2. Copy the DLL from the editor class library in `Assets\Plugins` (if required — .NET only).

 Although not critical, it's best to name the two DLLs and any others you create for other platforms using the same DLL name. This just makes it easier to manage later if you need to add more to the plugin.

With your DLLs now in your project, you can access the plugin from anywhere in your Unity project by calling the following code:

```
string WhatsMyPlatform =
    MyAwesomePlugin.MyPluginClass.GetPlatform;
```

When you run the project from the editor, this will return in the following manner:

**This is the Editor**

However, when you run this on an actual Windows 8 machine, this will return in the following manner:

**Welcome to Windows 8**

# Native plugins (Pro only)

The last integration approach is the one that takes the most effort but can have the most benefit—it also has the advantage of being the most reusable.

If you are running the Pro version of Unity, you can import the native C++ DLLs and their corresponding functionalities into Unity3D. Generally, this is used to access a third-party function library such as Physics and Math or Physics. Some assets on the **Asset** store also ship with native plugins to enable them to be as fast as possible (and as a by-product, they ensure that you cannot copy their code from a compiled library):

The plugin, once created, should be placed in the `Plugins` folder mentioned previously, and then called from the code as follows:

```
[DllImport ("PluginName")]
private static extern float FooPluginFunction ();
```

This effectively gives you a pointer to the code that will run outside of Unity3D. By calling the previous function, Unity interprets this and passes it on to the external library to process and return from.

The advantage of using the native plugins is mainly speed. You get direct access to a native platform and all the performance boosts it provides. It is by far the most complicated way to enable such features, and deciding on using it would simply come down to if you need that level of power.

In some cases, native plugins are the only way to access the underlying features of a platform, especially if it is a feature that Unity itself does not support.

Additionally, native plugins can be created to be used on all platforms so long as they are not using platform-specific features; in which case, you would still need one plugin per platform.

One very cool feature with native plugins is that you can even interact with Unity3D's own rendering engine, just in case you feel adventurous and want to spice it up a bit. For more details on this, check out the Unity scripting guide at `http://docs.unity3d.com/Documentation/Manual/NativePluginInterface.html`.

For more information about the native plugins, refer to the Unity scripting reference guide at `http://docs.unity3d.com/Documentation/Manual/Plugins.html`.

# Pushing code from Unity3D

Unity provides several post-processing capabilities that allow you to both intercept and override and also add your own processing to just about anything in the Asset pipeline, anything from assets, scripts, and even the build process itself.

## Processing assets

Post- or pre-processing of assets is very useful if you have custom-made or complex assets that need additional work once they are imported in Unity. In most cases, this is not needed as Unity does a lot of work for you by processing assets already.

If you do create any asset-processing scripts, remember they need to be placed in `Assets\Editor`.

We won't go into too much detail here as it is a very large area; this section is mainly to highlight its existence for those who were not aware. It is well-worth reading and checking up on.

For more information about asset processing, refer to the Unity scripting reference guide at `https://docs.unity3d.com/Documentation/ScriptReference/AssetPostprocessor.html`.

For a nice and clean example of an asset processor, see the post on using Unity to make a simple FBX model post processor at `http://forum.unity3d.com/threads/53179-Simple-AssetPostprocessor-example`.

# Processing the build

A more interesting area for study, especially if you are working with many platforms and find yourself doing repetitive tasks on each platform (or when you create your Unity assets and need to copy files to a platform to work), is the ability to extend Unity3D's own project build process.

Simply create a normal class script in `Asset\Editor`, and then create your build action function with the `[PostProcessBuild]` attribute and the build function signature, as follows:

```
using UnityEngine;
using UnityEditor;
using UnityEditor.Callbacks;

public class MyBuildPostprocessor
{
  [PostProcessBuild]
  public static void OnPostprocessBuild(BuildTarget target, string
    pathToBuiltProject)
  { }
}
```

The attributes from the build processing give you the following information:

- `BuildTarget`: This tells you which platform is currently being built using the `BuildTarget` enumeration.

- `Path`: This gives you the output path where the build project is being written. This is useful if you want to copy additional files to it.

You can also control the order in which this function is processed by adding parameters to the `[PostProcessBuild]` attribute as follows:

```
[PostProcessBuild(10)]
public static void OnPostprocessBuild(BuildTarget target,
  string pathToBuiltProject)
{ }
```

The order number is a definition of priority: the higher the number, the lower the priority. By default, all scripts have a priority of 1. Scripts with lower numbers are executed first (even negative numbers such as -10 are allowed for ultimate priority), whereas scripts with higher numbers are executed last.

This is especially useful if you want to have several actions execute on a successful build and want to control the order in which they are executed.

> You can also copy code files directly to the target solution, if you wish, from your Unity project. If you do not want those files to be read or executed by Unity, then simply suffix them with `.ignore`, and Unity will ignore them. Just remember to rename them when copying them to a platform.
>
> For example:
>
> `MyPlatformClassFile.cs.ignore`

For more information about build processing, see the Unity scripting reference guide at `http://docs.unity3d.com/412/Documentation/ScriptReference/PostProcessBuildAttribute.html`.

> For a very full-featured example of highly customized build processing, check out the AdRotator Unity plugin, which is open source, on GitHub at:
>
> `https://github.com/Adrotator/AdrotatorV2/tree/master/AdRotatorUnityPackage`
>
> Just check in the `AdRotatorUnitySDK.Assets\Editor\AdRotatorPostBuild.cs` script.

# Building your assets

What may seem daunting is actually one of the simplest tasks to perform in Unity because it is just a two-click job.

If you recall in *Chapter 2, Character Building,* I said you will create a package that contains all the default folders you can use for any project; so, let's do that.

First, create a new project (just because it's best to start from scratch) and then add in whatever folders, assets, scripts, and so on that you need in your asset package. In this case, just all the folders we will commonly use in any Unity project are shown here:

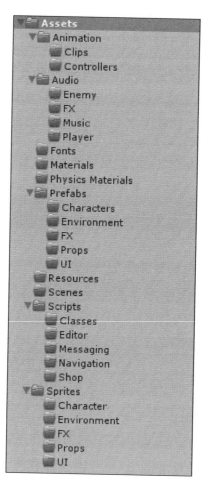

With that in place, just navigate to **Assets | Export Package** from the Unity editor menu, and you will be presented with the following window:

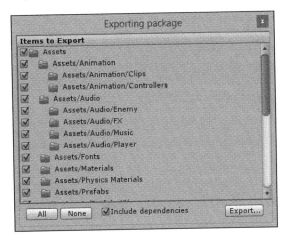

Here, you can select all the assets currently in your project that you want bundled up in your own reusable Unity asset package. Once you are happy with your selection, just click on **Export...**. Then, Unity will simply ask where you want your package to be created:

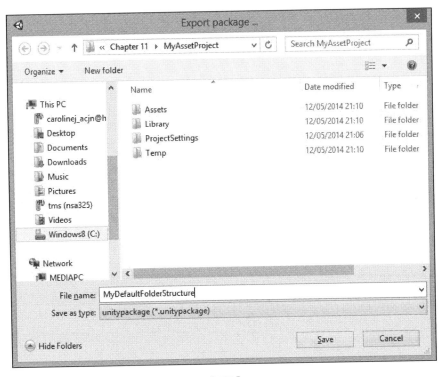

There you have it! Once saved, you will simply have your new asset package that you can reuse on every project or even publish to the asset store and make millions (well probably not if it's just a bunch of folders, you might need a bit more than that). This package can be named as follows:

```
MyDefaultFolderStructure.unitypackage
```

# Packaging gotchas

You have your game running fine in the editor, and you finally come to start testing it on a platform. Life is good and surely you must be ready to deploy; sadly, this is just the point where your next journey begins.

Actually, shipping your title brings to light a whole raft of new challenges. What follows is a list of tips, tricks, and gotchas I've encountered while working with many different teams and events:

### Just because it runs in the editor DOES NOT mean it will run on a platform

I've come across too many teams that finish their game in the editor without even trying to run it on at least one target platform. This can cause serious rework later on as you may find that the code will simply not run on some platforms.

Another issue that can sometimes rear its head is when you have written code that depends on the editor but you have not placed it in the Editor folder. When you run it in the editor, it will work fine, but on a platform it will either crash or give you a spurious message (worse on some platforms than others.)

If you are targeting the Web, then beware of the limitations of deploying to that platform.

The best advice is to build to a platform at regular intervals, and make sure that it actually compiles and will deploy to a device.

### Just because it works for one platform DOES NOT mean it will work for all

Unity obviously supports many different platforms, and each has its own peculiarities. If you mean to target multiple platforms, always check periodically whether you can build and deploy to the various platforms. It doesn't have to be too often, just find the right balance for you. See whether you can automate it through the Unity command-line tools.

What is often missed is how each platform behaves; Windows/Windows Phone/Windows 8 all run on the NET platform directly; however, iOS/Android/Mac/BlackBerry all run using the Mono framework (which is an interpretation of .NET for those platforms). They are both different in their own ways and handle similar situations differently. Don't assume just because it works for one, it will work for all. This is true for both JavaScript and C#.

As stated already, the Web is just different from everything else.

### For maximum exposure, try to focus on the lowest common denominator

It's always attractive to build to the highest resolution and target really high spec'd machines; however, this is going to really limit your target audience.

When working with mobile projects, it is better to test and target minimum specifications or devices, and make it run acceptably on that device. Any higher spec device, and it will just fly.

If you are feeling adventurous, then build your game to switch on higher spec features/assets when a high spec machine is detected. However, this will also potentially increase the size of your final download, which may also put your game out of budget for low spec devices.

It is a hard challenge and requires a different approach to tackle for each game you make, so think hard about it.

A last resort (which most developers shy away from) is to build two versions (a PRO HD version and a Basic low res version). There is no one right answer, so just pick a path that fits your game, budget, and time.

### Assets from the store can be your savior; they can also be your downfall

Be aware of what assets you are downloading in the scope of your title; check what platforms it supports and make sure it's maintained.

There have been quite a few horror stories about not being able to move to platform X because the plugins won't even compile, and finding an alternative is very difficult because of the particular plugin that is integrated in a project.

It all comes down to balance—ask why you are using a certain asset, make sure you understand why you are using it, and assess its long term fit before committing yourself to it.

### Beware of the platform requirements

Certain platforms have very specific requirements when it comes to games and/ or apps. Some have limits on project sizes, others (such as Windows Phone) have certain operating restrictions (Windows Phone has a hardware Back button, which must always "go back" for example).

Others have restricted device capabilities or require enforced policies to be in place before you can target certain markets.

In the end, it comes down to assessing your titles fit for a certain device/market or operating system, and making plans before you go all-in to adopt it. Make a plan, understand what you are getting into, and then move forward.

# Marketing your game

If you are the adventurous sort, try expanding your project to add the following features:

- Start a developer blog (go wild)
- Build an end-to-end story for a title you have been dreaming to make
- Make your dream a reality and ship a game

# Summary

Rounding out our last technical chapter, we have been through an interesting ride to finally complete and get your project out there. We also dug deeper into how Unity can interact with the platforms you deploy to, above all when involving the platform, and have a plan on how you will implement that same feature on all the platforms you want to deploy to, or else users will notice that some versions (yes, quite a few have multiple) lack more than others.

So, we covered extending your Unity project onto the platform, plugins and their extensions, building your very own reusable assets, and tips and tricks for marketing your title.

Something you can try when you engage with a platform is to look at engaging across platforms, building titles that work cooperatively, enabling either a true multiplatform, multiplayer experience, or even building cooperative apps/games (where the phone version of a game can act as a second screen for your tablet/console version), as this is where dreams truly become alive!

# Additional Resources

In the previous chapters, you worked toward building a 2D RPG game. We've covered lots of tips and tricks with a lot of scripts and a couple of assets to boot. The Unity community, however, is very helpful, and there are a lot more resources available, not just the ones on the asset store.

In this appendix, I'll highlight a lot of exciting places to go to and get more assets for your title, scripts, and other noteworthy tutorials that will help you grow on your journey through Unity.

We will cover the following topics:

- Scripting resources
- Useful assets
- Sources of art and SFX
- Highlights of the Web

## Scripting resources

Scripting in Unity is a large part of what goes into making a game. As this title has shown, there are some good ways to script and some not so good ones. In this section, you will find several resources that extend what has already been shown and offer you more places to look and learn from.

## Extending the editor

The editor is by far the most underutilized feature of Unity, partly because while building your game, you focus on what goes into it, and partly because the documents surrounding the editor are quite sparse.

However, many a brave soul has ventured into this domain and extracted the secret sauce. I've shown you the basics, so continue on to more advance uses of this hidden tool by going through the following links:

- An interesting article by Mana Break walks through the process of transforming the Unity editor into your own level-creation system, which is well worth a read. It is available at `http://mana-break.blogspot.co.uk/2013/12/howto-use-unity3d-as-level-editor-for.html`.

- A good friend of mine, Jamie Hales (of Pixelballon), gave a talk in the UK on extending the editor, and he was kind enough to share it. He provided a lot of information to the audience about interesting tricks to extend the editor (even adding context menus). You can view the deck for the presentation and the associated code at the following links:
    - `http://t.co/VaiQjjFLHg` (PowerPoint)
    - `https://t.co/AiNj2XVSVm` (sample code)

- Catlike Coding has an awesome array of Unity articles with very interesting results. I checked out the rest of the articles, but there was one in particular that highlighted some great use of editor features for asset editing in the scene. Visit `http://catlikecoding.com/unity/tutorials/editor/star/` to read more about this article.

# Even more AI

AI is a tricky subject at best; the following are a few extra tips and tricks for Unity on how to build on the AI elements in this title:

- There is a great article on the use of NavMesh in Unity, valid for both 2D and 3D, at `http://blackwindgames.com/blog/pathfinding-and-local-avoidance-for-rts-rpg-game-with-unity/`.

- `UnityGems.com` is a wealth of content for Unity developers, like the beginner's tutorial to develop a character AI, which is available at `http://unitygems.com/basic-ai-character/`.

- AI Gamedev is one of the biggest sites for AI in game development. Its resources reach far and wide. Some content is free, but for most, there is a subscription fee. You can visit `http://aigamedev.com/` for more information.

# Procedural generation

Procedural generation is a passion of mine; I wished there had been enough pages to do justice to it in this title. If you are looking to get into this fascinating subject, the following are some really handy and practical places to look:

- First and foremost is the Procedural Content Generation Wiki, not really about wiki but procedural generation's techniques and guidance. It is a great place to refer to when you're curious or stuck. Visit `http://pcg.wikidot.com/` for more information.

- Another fascinating post on the Catlike Coding blog shows an implementation to generate procedural worlds using fractals. You can see the post at `http://catlikecoding.com/unity/tutorials/constructing-a-fractal/`.

- At `tutsplus.com`, they have a wide array of game development tutorials in lots of frameworks/platforms and languages. One such article is on procedurally modifying game assets. Check it out and the rest of the site at `http://gamedevelopment.tutsplus.com/tutorials/how-to-procedurally-customize-your-unity-game-assets-with-code--gamedev-12324`.

- As mentioned earlier in *Chapter 6*, *The Big Wild World*, if you want some fascinating procedurally generated maps for your game, check out `http://donjon.bin.sh/fantasy/world/`.

# Advanced coding

Coding doesn't need to be hard. The following are a few helpful sites to keep you moving:

- Coding Jar has a number of advanced coding-style posts and tutorials. There is one such tutorial that particularly stands out to deal with Advanced Serialization, which is well worth a look. It is available at `http://www.codingjargames.com/blog/2012/11/30/advanced-unity-serialization/`.

- We discussed messaging and other systems in this title, so it's worth checking out SignalChain, which is a much improved messaging engine for Unity. You can visit `https://github.com/sebas77/SignalChain` for more information.

- IOC and dependency injection is a particularly interesting and advanced topic that can simplify your project immensely (however at a cost of increased technical understanding). If you feel so inclined, you can check out the full free implementation written specifically for Unity at `https://github.com/strangeioc/strangeioc`.

- Another view on abstraction and interfaces can be found on the blog (not for the faint hearted) at `http://victorbarcelo.net/using-abstractions-interfaces-unity3d/?goback=%2Egde_3383466_member_5818738285761015811#%21`.

# Other scripting resources

The following sites simply have large collections of scripts that you can freely use and learn from. Some have already been mentioned in this title, but it is worth calling them out here specifically:

- One of the best collections of scripts in one powerful library is maintained by a former XNA developer, Nick Gravelyn. UnityToolbag is chock-full of tried and tested scripts that are essential for any Unity developer. You can visit `https://github.com/nickgravelyn/UnityToolbag` for more scripts.

- I've mentioned Unity wiki on several occasions in this title—always keep its location close at hand. The script also has a wealth of information on other aspects of Unity. It's community-driven, so keep that in mind. The scripts wiki is available at `http://wiki.unity3d.com/index.php/Scripts`.

- Game produce a lot of valuable resources; at one a Free Achievement Framework for Unity was born. It is worth reading and looking into. Visit `http://www.stevegargolinski.com/progress-a-free-achievement-framework-for-unity/` for more information.

# Useful assets

The asset store holds a vast array of good and not so good offerings, some free, some reasonable, and some just down right ludicrous.

Based on what we have covered in this book, the following are some prebuilt alternatives you can use if you don't want to roll your own; above all, they are highly rated and reviewed:

- LeenTween isn't just a powerful tweening solution (a framework that will create transitions smoothly between two points, like animations), but it also has a very robust and easy-to-use messaging system bundled with it. It is available at `https://www.assetstore.unity3d.com/#/content/3595`.

For more details on how to use LeanTween or its event dispatcher (messaging), visit the DentedPixels website, `http://dentedpixel.com/`.

You might also find some other interesting topics there (my favorite being procedural textures scripts).

 Also what's noteworthy on the store is a very in-depth review of all the competitor tweening solutions and the pros/cons of each. It is there at `http://dentedpixel.com/video/leantween-speed-comparison-to-itween-and-hotween/`.

- Dialoguer is quite fantastic for the price and offers not only a full conversation and UI system, but also a rich node-based editing tool for crafting conversations. It is available at `https://www.assetstore.unity3d.com/#/content/14854`.

- Another engine that is fairly full featured is called **Conversation Engine**. Similar to dialoguer, it has a node-based editor and UI features and includes video tutorials on its use. It can be found at `https://www.assetstore.unity3d.com/en/#!/content/11967`.

If you haven't had the time to build your own, it can be worth shopping around; remember that you can always extend what you get with the lessons you have learned in this title.

- A great post as a rundown of the top editor extension assets on the store that is well worth a read is available at `http://blogs.unity3d.com/2014/04/17/extend-the-editor-to-infinity-and-beyond/`.

- Managing multiple languages within your project can be a hassle, but as it turns out, there are assets to help you deal with this; the most notable one is Language Manager Asset. For full details, check out the author's post about the asset at `http://thecreativechris.wordpress.com/2014/04/03/localization-support-with-unity/`.

- If you like Voxels (scenes made up of thousands/millions of tiny cubes) such as MineCraft, you might want to try out Cubiquity. It's a full Voxel engine that you can use to build your games with mountains of power as it's implemented in C++ and available at `https://bitbucket.org/volumesoffun/cubiquity-for-unity3d`.

# Sources of art and SFX

It's well known that programmers don't do art (except for a very talented few): more often than not, we end up with either bad code or programmer art. However, there are many great resources to get assets for your title, even if they are only placeholders until you find a designer who is worthy of your vision. The following are some of the best places to start your journey from:

- One of the latest marketplaces to spring up plenty of assets is the new GameDev Market. It is chock-full of 2D, 3D, textures, and even sample GUI art of which some are paid and some free. If you wish, you can also sell your own assets. The store is available at https://www.gamedevmarket.net/.

- If free art helps you begin your title (sometimes even finish it), then one of the biggest sites is the OpenGameArt site. It has hordes of free-to-use assets, from spritesheets to textures and even audio, and it is available at http://opengameart.org/.

- The VG resource is a forum-based art system where you can download or even request art and SFX. It is well worth a look (so long as you wear shades) and is available at http://www.vg-resource.com/.

- Another source of freely available assets under a creative commons license is the aptly named search site, http://search.creativecommons.org/.

- As we had an entire chapter in this title where we worked with maps, it only seems fair to point out this free resource for maps at http://freefantasymaps.org/.

- A good review of some of the other most common map solutions out there for titles can be found at http://nevermetpress.com/six-rpg-map-making-solutions-for-your-game#.U6V1LvldURq.

- Inspiration is hard to come by at times, so the following sites are well worth browsing for the next big idea (some assets can be used, just check the license):
    - http://commons.wikimedia.org/wiki/Main_Page
    - https://www.tumblr.com/
    - https://www.pinterest.com/

- If you are looking for some cool effects, visit http://dm4331-sidm-s1-2012-06.blogspot.co.uk/2012/07/updates-for-healing-and-fire-effects.html. I used assets from this site for the blood splatter effects in *Chapter 9, Getting Ready to Fight*.

- Finally, sometimes projects don't go well and sometimes they die. However, if you are like these guys, you can share your content from your title. The following two links contain gigs of assets from `http://www.glitchthegame.com/`, which met its demise; however, the authors of these links gave all the game assets away for free:

  ° `https://github.com/ThirdPartyNinjas/GlitchAssets`

  ° `https://github.com/ThirdPartyNinjas/GlitchAssets-Inhabitants`

# Highlights from the Web

The following are just a general collection of respected resources out on the Web to help the budding Unity developer hone their skills:

- The Unity3D learn site is an ever growing set of tutorials and videos to help you out; it's always worth checking them out every so often. It can be found at `http://unity3d.com/learn`.

- What's specifically worth calling out on the Unity site is the live training session and its archive. Here, the Unity learning team takes requests and then transfers them into live recorded sessions. Keep watching! There's always something to learn from these videos. The videos are available at `http://unity3d.com/learn/live-training`.

- On my blog, there are two major posts worthy of mention, which contain links to just about every interesting thing I find useful for budding game developers. I keep them updated as often as I can (you can also check the rest of my blog as well). The blogs can be found at:

  ° `http://darkgenesis.zenithmoon.com/so-you-want-to-be-a-unity3d-game-developer/`

  ° `http://darkgenesis.zenithmoon.com/monster-set-of-free-resources-for-game-design/`

- The indie resources site is a wealth of information, and the assets can be freely used in any game. Visit `http://www.pixelprospector.com/indie-resources/` for more information.

- There is a fascinating post with information on the recent release of Unity 4.5, useful tips, and changes in the latest update; it is available at `http://va.lent.in/interesting-things-in-unity-4-5-you-probably-didnt-know-about/`.

- Then, there is a post that should not be far from your reading list; one that contains huge number of tips from experienced Unity developers sharing their woes and how they overcame them; additionally, it provides some very useful tricks of the trade. It is available at `http://www.reddit.com/r/Unity3D/comments/1r63tq/new_unity_users_if_i_knew_then/`.

- Some final hints and tips with the Top 50 best practices when working in Unity are given at `http://devmag.org.za/2012/07/12/50-tips-for-working-with-unity-best-practices/`.

# Index

enemy
adding 231-235
beefing up 328
controller, creating 329, 330
enemy profile, setting up in code 333
Goblin prefab, updating 332, 333
profile, creating 329, 330
**Enemy class 37**
**EnemyController class**
selection logic, adding to 335-339
**enemy profile**
setting up, in code 333
**Entity class 39**
**Entity object**
about 38
implementing 38, 39
**event systems**
fixed systems 220
planning 219, 220
random generation 220
**expansion tips, sprite animation 85**
**Expression design**
URL 387
**extension methods**
URL 199
**extra scenery 92-94**

# F

**fading process**
starting 213
used, by level loading update 215
**FBX model post processor**
URL 421
**fill rate 260**
**Finite State Machines**
(FSM). *See* **state machines**
**fixed maps**
about 184-186
URL 185
**fixed systems 220**
**FixedUpdate method**
about 102, 247
and LateUpdate method,
comparing 102, 103
and Update method, comparing 102, 103

**float parameter**
updating 80
**flocking, AI 223**
**FollowCamera script 107, 108**
**foreground objects**
adding 120
**Free Achievement Framework**
URL 432
**Freemind**
URL 387
**free resource, maps**
URL 434

# G

**game**
marketing 428
settings 385
**GameDev Market**
URL 434
**game object**
tagging 113
**GameState class 243**
**game structure**
common game object 38, 39
**general techniques, procedural generation**
Diamond-square algorithm 189
iterated function systems 189
L-systems 189
midpoint displacement algorithm 189
perlin noise system 189
simplex noise system 189
**generated maps**
about 184-187
in-game generated maps 187, 188
**generators**
URL 386
**generics**
URL 391
**GetComponent function 33**
**GetRouteInfo 117**
**GetWindowWithRect function 370**
**Gimzo-driven design tutorial**
URL 373
**GitHub**
URL 23

# W

**WaitForEndOfFrame function 241**
**Web**
  highlights 435
**web backend**
  benefits 401
  implementing 401-403
**while loop 240**

**world space 190**
**WWW class**
  URL 403

# X

**XML serialization 390**

Thank you for buying
# Mastering Unity 2D Game Development

## About Packt Publishing

Packt, pronounced 'packed', published its first book "*Mastering phpMyAdmin for Effective MySQL Management*" in April 2004 and subsequently continued to specialize in publishing highly focused books on specific technologies and solutions.

Our books and publications share the experiences of your fellow IT professionals in adapting and customizing today's systems, applications, and frameworks. Our solution based books give you the knowledge and power to customize the software and technologies you're using to get the job done. Packt books are more specific and less general than the IT books you have seen in the past. Our unique business model allows us to bring you more focused information, giving you more of what you need to know, and less of what you don't.

Packt is a modern, yet unique publishing company, which focuses on producing quality, cutting-edge books for communities of developers, administrators, and newbies alike. For more information, please visit our website: www.packtpub.com.

## Writing for Packt

We welcome all inquiries from people who are interested in authoring. Book proposals should be sent to author@packtpub.com. If your book idea is still at an early stage and you would like to discuss it first before writing a formal book proposal, contact us; one of our commissioning editors will get in touch with you.

We're not just looking for published authors; if you have strong technical skills but no writing experience, our experienced editors can help you develop a writing career, or simply get some additional reward for your expertise.

**Unity 4.x Game AI Programming**

ISBN: 978-1-84969-340-0     Paperback: 232 pages

Learn and implement game AI in Unity3D with a lot of sample projects and next-generation techniques to use in your Unity3D projects

1. A practical guide with step-by-step instructions and example projects to learn Unity3D scripting.

2. Learn pathfinding using A* algorithms as well as Unity3D pro features and navigation graphs.

3. Implement finite state machines (FSMs), path following, and steering algorithms.

**Practical Game Design with Unity and Playmaker**

ISBN: 978-1-84969-810-8     Paperback: 122 pages

Leverage the power of Unity 3D and Playmaker to develop a game from scratch

1. Create artificial intelligence for a game using Playmaker.

2. Learn how to integrate a game with external APIs (Kongregate).

3. Learn how to quickly develop games in Unity and Playmaker.

**Grome Terrain Modeling with Ogre3D, UDK, and Unity3D**

ISBN: 978-1-84969-939-6       Paperback: 162 pages

Create massive terrains and export them to the most popular game engines

1. A comprehensive guide for terrain creation.

2. Step-by-step walkthrough of Grome 3.1 and toolset.

3. Export terrains to Unity3D, UDK, and Ogre3D.

Grome Terrain Modeling with Ogre3D, UDK, and Unity3D

Create massive terrains and export them to the most popular game engines

Richard A. Hawley

**Unity 2D Game Development**

ISBN: 978-1-84969-256-4       Paperback: 126 pages

Combine classic 2D with today's technology to build great games with Unity's latest 2D tools

1. Build a 2D game using the native 2D development support in Unity 4.3.

2. Create a platformer with jumping, falling, enemies, and a final boss.

3. Full of exciting challenges which will help you polish your game development skills.

Unity 2D Game Development

Combine classic 2D with today's technology to build great games with Unity's latest 2D tools

Dave Calabrese

Please check **www.PacktPub.com** for information on our titles

Made in the USA
San Bernardino, CA
17 May 2015